MARY THOMSON'S
EVENTING YEAR

MARY THOMSON'S EVENTING YEAR

A month-by-month plan
for training a champion

Debby Sly and Mary Thomson

David & Charles

To
GILL ROBINSON
The owner of my horses: thank you for your kindness, generosity
and endless enthusiasm over the years – I owe my success to you

A DAVID & CHARLES BOOK

Copyright © Mary Thomson and Debby Sly 1993

First published 1993

Mary Thomson and Debby Sly have asserted their right to be identified as authors of
this work in accordance with the Copyright, Designs and Patents Act 1988.

A catalogue record for this book is available from the British Library.

ISBN 0 7153 0065 2

Typeset in Goudy
and printed in Italy by Ofsa SpA for
DAVID & CHARLES
Brunel House   Newton Abbot   Devon

CONTENTS

INTRODUCTION

The 1992 horse trials season saw Mary Thomson poised to tackle the highest level of three-day eventing – the Olympics. The previous season she had been selected for the British team for the first time when she rode in the European Championships at Punchestown. She won the British Open Champion title for the second year running at Gatcombe, and finished the year by winning three major three-day events in a row, on three different horses.

As a child, Mary was no different from any other pony-mad youngster. She had begged and borrowed ponies from the age of six, starting with Magpie, the local vicar's pony; by the time she was twelve her parents finally relented and Mary was allowed a pony of her own. The pony, Butterboy, took her successfully through Pony Club. Mary's family had moved to the tiny village of Salcombe Regis when Mary was a baby; her father had suffered a terrible motorcycle accident and had been pensioned out of the navy, and the move to Salcombe Regis was so that he could take up the position of verger. The church cottage is pretty small with no land, and there was simply no room to accommodate a pony for Mary. However, the vicar provided a stable for Butterboy and a local farmer allowed Mary to use one of his fields.

When Mary left school she sold Butterboy and spent two and a half years working for Sheila Willcox, the first lady event rider to be exceptionally successful –

King Boris, who gave Mary her first British Open Championships victory

6

● *King William on his first visit to Badminton in May 1991*

she won Badminton three times on her two horses, High and Mighty, and Airs and Graces. Here Mary learnt an enormous amount, particularly in the art of dressage and bringing on young horses.

Mary then took a break from horses to do a Cordon Bleu cookery course, and to work as a chalet girl in Switzerland for a winter ski season. However, when she returned to England she was determined to compete successfully in eventing; by doing a variety of part-time jobs she was able to keep two event horses, and also purchased a third horse specifically to 'bring on' so as to sell at a better price. One horse – Boris – was bought with the help of her boyfriend, David King: and for a bit of fun they called him King Boris. Then the next horse Mary bought was called Arthur, a name which naturally asked for 'King' to be put in front of it; and so Mary's royal family grew from there. 'My odd jobs included a butcher's delivery round, working in people's gardens, cleaning the local campsite loos, anything I could think of. To fit all the work in it sometimes meant riding the horses in the dark!' says Mary.

From these early beginnings Mary's talent and perseverance has enabled her to build up a string of quality horses. With the very generous support of Gill Robinson, her dream to compete at the highest level in the world of eventing is now a reality.

The 1992 season brought the chance for Mary to be selected to ride at the Olympic Games in Barcelona; her Olympic hope was King William. This book follows the fortunes and progress of three of Mary's horses – King William, King Kong and King Basil – through the 1992 season, and the reader will soon appreciate that although the Olympics offered Mary and King William the greatest opportunity of their lives, the aims and ambitions of her less experienced horses were just as important: they could become the champions of the future.

INTRODUCING THE HORSES

KING BASIL

Basil, as he is known to his friends, was born in 1986. He is a 16.3hh bay gelding, a $^{15}/_{16}$ Thoroughbred by the successful event horse National Trust; his mother appropriately named 'Just Mary', was by Spiritus, also a successful eventing sire. Mary bought him as a five-year-old, and observed that: 'Basil had less experience than the horses I normally buy, but he had good paces, a nice temperament and a very purposeful air about him.'

Basil has a very soft, gentle, friendly nature and for a young horse is surprisingly calm. 'It will be interesting to see if that changes once he is introduced to the thrill of eventing', says Mary. When Basil arrived in Mary's yard in 1991, all he had done was some light hacking and little bit of work over trotting poles. Mary set about improving his flatwork, and introduced him to jumping; she hacked him out on his own, taught him to cope with traffic on the road, and about going through water. He did a local hunter trial as a 'pair' with a more experienced horse, and also went indoor showjumping; he then had a few weeks' rest over Christmas.

He was brought back into work, together with all Mary's horses, on 1 January.

Although he is a big horse, at this point he was very soft and loose in himself, and really needed to be a bit stronger; he also needed to be more positive about everything, though Mary expected this would happen naturally as he matured. Because he was quite inexperienced, Mary's intention was to ride him in a few Pre-Novice classes rather than to go straight into a Novice event; ultimately she hoped that he would upgrade to Intermediate standard during the autumn.

KING KONG

'Conker is one big bundle of energy and naughtiness', says Mary. Born in 1985 in Cornwall, he is a 16.2hh dark brown gelding, out of a $^7/_8$ Thoroughbred mare and by the Thoroughbred stallion Newski. He came to Mary as a six-year-old, having already won £60 in BSJA showjumping classes. 'His flatwork needed a huge amount of attention. Because he had showjumped, his canter was very good but his trot was all over the place. He is a very compact horse and very full of himself, especially when out hacking. Although he is very friendly and gentle in the stable, as soon as he comes out

● *King Basil accurately jumping the Corner at Peper Harow*

his eyes start to twinkle. In fact initially I was worried that he might be too much of a lively character to cope with the discipline of eventing,' says Mary.

Mary therefore worked him quietly at home, insisting that he remained steady and in a level rhythm, and his trot work has gradually improved. He went on to win three Novice events in a row, and also his first Intermediate event; he ended his first year with Mary by winning Osberton three-day event which upgraded him to advanced level with a total of 74 points. His aim for 1992 is Windsor three-day event in the spring, and Blenheim in the autumn.

KING WILLIAM

William is a much more grown-up character than Basil and Conker. He came to Mary from a showjumping yard as a five-year-old, and rapidly established himself as an eventing star. He won his first Novice event and upgraded to advanced while he was still only six.

'He is a very aloof but cool character, and although he is very bold he is also quite sensitive and hates men!' says Mary. His sire was an Irish Thoroughbred called Nickel King, and he was born in 1984; he is probably 7/8 Thoroughbred. He is 16.3hh, and dark brown with a distinctive white blaze. 'As a young horse he was always ahead of himself. When I schooled him it was a case of "Hey, wait for me ,William".' Mary was worried that he would become too strong as he is such a big, tall horse and very eager to get on with his work, but by doing plenty of dressage with him to steady and calm him she has managed to remain the boss so far!

● (above) *King William: head and shoulders above the rest*
(right) *King Kong: his natural talent makes him an exciting prospect for the future*

William attempted Badminton for the first time in 1991, a year which proved to be full of ups and downs for him. He performed a good dressage test, but although he actually jumped clear across country, he slipped up on the flat on the turn out of Huntsman's Close and was given 60 penalties for a fall. Nor was his showjumping very brilliant: in the autumn of 1990 it had got steadily worse – at Blenheim he had knocked three show jumps down, thus falling from 3rd to 9th place – and the problem was still with him at Badminton, when he again had three fences down. However, with the help of Captain Mark Phillips and Stephen Hadley, Mary worked hard to sort out their problems. In exoneration, William produced fabulous showjumping and cross-country rounds at Gatcombe in 1991 to win Mary her second British Open Champion title.

It was with William that Mary represented Britain for the first time in her career when she was selected to ride at the European Championships in Punchestown. William led after the dressage, and it *should* have been a fairytale ending, as he and Mary looked set to be the only combination to get round the cross-country course within the time – but disaster struck at the water jump, a few fences from home. The fence involved a huge drop into water and William produced such a

● (opposite) *King Samuel thoroughly enjoying the cross-country challenge.* (above) *Star Appeal, a promising young advanced horse whose 1992 target is Bramham three-day event*

bold leap that his legs just went from under him as he landed in the water. Mary was thrown off, and although they completed the course, an injury to her knee prevented them from showjumping on the final day. Despite this the British team still managed to win the gold medal.

'I have ridden that fence over and over in my mind since then, and I am doing it quite beautifully now!' says Mary. 'If only I had slowed down to a trot so that William was not able to jump so boldly, things could have been very different.' If only…

William has been longlisted for the Olympics, and he will compete at Badminton in the hope that he will be selected for the Olympic team. The most important year in his life has begun.

MORE KINGS AND COURTIERS

Mary has three other horses to fit into her busy schedule: **Star Appeal**, a seven-year-old who is aimed at Bramham and Blenheim; **King Samuel**, who has qual-

● *Annie (left) and Tina, keeping up with the less glamorous side of their work*

ified for the European Cup in Italy; and **King Boris**, who won Mary's first British Open Champion title. Boris is now thirteen years old – he suffered quite a bad ligament injury at Badminton last year, and will probably retire at the end of the season. Mary is also looking for another young horse so that Basil will have some company around the novice tracks. Gill Robinson owns all the 'royal' horses, with Mary's boyfriend having a half share in King William. Star Appeal is owned by Mrs Angela Pinder.

THE STABLES AND YARD ROUTINE

Mary's yard consists of several old Devon barns which she has converted into nine luxuriously large and airy loose boxes. The whitewashed tackroom and colourful hanging baskets add to the relaxed atmosphere. Out at the back there is a dry feed store, a manège, and about three acres of paddocks.

Mary is helped by Annie Collings who works full time. 'Annie is my headgirl, although she hates being called that,' says Mary. 'She has been with me since 1985. I also employ a working pupil, this year a girl called Sarah Tancock. We have a different working pupil each year, and luckily there is quite a long queue of them lined up for the job! All my staff have to live locally, as there is no accommodation here for them. During the year there is extra help on hand from Tina Court; Tina has been helping me since 1984 and works about three mornings a week – she also looks after any horses left behind when we are away at events.

'The girls come into work at 8am – we're very civilised down here! The horses are fed straightaway, their rugs are straightened and their legs felt quickly for any sign of injury. If the day promises to be busy I will work a horse before its breakfast, otherwise the girls go ahead and muck out. My own morning starts by sorting the post and paperwork, and normally the horses don't see me before about 9am. I try to make sure that they are all worked by lunchtime – I do all the schooling and jumping, but the girls help with the roadwork and much of the fast work which is needed to keep event horses fit.

'Lunch is from 1pm until 2pm and the afternoons are spent doing all the other work that horses create – grooming, tack cleaning, mane and tail washing and pulling, tidying the yard etc. At the end of the afternoon they are skipped out and water buckets are filled for the night. The girls normally manage to leave the yard by 5pm. All the evening feeding is done by me, as it gives me a few moments alone with each horse. They have their hay at about 5.15pm and their last feed at 6pm. All the horses have two buckets of water in their stables so they never go thirsty.'

● *The lorry needs to be as well-equipped as the yard; Annie loads up ready for another equine outing*

WHAT IS EVENTING?

The sport of eventing, or horse trials, is the ultimate test of a horse and rider's courage, skill, discipline and fitness. Unlike most other equestrian sports where competitors specialise in one aspect, such as showjumping, dressage, race riding or team chasing, eventing encompasses all these skills in one major test of the horse and rider.

The ambition of most event riders is to compete at the highest level in the sport, which is the three-day event. As the name suggests, this is a competition which is held over a minimum of three days. On the first day every horse and rider completes a pre-set dressage test – the scoring at events is done on a penalty basis, so the horse with the lowest dressage score takes the lead. The second day is what the sport is all about: the speed and endurance test, a test of the horse's stamina and courage. It comprises four phases: the competitor sets out on Phase A, the roads and tracks which involves riding a set route over varying country within a set time – it works out at about 220mpm. At the end of Phase A is the start of Phase B, the steeplechase, a course of about eight point-to-point fences, also to be completed within a set time – the speed is between 640 and 690mpm (about two-thirds racing speed) depending on the star rating (severity) of the event; exceeding the set time incurs one penalty point for every second over. The end of the steeplechase is the start of Phase C, another section of roads and tracks also to be ridden at an average of 220mpm; this brings horse and rider to the 10-minute box, a designated area near the start of Phase D, the cross-country course. The horse is first trotted up and checked over (pulse and respiration) by a panel of vets who then decide whether he is fit to continue the test. If he passes, horse and rider are allowed to rest in the box for 10 minutes; they then set off round the cross-country jumping course, where the ultimate aim is to achieve a clear round within the time set; the speed for a three-day event is between 520 and 570mpm. Again, time penalties are awarded for exceeding the set time; also 20 penalties for a first refusal, 60 for a fall, and so on.

All the penalty points incurred on the speed and endurance phases are added to the dressage score. – there are not many who finish without any at all! On the third day, the horse is again trotted up and inspected by a panel of vets; if he is judged fit to continue he can be presented for the final phase of the three-day event: the showjumping test.

The three-day event is the goal which most riders work towards, and there are events of varying severity, star-rated 1 to 4, to suit all levels of experience. Obviously such competitions involve a huge amount of organisation and voluntary help, so there are only a limited number on the horse trials calendar for the year, certainly when compared with the number of one-day events run throughout the country. The three-day event is also extremely tiring for the horse, and he would not be expected to compete in more than two or three such competitions each year. So in between these major events, the horses and competitors can gain experience at one-day events, which are an abbreviated version of the above. At a one-day event the horse would be presented for a dressage test, a showjumping test and a cross-country test all in the same day. The courses are shorter than they would be at a three-day event, and there are *no* roads and tracks, and steeplechase phases at all. Some horses and riders do not aspire to the demands of the major three-day events; for them, the one-day events provide a great deal of fun, experience and satisfaction, and are a sport in themselves.

When a horse is placed at an event he wins a number of horse trials *points*. The rider keeps a record of these, because they determine the level of competition at which the horse may compete. Thus event horses are graded into four levels depending on the number of points they have won: Pre-Novice, Novice, Intermediate and Advanced (see table below).

GRADING OF EVENT HORSES

Grade:	Pre-Novice	Novice	Intermediate	Advanced
Points:	No points	Less than 21	21–60	61 or more

ONE-DAY EVENTS: POINTS AWARDED

Place	Number of starters	Novice/ ON	Intermediate/ AI/OI	Advanced
1		6	12	24
2		5	10	22
3		4	8	20
4	over 15	3	6	18
5	over 19	2	4	16
6	over 23	1	2	14
7	over 27	1	2	12
8	over 31	1	2	10
9	over 35	1	2	8
10	over 39	1	2	8

and so on

THREE-DAY EVENTS AND BRITISH CHAMPIONSHIPS: POINTS AWARDED

Place	Starters	Brit Champ N	I	Open	CCI*	3-day event **	***	****
1		9	15	30	10	30	50	70
2		8	13	27	9	28	45	65
3		7	11	24	8	26	40	60
4	over 15	6	9	21	7	24	35	55
5	over 19	5	8	18	6	22	30	50
6	over 23	4	7	15	5	20	25	45
7	over 27	3	6	14	4	16	20	40
8	over 31	2	5	13	3	13	15	35
9	over 35	1	5	12	2	13	15	30
10	over 39	1	5	12	2	13	15	25

and so on

Additional points for competing cross-country without jumping penalties — 5 10 20

This system means that it is horses of the same experience that compete against each other, irrespective of the level of experience of their rider. This means that at your very first event you could find yourself competing against Mary Thomson! You may think it is unlikely that a novice rider would have any chance at all against such experienced competitors, and this is often the case! But eventing is a sport full of surprises, and if you do succeed, it is all the more worthwhile and exciting for that reason.

As well as classes for the four grades already mentioned, there are also 'in-between classes' for horses that have just upgraded from one level to another. First, there is the Open Novice class for horses with up to 36 points, where the dressage and showjumping tests are of Intermediate standard, but the cross-country course is Novice standard. Then there is the Open Intermediate competition, which uses the same speeds and fence dimensions as an ordinary Intermediate class, but is open to Advanced horses as well. So if a horse has upgraded but finds he is struggling at Advanced level, he can enter an Open Intermediate class to help him regain his confidence. In 1992 an Advanced Intermediate class was introduced, which works on the same principle as the Open Novice: Intermediate and Advanced horses can enter this and do an Advanced dressage and showjumping test, but they have an Intermediate cross-country course.

Three-day events are run at four different levels and can be either national or international competitions; they are described as follows:

National	International
Novice (CCN*)	CCI*
Intermediate (CCN**)	CCI**
Advanced (CCN***)	CCI***
Championship (CCN****)	CCI****

CC stands for *concours complet*, followed by either N for National or I for International. Badminton is considered by most competitors to be the ultimate challenge: it is a CCI****, as is Burghley. Bramham and Blenheim are CCI***, and two-star events include Windsor, Osberton and Blair Castle. One-star events are Holker Hall and Tweseldown. There are also a number of three-day events held in Europe, USA, Australia and New Zealand including Boekelo (Holland), Lion d'Angers (France), Gawler (Australia), Taupo (New Zealand) and Lexington (USA).

Three-day eventing is a very expensive and time-consuming sport. The event horse and rider require a greater degree of fitness and schooling in all the riding disciplines than in most other sports. Once you are competing with more than two or three horses it is almost impossible to manage on your own, and sponsorship or some other income must be sought.

•Coping with the elements is all part of the job; Mary and Mark Todd at the South of England horse trials, 1991

THREE-DAY EVENTS – FENCE DIMENSIONS (1992)

Speed and Endurance

	1 Star	2 Star	3 Star	4 Star
Heights, Phase B (steeplechase):				
Fixed	1.00m	1.00m	1.00m	1.00m
Brush	1.40m	1.40m	1.40m	1.40m
Heights, Phase D (cross-country):				
Fixed	1.10m	1.15m	1.20m	1.20m
Brush	1.40m	1.40m	1.40m	1.40m
Spreads, Phases B and D:				
Highest point	1.40m	1.60m	1.80m	2.00m
Base	2.10m	2.40m	2.70m	3.00m
Without height	2.80m	3.20m	3.60m	4.00m
Drops, Phase D:	1.60m	1.80m	2.00m	2.00m

Speeds and Distances

	1 star	2 star	3 star	4 star
Phases A and C	220mpm	220mpm	220mpm	220mpm
	40–55min	50–65min	60–75min	70–85min
	8,800–12,100m	11,000–14,300m	13,200–16,500m	15,400–18,700m
Phase B	640mpm	660mpm	690mpm	690mpm
	3.5min	3.5 or 4 min	4 or 4.5min	4.5 or 5 min
	2,240m	2,310 or 2,640m	2,760 or 3,105m	3,105 or 3,450m
Max jumping efforts	6–8	6–8	6–8	8–10
Phase D	520mpm	550mpm	570mpm	570mpm
	7.5–9.5min	9–11min	10–12min	12–14min
Max jumping efforts	30	35	40	45

The Showjumping Course

	1 star	2 star	3 star	4 star
Heights:	1.10m	1.15m	1.20m	1.20m
Spreads:				
Highest point	1.40m	1.60m	1.80m	1.80m
Base or triple bar	1.90m	2.10m	2.30m	2.30m
Water	2.50m	3.00m	3.50m	3.50m

Speeds, Times and Distances

1 star	2 star	3 star	4 star
350mpm	375mpm	400mpm	400mpm
102–120sec	104–120sec	105–120sec	113–128sec
600–700m	650–750m	700–800m	750–850m

0.25 penalties for every second over time allowed

ONE-DAY EVENTS

The Showjumping Course

	PN	Nov	Int	Adv
Max height:	1.10m	1.15m	1.20m	1.25m
Max spread at highest point:	1.20m	1.20m	1.50m	1.80m
At base:	2.15m	2.15m	2.45m	2.80m
Water:	–	–	2.60m	3.00m
Max length:	500m	500m	500m	550m
Speed:	320mpm	320mpm	320mpm	350mpm

Penalties:
Knockdown: 5 penalties
First refusal: 10 penalties
Second refusal : 20 penalties
Third refusal: elimination
Fall of horse or rider: 30 penalties
Second fall: elimination
One time penalty for every 4 seconds over the time

The Cross-country Course

	Novice/ Pre-Novice	Intermediate	Advance
Max height:	1.08m	1.15m	1.20m
With height and spread			
Max spread at highest point:	1.20m	1.60m	1.80m
At base:	2.15m	2.45m	2.80m
With spread only Max spread:			
– dry ditch	2.74m	3.05m	3.50m
– water	3.05m	3.65m	4.00m
Drop fences max drop:	1.68m	1.83m	2.00m
Jump into and out of water, max depth of water:	0.30m	0.30m	0.50m

Distances and speeds

	Novice/ Pre-Novice	Intermediate	Advance
Length	1,600–2,800m	2,400–3,620m	3,250–4,000m
Speed	520m/min 490/minPN	570m/min	600m/min

Penalties:

First refusal or runout	20 penalties
Second refusal or runout at the same fence	40 penalties
Third refusal or runout at the same fence	elimination
Fall of horse or rider	60 penalties

One time penalty for every three seconds over optimum time.

The above information is supplied courtesy of the British Horse Society, Horse Trials Rules 1992. The BHS takes no responsibility for any of the contents or opinions expressed in this publication.

JANUARY

This month is the beginning of what I feel is going to be the most important year of my eventing career. I start it with a feeling of excitement and great expectation as to what it might have in store; though at the back of my mind there is always the knowledge that with horses, even the best laid plans can backfire.

Over the last few years I have built up what I think is the best team of horses I have ever had, so the possibility of success is on my side – but with a never-ending list of things that can go wrong, I am trying not to build up my forever ambitious hopes!

The horses had wintered well. My January diary follows William, Conker and Basil through their initial fittening work, starting with walking on the roads and gradually building up to include flatwork and jump training in their exercise programme. I have three other advanced horses as part of my team for this year as well: first there is King Boris, my old faithful, who has retired from three-day eventing following a suspensory ligament injury at Badminton last year, who will continue to 'play' at one-day events. Then King Samuel, who won the Lion d'Angers CCI in France last autumn, and has therefore qualified for the Continental Cup Final which is being held in Italy at the end of May. These five horses are owned by Gill Robinson, although my boyfriend, David King, has a half-share in William. Star Appeal, otherwise known as Apple, makes up my team of six horses, and is owned by Mrs Angela Pinder. Apple is a 7-year-old and is being aimed at Bramham three-day event in June.

During January my personal diary had rather more variety than that of the horses. It started with a very amusing recording for the television programme 'A Question of Sport': with partners Bill Beaumont and Alan Lamb, with Ian Botham, Rob Andrew and Gordon Drurie forming the opposition. The show is recorded four weeks before it is shown on television. This occasion was slightly quieter than my first appearance when I was in a team with Frank Bruno but this time our team won! Television is quite an eye-opener for the person involved, as you never look or sound the way you think you do.

In fact London called again on two more occasions; the first was for a press conference, and here it was announced that I, amongst others, would be invited to ride in a flat race at Kempton Park in June – this sounded like fun, too! The second trip was for a live Radio 4 recording for 'Woman's Hour' about women in sport. Actually I enjoy doing this sort of thing, especially if there is time for a bit of a shopping spree!

Teaching and giving lectures also kept me fairly well occupied through January. A two-day clinic at the Duchy College of Agriculture Equestrian Centre in Cornwall helped to boost my winter income, as did a lecture demonstration at the end of January. Besides these I gave a series of evening lectures on Romania's orphans – Riders for Romania is a charity with which I am actively involved – and concerning horses generally.

Whilst most people enjoy a holiday on New Year's Day, the first day of January marks the end of a holiday for Mary's horses, and the start of their preparation for the new eventing season.

Once each horse has completed his last event of the season, he is turned out for a rest for several months; all the horses are left out, day and night, and allowed to unwind completely – it is a chance for them to get back to as natural an existence as possible. When they are brought back in from the fields they look like a small herd of wild, shaggy ponies, and nothing like the string of smart event horses that they are meant to be – and will soon become!

THE IMPORTANCE OF CORRECT SHOEING

The correct maintenance of a horse's hooves is of paramount importance. Bad shoeing can not only cause problems such as corns, nail binds and pricks, it can also increase the chance of injuries such as strains, sprains and bruised soles. We owe it to our horses to look after their feet properly so that they can achieve their best.

A good farrier should balance the hoof correctly so that a straight foot/pastern axis, from both the front and side view, is maintained (see diagram). The base of the hoof should be as level as possible, ideally with the heels equal, and the coronary band horizontal. Obviously any abnormalities of the conformation of the leg must be taken into account.

Shoes should be long enough at the heel to give as much support as possible to the structure of the hoof and leg. If the heels of the shoes are left a bit long they are unlikely to get pulled off, providing they are correctly fitted and the hoof is balanced properly. Shoes that are too short can do untold damage, causing the horse's heels to collapse, and unnecessary stress being put on the structures of the leg.

My horses have front shoes with rolled toes. The aim is to advance the 'break over' point, allowing the foot to leave the ground more quickly, lessening the chance of an overreach injury, and reducing the stress on the tendons and ligaments. My larger horses, eg William, Boris and Apple, and those with weak heels eg Basil, have front shoes made from metal which is wider than normal, thus providing a greater weight-bearing surface.

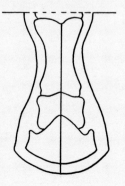

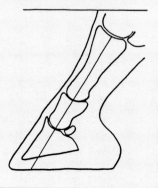

BASIC MANAGEMENT

When the horses come in, their first week in work involves a whirlwind of activity for the grooms! They still have their thick heavy coats so are not rugged up at all until they are clipped, and this is not done until they have been in for about a week and the worst of the grease and dirt removed from their coats. The most important of the initial jobs is shoeing, and Mark Malin, Mary's farrier, comes and fits all the horses with a full set of shoes. 'I do not have stud holes put in until they start eventing; as a rule I

do not use road studs for everyday work because I feel they unbalance the foot,' says Mary.

Once the farrier has dealt with his end of the horses, John Fowler, Mary's vet, comes to sort out the top end – their teeth. All the horses have their teeth rasped at the beginning of the year, to remove any sharp edges which might prevent them eating properly, and which may hurt once they have a bit in their mouth and are being worked again. Conker is the only horse that really objects to this visit by the 'dentist'. 'He is genuinely frightened,' says Mary. 'We realised this the first time, and so rather than

have a fight with him which would have made him even worse to do the following year, the vet gave him a sedative to tranquillise him. As Conker is very ticklish at the best of times, we took advantage of his sleepy state and pulled his mane and tail at the same time!'

One by one the horses' manes and tails are brought under control by pulling and washing them. The hair around their heels and coronary band (the top of their hooves) is trimmed with scissors and, with great care, so is the hair around their ears.

Although the first events do not start until

● *William and Conker at the end of their winter holiday*

23

PULLING MANES AND TAILS

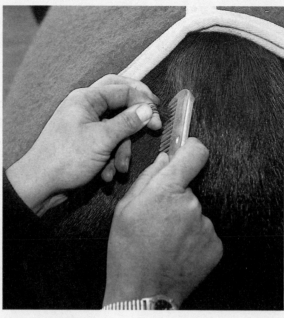

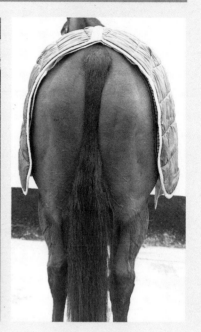

● **Tail pulling:** *The tail is pulled by thinning the hair from the sides of the dock*

● ***Mane pulling:*** *The mane is pulled by taking small amounts of hair from the underside of the mane. The comb is run up through the hair to the appropriate length, and a sharp downward tug will remove the unwanted ends*

the spring, the horses have to be brought into work several months beforehand so as to get them fit enough to compete. The fitness programme begins by just walking the horses out for the first two weeks; this helps to harden up and strengthen their legs and tendons in particular so they can cope with the hard work that is to come. For the first few days these walks only last about three-quarters of an hour, but this is gradually built up until by the end of a fortnight they are walking out for one and a quarter hours.

During the horses' second week in work the daunting task of clipping off their winter coats must be tackled, otherwise they would become very hot and sweaty when working and it would take them several hours to dry off and feel warm again once they were back in the yard. William and Conker are given a hunter clip, where only the hair on their legs and a 'saddle patch' is left for warmth and protection. Basil has a blanket clip, in which the hair on his back and hindquarters is left on, as well as the hair on his legs. As he is the youngest he is usually turned out in the field for longer than the others, and this type of clip helps keep him warm.

Once clipped, the horses obviously need to wear rugs in the stable to keep them warm. Each horse wears a summer sheet (a lightweight cotton rug) next to his skin (this is washed every two weeks), on top of which he has between one and four blankets depending on how cold it is – Mary buys her blankets very cheaply from the local Oxfam shop. On top of all this he will wear a quilted rug fastened by cross-over surcingles (two straps which cross under the horse's tummy, a secure and comfortable way of keeping a rug in place).

When the horses are taken out on exercise their hindquarters are kept warm by putting a light woollen day rug on over their saddles; during the cold winter months this also means the girls have something nice and warm to sit on! In fact purpose-made exercise rugs are available, designed to be worn under the saddle, but this would mean extra expense.

Out on a ride the 'three boys' are expected to walk out energetically and to behave. Says Mary, 'We ride the horses up to a contact, but do not expect them to be on the bit as we often use a hack as a reward and a relaxing break after a schooling session.'

Basil, Conker and William are all turned out for at least an hour every day to stretch their legs and enjoy some fresh air, freedom and grass.

CLIPPING

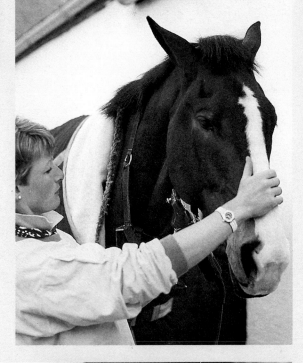

● William's head is carefully clipped. Small dog clippers are used to remove the whiskers.

● A hunter clip involves leaving the hair on the legs and just a small area on the back to protect the saddle area

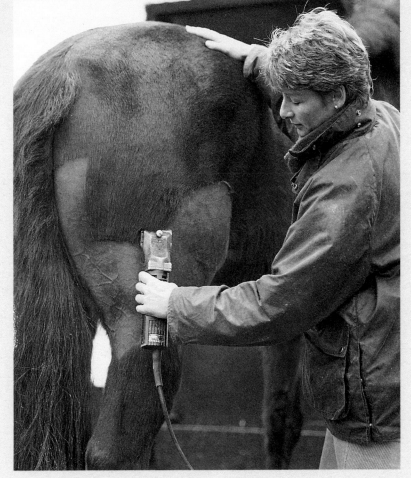

They wear a waterproof New Zealand rug with one or two under-rugs if it is cold, and brushing boots on their legs to minimise the risk of injury. These boots are also worn when the horses are being ridden, as they offer some support and protection against the horse knocking one leg against the other.

By their third week of fitness training the horses are asked to work a bit harder and a little trot is included out on their rides. Mary lives in very hilly countryside, and whichever direction you take from her yard involves a 600ft (182m) hill within a mile. This means that even quite short rides can be very strenuous and when it come to getting horses fit, effort is more important than distance.

'We start building up the horses' exercise by increasing the hill work and including a bit of trot work, always uphill as this avoids unnecessary concussion on the horses' front legs. The horses go on a different ride each day to help keep them interested in their work. They are all taught to ride and lead as this can save a lot of time when you are trying to get them fit, but you do need to take care,' warns Mary. It is important to practise riding and leading somewhere safe before venturing out in public. Some horses simply will not work together, and it important to find this out at home – not on the roads. The led horse should always be on the nearside of the ridden horse so that he is shielded from the traffic. He should wear a bridle and be led by the reins or from a chain and lead rope clipped to the bit rings.

All the horses have a day off each week. The night before they are given more hay than usual, but have a smaller feed; on their day of rest they are turned out before breakfast and left until lunch-time. They then come back in and have a normal lunch and tea, ready for work the next day.

Every six weeks throughout the year the horses are wormed. Mary varies the wormers she uses, but considers Eqvalan the best; however, it is also expensive, so she uses this every third worming, and in between uses Strongid P or Panacur. The worming round is done just before the horses are given their evening hay – if they have got any bits of food or hay in their mouths it is easy for them to spit the wormer out along with the mouthful. Each horse's head is held and the wormer is squirted out of a syringe into the back of his mouth; his head is then held up in the air until he swallows the mixture. He is allowed his hay immediately after, to take the taste away.

KING BASIL

Normally Mary would not start to school any of the horses until they had done three or four weeks' work, but as Basil had had a shorter holiday than usual over Christmas and was still relatively fit, schooling began in the second week.

'Because Basil is young and inexperienced he finds it hard to work on an even, soft contact with the bit,' explains Mary. 'His schooling sessions begin simply by loosening him up – he is worked for some time in a longer, rounder outline in trot, and canter, and this work is done on each rein and without too much interference from me as a rider.

'Once he is settled, the aim of the lesson is that he keeps a constant contact with the bit,

● (opposite above) *In the stable the horses wear a cotton sheet, a number of blankets and a quilted rug*

● (opposite below) *Once the horses are clipped waterproof New Zealand rugs protect them from the elements. Basil and Cuthbert enjoying their daily turnout*

● *Training horses to ride and lead can save a lot of time in a busy yard – in this case William and Conker*

and I insist on this: if he comes above the bit by raising his head, I gently widen and lower my hands to ask him to bring his head down. If he goes behind the bit by tucking his head in and becoming overbent, I send him forwards again with my legs and ask him to raise his head by lifting my hands.

'It is very easy to think that a horse knows what you want him to do, but a young horse is very ignorant. The only way he can learn what you want is if you correct him when he is wrong, and reward him when he is right.'

Mary works Basil on a circle at trot; it is easier for a horse to keep a steady contact when he is on a circle. Only when he is going well does Mary ask him to do a few changes of direction, figures of eight and serpentines, while trying to keep the

● (top) **Early flatwork:** *Mary encourages Basil to work in a low, rounded outline before gradually asking him to lift up in front and engage his hindquarters*

● (middle) **Early jumping:** *Basil shows his greenness by spooking at the crossbar on the approach amd jumping overcautiously*

● (bottom) **Gridwork:** *Mary concentrates on keeping Basil going forwards and in a straight line through the grids*

same even contact throughout these exercises.

Basil's first flatwork session was followed the next day by some show-jump schooling. Whichever horse Mary is riding, she always starts a showjumping session by trotting him over a small cross-pole with a placing pole in front of it – a pole on the ground about 9ft (2.7m) away from the base of the fence which helps bring the horse to the correct take-off spot so that he can tackle the fence comfortably. With William and Conker the placing pole would be put a little nearer to the jump to bring them in a bit deeper so that they really have to be quick with their front legs and 'bascule' over the fence. As Basil is still learning, the placing pole remains at 9ft (2.7m) so that he is not put under too much pressure. Trotting into the

fence helps to teach Basil to approach the jump steadily and without getting over-excited. When he lands over the fence he must continue forward calmly and in a straight line.

This exercise is repeated until Basil is settled and concentrating, and then the cross-pole is made into an upright fence, still approached in trot. If all is going well, the fence is gradually made higher until Basil is jumping about 3ft 9in (1.2m) from trot. A horse can jump surprisingly high from trot, and this exercise encourages him to jump neatly and to really push off the ground, lift his shoulders and fold his front legs.

As part of the preparation for his first indoor show of 1992, Mary went on and worked Basil over single fences at canter, linking them u p to make a small course. Mary then took Basil to Woodspring Equestrian Centre, near Bristol, where there were showjumping classes held in the spacious indoor arena. Woodspring is a one-and-threequarter-hour drive, and it is one of the times that Mary wishes she did not live in deepest Devon. The atmosphere at any show tends to distract even the calmest of horses, so Mary rode Basil quietly around the outdoor practice arena to help settle him down and let him take in the excitement and the strange surroundings. After some trot and canter work, she trotted him over a cross-pole. At affiliated competitions you are not allowed to use a placing pole as Mary does at home.

'I'm not very brave about trotting to fences without a placing pole,' says Mary, 'so at a competition I would only ask a young horse to trot over a cross-pole, and then he is cantered to an upright.' This fence is gradually put up to the height he will be asked to jump in the competition, which in this case was about 3ft 3in (1m). Mary would then jump the horse over the other practice fence, which is always a spread fence, gradually increasing the height and width. Just before he is due into the ring, Mary would pop him over the upright fence, which she will have raised to a few inches higher than the jumps in the ring; this is so that the competition fences will feel easier to the horse and give him confidence. In fact at one-day events you are not allowed to do this – the practice fence can be no higher than the biggest fence in the class you are competing in.

Once in the ring, things on this occasion did not go quite to plan. The Christmas trees and decorations were still up and Basil found these rather fascinating; in fact he was so busy looking at them that he crashed through the first fence, and this upset him for the rest of the round. So before he went back in to do his second class, Mary jumped him over the practice fences more than she would normally, to help restore his confidence, Obviously this worked well as he went back in and jumped a clear round – so he was able to go home and tell William and Conker what a good chap he had been.

As Basil became fitter, his education continued to include simple gridwork to improve his jumping. Mary always varies the jumping exercises so that the horses learn to look at the problem ahead of them and to think about how to tackle it. One exercise might be a placing pole to a small bounce combination (with the second fence slightly higher than the first one so that it is not hidden from the horse), followed by a one-stride distance to a parallel. When riding through a line of fences, Mary concentrates on staying in balance with the horse and keeping him straight: then the jumping can be left to him.

At this stage Basil was given his first experience of cross-country schooling on his own. He had been bold and fluent at the hunter trial the previous autumn and so Mary took him to a small practice course where she knew that most of the fences would be quite straightforward, and only about 2ft 6in (0.7m) high. She took him round quietly, and was pleased with his calm but keen approach. Anything that he was not too sure about she popped him over again until he was confident, making a big fuss of him all the time and telling him what a good boy he was, particularly as this was his first solo performance.

To complete this part of his education Basil visited a nearby river so he could practise jumping into, and going through water. In this respect Mary and her horses are extremely for-

● (opposite) *Basil is quietly introduced to water*

● *Early days: cross-country schooling for Basil. A strong lower leg position is essential for cross-country riding, as shown here*

FEEDING

In the past Mary always mixed up her own feeds from a variety of different ingredients such as oats, barley, sugarbeet and so on, but this year she has been offered a range of Spillers compound feeds to try.

When deciding what and how much to feed her horses, Mary considers their condition and then assesses whether they need to lose weight or to put it on. They are given three concentrate feeds a day, but are only given haynets (which have been soaked) with their morning and evening feeds. Mary then matches the type of concentrate feed each horse is given, to the amount of energy she thinks it needs, and alters the amount of hay it has according to whether it needs to lose or gain weight. She has three different sizes of haynet for this purpose: medium (3½lb), large (5lb) and extra large (7lb)!

When the horses were brought back into work on 1 January, William and Conker were quite fat, whereas Basil needed building up a bit more. Thus William and Conker started off on the same level of feed: in the morning they each had 2lb (1 scoop) Cool Mix and a handful of Provider Plus; their lunchtime feed was 3lb (1 scoop) of Horse and Pony Cubes each, and in the evening they both had another 3lb (1½ scoops) of Cool Mix and a couple of handfuls of Provider Plus. As Conker is rather a fatty he is restricted to a medium haynet morning and evening. William has two large haynets.

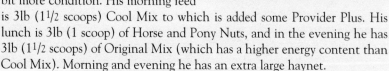

Basil was given more hay and feed than the others to help him build up a bit more condition. His morning feed is 3lb (1½ scoops) Cool Mix to which is added some Provider Plus. His lunch is 3lb (1 scoop) of Horse and Pony Nuts, and in the evening he has 3lb (1½ scoops) of Original Mix (which has a higher energy content than Cool Mix). Morning and evening he has an extra large haynet.

tunate, as they are within hacking distance of the beach and are surrounded by rivers and streams. On this occasion Mary started by letting Basil just walk down the shallow banks into the water; then she asked him to trot through and out the other side. In fact he was so confident that they finished up jumping off the top of the small banks straight into the river.

All in all, Mary was pleased with Basil's progress. Even though she had given him a great deal to think about over the past week or two, he was feeling very confident and happy about life.

KING KONG

Conker is altogether more experienced than Basil, and was therefore soon put to more demanding work, with some serious schooling sessions. Although he is more advanced in his flatwork than Basil, his trot still needs improving – he has very loose paces, and because he is quite sharp and excitable it does not take much for him to tense up and so upset his own rhythm and balance. Like Basil, he is not very good at staying on a steady contact so his early training sessions are similar to Basil's, with Mary insisting that he stays in a steady, even rhythm, and correcting him when he goes either above or behind the bit.

In his early schooling sessions, Conker's technique and attitude are always much improved by lungeing. A horse is often more relaxed and willing to be corrected when the rider is on the ground rather than on his back. Lungeing a comparatively excitable horse like Conker can mean that an unnecessary battle with his rider is avoided.

Conker is lunged with his saddle and bridle on, and brushing boots to protect his legs. As he is quite experienced, Mary puts the lunge-rein straight onto the bit-ring; with a younger horse she would use a lungeing cavesson over the top of the bridle. He is also lunged with side-reins attached from the bit to his girth: side-reins provide a constant even contact for the horses to be driven into.

The side-reins are not attached until Conker has had a few minutes to warm up and settle down on the lunge. Mary insists on complete obedience when lungeing: Conker must stand still while she walks away from him, gradually letting out the lunge rein, and only move on when given the command to walk. Once he has walked, trotted and cantered on each rein, the side-reins are attached. As Conker tends to come above the bit, the side-reins are fitted just below the saddle-flaps and are buckled up just tight enough to keep his head in the correct outline while he is standing. After a few walk strides he is then sent straight into trot as it is quite hard for a horse to walk properly with side-reins attached. Mary uses transitions from walk to trot, trot to walk, walk to canter and so on, to make Conker really work and use his hindquarters properly. The steady contact offered by the side-reins encourages him to accept the bit, and if he is still finding room to come above the bit, Mary tightens the side-reins a little more. When a horse is being worked in side-reins it is very important to make him really go forward into the contact, and not to allow him to avoid the contact by becoming overbent.

Training with the professionals

Basil and Conker enjoyed a break from their routine when Mary took them up to see Ferdi Eilberg, her dressage trainer, for two days. 'It is always helpful to have someone else watch you work the horses, as they notice faults that you do not always realise are developing,' says Mary. 'Basil was the first to come under Ferdi's watchful eye, and he asked us to work on 20-metre circles in trot and canter; I needed to encourage the horse to engage his hocks more. More activity and engagement is created by the rider using seat and legs, but initially Basil did not really understand what was being asked of him and tended to lean on the bit and feel heavy in front. In fact he had to learn to allow the extra activity created by my seat and legs to go from his hindlegs through his body so as to lift his shoulders – he can then step forward more freely with his front legs. The aim is to get his hindlegs to step further under his body so that they are carrying its full weight, and not just propelling his weight forwards, through the shoulder and "out of the front door", which means he ends up just going faster rather than working more actively.

'Conker was too full of himself to learn very much at all, and was only just settled by the end of the last lesson. When he is excitable and unsettled there is no point in trying to attempt more difficult work. We just kept him cantering in 20-metre circles on each rein until eventually he started to relax, though he was still being very

strong, and kept coming above the bit and going faster. For the next lesson we put him in a Magenis snaffle which is a bit stronger than his usual snaffle, and he did respect this a little more. However, he has to learn that after he has been allowed to loosen up – during which time he can have a little play – he must still behave when I start to ride him up together a bit more.

'It was Conker's first outing since winning Osberton three-day event the previous season, so he was bound to be excited. However, it is important not to get cross when a horse is feeling like that: you have to be cool, insistent and patient.'

On the way home from Ferdi's, Mary stopped off at Woodspring for another showjumping competition. Basil jumped two super clear rounds, and Conker found an outlet for his endless energy and also jumped clear in the bigger Newcomers class. Mary did not take him in the jump-off as he had worked hard that day with his dressage. 'It's given them something to think about while I'm away ski-ing next week,' said Mary.

KING WILLIAM

William needs to be the fittest of all the horses to compete at Badminton in May, although in the first week or two he will just quietly continue with roadwork to build him up gradually. He requires less schooling than the others as he is already quite experienced and does not forget what he has learnt in the past; it is more a case of keeping him fit, supple, obedient and inter-

● *Lungeing with side-reins gives the horse an even contact to go forward into*

● *William stops for a chat during his roadwork*

ested in his work, and there are ways of keeping an advanced horse alert. If you looked at a list of the different dressage movements and thought about the situations in which they can be used and combined, you would find yourself spoilt for choice. But so often a rider produces a schooling session made up of a few 20m circles, a bit of shoulder-in, some medium work across the diagonal and the occasional change of rein – no wonder horse and rider become bored! Before you start a schooling session you should have in mind a variety of movements and some idea of how to build them up and string them together. Use your imagination and you will both find inspiration!

Towards the end of the month Mary starts to school him quietly. The aim at the moment is just to supple him up and help him to build up his muscles correctly – schooling a horse properly will improve his 'top line', that is, the amount of muscle he has over the top of his neck and hindquarters.

Jumping exercises also help to make the horse supple; by this time William would have his first jumping session of the season. Although he is more experienced than Basil and Conker, the same approach to jumping is used for him: that is, quiet trotting over a placing pole to a cross-pole and then to an upright fence. By the end of the session the placing pole would have been moved in a bit closer to the jump; this encourages the more experienced horse to be quick off the ground and neat with his front legs.

FEBRUARY

*I*n the first week in February I had a fabulous skiing holiday in Chamonix, managing to return in one piece to start some intensive work with the horses. I was really looking forward to getting going properly, and the horses gave me the impression that they were, too; they had become a bit bored with just hacking out on the roads, and were eagerly awaiting their turn for a trip in the horsebox.

I had booked some jumping lessons with both Steve Hadley and Captain Mark Phillips, and these proved invaluable, giving the horses and me a great start by providing a correct base on which to build. I then had to try and put all I had learnt into practice when I took the horses to compete in the showjumping classes at Woodspring Equestrian Centre near Bristol, which was not so easy! I also organised a couple of sessions with Ferdi Eilberg; and not only were these a sharp reminder to us as to the discipline we needed to maintain and improve our flatwork, but they also made me realise that skiing does not keep you fit! However, I was thrilled with the way the horses shaped up during this month, and started to get very excited at the thought of the first event creeping nearer.

I had been quietly looking for another young horse to bring on with Basil, but had had no luck in finding anything I really liked. Then Janice Burrough, a friend who lives up the road, asked if I would ride her novice horse 'Borcombes Masterblend' (Mars) this spring, as she was going to have a baby and did not know what to do with her horse. I tried him out and found him to be a smashing type, with good movement and a careful jump (although rather a strange style), and so accepted the ride. Mars is an Irish-bred 16.1hh chestnut gelding – starting out on his eventing career as an eight-year-old means he has a bit of catching up to do, but I think he will relish the challenge.

During February I had to sit down and work out a provisional programme for each horse for the spring. This needed a great deal of thought and care, as I knew that my decisions were crucial to the future careers of my horses. Being over-ambitious can dishearten a horse and ruin its confidence; but equally, being cautious, although perhaps resulting in many fun, but undemanding rides, can put unwanted wear and tear on a horse's legs without it gaining any extra experience – and if you are aiming for the top, this is not what you want! The first lot of entries had to be sent during the second week of February.

Plans of quite a different nature were also made in this month: I am a member, with ten other event riders, of a charitable organisation called 'Riders for Romania', chaired by Lucinda Green. At the end of the eventing season in 1990 and 1991 we drove three horse-boxes and two lorries full of essential supplies out to some of the orphanages in Romania which desperately needed support. We had a meeting in February and it was decided to mobilise a third convoy to leave the UK on 14 October 1992. This will entail raising £50,000, and we intend to collect forty tonnes of supplies between now and then; however, with Lucinda's endless enthusiasm and energy I am sure we will reach our target!

FASTWORK FIELD

Short side: 225m
Middle: 270m
Long side: 365m
Along bottom and up long side: 560m
Long side: 200ft incline
Short side and middle: 150ft incline

In the first week of February Mary was able to steal away for a week's skiing in France. It was the horses' fifth week in work, and by this time they were well settled into their routine; besides there would still be a month in which to make the final preparations for the first event of the season after her return – as long as she returned in one piece.

FITNESS TRAINING

While skiing was keeping the edge on Mary's fitness, William, Conker and Basil continued their fitness routine with more strenuous roadwork. It was a comparatively relaxing week for them, since in Mary's absence they escaped any schooling or jumping sessions.

Because of the exceptionally hilly terrain around Mary's yard the horses can be kept fit quite easily without too much trotwork on their hacks – an active walk for an hour to an hour and a half around the steep lanes is sufficient. In their second month in work the trotwork is increased very slightly, but it never makes up a very large proportion of the ride.

In the middle of February all the horses normally start their fastwork. Fastwork is carried out in one of two ways: either galloping on two or three days a week for a certain length of time on a piece of suitable ground; or using *interval training*, which involves usually two or three timed periods of canter work with a certain period of rest in between – according to the horse's pulse and recovery rate, monitored after each session, the periods of canter work are increased in length and speed, and the rest period or slow work decreased within each session. Mary does not use interval training, but prefers to gallop the horses in a local farmer's field in the next valley; the field is large and sloping and Mary uses it like a racehorse gallop, but never at full speed!. The amount of fast work in each session is built up gradually: for their first session in February the horses just go up the middle of the field once in a strong canter; by the end of the month they are working up the middle of the field twice at $3/4$ speed. William and Conker are worked at $3/4$ speed every four days; Basil only gallops about once a week as he does other fast work, for example in his cross-country schooling sessions. And after a fastwork session the horses can't relax completely because they face a 25-minute walk home, back up 600ft! But this offers a good opportunity for them to cool down and unwind.

● *William starting the long pull up the hill in the fastwork field*

FEEDING FOR PERFORMANCE

Correct nutrition goes a long way towards helping the horse achieve optimum performance and fitness. However, first of all it is important to understand how the horse uses the nutrients he is given, and how much he needs to be fed. His total daily feed intake should equate to approximately 2½ per cent of his bodyweight. Bodyweight can be calculated by measuring his girth and height, and checking the measurements against the table below:

Height guide (approx)	Girth (cm)	Bodyweight guide (kg)	Total daily ration(kg)
	160	350	8.8
14hh	165	390	9.8
	170	420	10.5
	175	460	11.5
15hh	180	490	12.3
	185	520	13.0
16hh	190	550	13.8
	195	580	14.5
	200	610	15.3
17hh	205	640	16.0
	210	680	17.0

(Table courtesy of Spillers Horse Feeds)

For a horse or pony in work, the total daily intake is usually made up of forage and concentrates, divided into three or four daily feeds, depending on stable management routine. The amount of forage (long fibre) in the horse's diet should never fall below 25 per cent of his total feed intake, otherwise the gut will not work properly and this will result in colic or other digestive disorders.

When the horse first comes into work it is usually best to give him a ration with a higher proportion of forage to concentrate feed; then as his workload increases, these proportions will gradually alter until, when at peak fitness and in hard work, he is receiving a higher percentage of concentrate than forage. You may need to stray from this generalisation if a horse either gains or loses weight rapidly, or if his temperament is such that he cannot take a large proportion of concentrate feed without becoming too excitable. Generally speaking, the forage-to-concentrate ratio might be:

Rest/light work: 75:25
Medium work: 50:50
Hard work: 25:75

Within the concentrate ration, the energy component is the most important for the event horse – the harder his work, the higher his energy requirement. Energy is available in two forms: carbohydrate and fat. Contrary to popular belief, the event horse's protein requirement is relatively low, at 12 to 14 per cent. Many compound feeds provide much higher protein levels than this, but excess protein is simply broken down or de-aminated. The resulting nitrogen then has to be excreted so wasting valuable energy and increasing water loss in the urine.

Carbohydrates are broken down in the small intestine and used as glucose or glycogen in the muscles; this is the traditional energy source for the event horse. But as the muscles work harder, they are likely to deplete the supply of glycogen quite quickly and a second source of energy may be required. Fat, as fatty acids, is this reserve fuel source. Fat releases 2.25 times more energy than the same amount of carbohydrate, and is readily digested in the small intestine, thus increasing the digestible energy provided by the feed. Adding fat to the diet means that the total volume of feed input can be reduced while still providing a high energy output. Since the event horse is required to perform at speed across country but with control and flexibility in the dressage and showjumping, he will be using both glycogen and fatty acids as energy suppliers.

The ideal ration for the event horse should include a sensible level of protein (under 14 per cent), a higher-than-average level of fat (up to 8 per cent), a large percentage of carbohydrate, and a low percentage of fibre. (The 25 per cent minimum requirement should come from forage.) High quality grains and traditional feeds supply most of these requirements, but they can vary in quality from batch to batch. Also, cereal diets tend to be low in oil and so extra fat may have to be added to the feed; this can be accomplished quite easily by adding vegetable oil to the feed

Compounded and extruded feeds have the advantage of being of a consistent quality; high pressure cooking, or 'extruding', feed increases its digestibility by up to 20 per cent over non-cooked feeds. It is also easier for the manufacturers to include higher levels of fat and minerals in extruded feeds than in cereal or complete feeds.

In summary, the horse's total daily intake should remain the same throughout training, though the harder he is worked, the greater the concentrate-to-forage ratio should be; equally, as his work increases, the carbohydrate and fat content of his feed should be increased.

FEEDING As the horses' work increases, Mary adjusts the type of feed they receive in order to meet their greater energy requirements. At the beginning of February in this particular year she started to replace most of the Cool Mix with the higher energy Original Mix. 'Conker does not have too much high energy feed as he is such a hothead,' says Mary, 'but Basil still needs to be stronger and has a higher energy requirement, so he gets the largest proportion of his feed as Original Mix.' This year however, having just got used to the new feeding régime, Mary was informed that the mixes she had been using were not guaranteed to pass a dope test; to be on the safe side, Mary changed the horses' diet so they were receiving the guaranteed feeds within the Spillers range. A nutritionist advised that the horses should have approximately 70 per cent Competition Cubes and 30 per cent Breeding Mix. 'Competition cubes can be fed as a complete diet, although humans always tend to think that horses would prefer more variety in their feed!' says Mary. Basil is also given stud cubes, as these are good for putting on weight.

Although compound feeds already have salt included in them, once the horses start their fast work Mary adds a teaspoon of extra salt to their evening feed. The horses are now on a middle energy-range diet – the energy input can be increased by changing to Competition Mix, for example, if this becomes necessary. Says Mary, 'I prefer to underestimate the energy requirement until the horses start competing and you know how they are going to react. I hate it when horses go over-excited at an event because of over-feeding.' William and Conker are now on about 9lb (4kg) of hard feed a day, while Basil is munching through about 11lb (5kg). This is fed in the 70:30 ratio that the nutritionist suggested, with Basil receiving an extra 2lb (0.9kg) of stud cubes.

The last three weeks of February were used to squeeze in as much instruction as possible from Stephen Hadley, Captain Mark Phillips and Ferdi Eilberg, as Mary felt this would give her a good base on which to build at home. It is always best to correct any mistakes in the horse or rider as early as possible – there is no point in putting a lot of work into the horses at home if things are going wrong, and you do not know where, or how to improve the situation.

KING BASIL
Training with Stephen Hadley

Basil was to experience his first 'serious' showjump training when he was taken, with William and Conker, to work for two days with Stephen Hadley in Warwickshire; Steve had not seen Basil in action before, and liked him very much. He began Basil's schooling session by asking him to canter to single fences, gradually building this up until he was tackling a small course which included a combination and a related distance. Basil is naturally very careful, and actually needs to be a bit stronger and more positive into his fences – Steve likes to see horses approaching a fence on a strong stride, with each stride increasing in impulsion. He explains it as being like bouncing a rubber ball: if you contain the height that the ball is allowed to bounce to, the power in the bounce is increased.

He advised Mary to ride Basil forwards quite strongly into his fences. Basil's actual technique over a fence is very good, but because he is younger and not as strong as the others, he needs more help from his rider in creating sufficient impulsion to really attack his fences. Steve thought that using this technique when schooling him at home as well as at competitions should help him to tackle his fences far more easily.

Cross-country

Once home from his travels, Basil's next challenge was a team chase, to be held locally at the weekend. To prepare for this, Mary took him water-schooling in the river a few days beforehand to make sure he would tackle any water obstacles at the competition; she also schooled around a small local cross-country course.

Stephen Hadley's advice was put into practice at Woodspring Equestrian Centre the following day when Basil produced a double clear in the Discovery class. However, Mary felt that Basil was still quite tired from his trip to Warwickshire during the week so she did not enter him in any other classes. This also meant he had a better chance of finding enough ener-

gy for his team chase the following day.

The team chase did Basil the world of good. It was a small course, about 3ft (0.9m), and an ideal confidence giver. Having schooled around fences on his own at home, on this occasion Basil had to cope with tackling a set course of fences at a good pace, and in the company of other horses. 'Annie was riding King Cuthbert, an ex-eventer of mine which Gill Robinson gave to Annie when I retired him from advanced eventing. Basil and I tucked in behind Annie and Cuthbert for the first few fences, but Basil was immediately very confident so I moved him up to the front so that he did not always have a lead – by the end of the course he was almost *too* strong and keen! He had obviously gained a lot of confidence, and would not need to repeat this exercise!' said Mary.

Training for his first event

In the middle of February Basil began his fast work training along with the other horses, in preparation for his first BHS event which was now only a fortnight or so away – a Pre-Novice competition at Stilemans one-day event, in Surrey. In the last week of February Mary made sure that Basil was as well prepared for this chal-

● *Exploring more ditches and streams helps prepare Basil for his first BHS event*

● (opposite) *The horses usually do their fastwork every four days*

lenge as he possibly could be. She marked out a 20x40m dressage arena in the field, and some of Basil's schooling work was then carried out within the confines of the arena. 'I do run through parts of the dressage test before an event,' says Mary. 'Some people do not like to do this as they think it teaches the horse to anticipate the next movement. However, if my horses start to do this they are schooled through it so they learn that, even when they think they know what's coming next, they must wait for an instruction from me.'

When an inexperienced horse such as Basil first enters the 'practice' arena, Mary will let him walk around and get used to the area in which he has to work. She makes sure he goes well into the corners, and then works him in trot and canter, making many turns and changes of direction. She then pieces together some of the movements from the test to be performed at the competition, and practises these. The aim of this sort of session is to teach the horse to keep his balance when working in the smaller confines of a dressage arena.

Some of Basil's hacks were also used to further his education and prepare him for his first event, and took in as many ditches and streams as possible. This sort of thing helps to teach a horse that he must be ready to tackle anything that his rider asks, even when just out on a ride.

For Basil the weekend before Stilemans entailed another trip to Woodspring, and a chance for him to become even more adept at tackling courses of showjumps. He obliged by showing a real improvement, and completed the Pathfinder and then the Newcomers class which was higher than any competition courses he had tackled before. This was most encouraging, and left Mary looking forward to March and the start of the eventing season.

ENTRIES AND BALLOTING

The ever-increasing popularity of horse trials has meant that many events are now oversubscribed. To cope with this problem a somewhat complicated system of balloting is used.

The eventing season is split into ten 'ballot periods'. Every event in the Horse Trials Group *Omnibus Schedule* has an opening and closing date for entries, and also a ballot date which is usually about four weeks before the competition itself; you must therefore decide about a month in advance which competitions you wish to attend, and send your entry to arrive by 9am on the ballot date. You need to take into account which events are most likely to be oversubscribed and ballot you out – an eventuality which will, of course, upset your competition programme. Competitors do have one official concession: except for Pre-Novice and all three-day events, each horse is allowed one 'Special Entry' sticker for each ballot period – this is a self-adhesive label bearing the horse's name and registration number and the number of the ballot period, and when attached to an entry form it gives that horse's entry priority over normal entries. This ensures that every competitor is able to run a horse in an event of his choice within each ballot period.

To prevent riders trying to overcome the effect of being balloted out by entering more events than they intend to compete in, a withdrawals system was introduced. If a horse is withdrawn before the closing, or ballot date, your entry fee will be refunded. There is then a final withdrawals date three days before the actual event and you can withdraw up until this date, for any reason, but you will forfeit your entry fee. If you are forced to withdraw during the last three days through injury to horse or rider, a veterinary or medical certificate must be sent to the Director of Horse Trials. If it appears that you simply did not bother to turn up then you are liable to be fined or suspended. Remember – once you have entered an event it is assumed that you intend to take part.

Some riders do still enter more events than they would normally wish to ride in, knowing that they may get balloted out of some. However, if you are lucky and not balloted out of any (as was the case with Conker and Basil in the early part of the season) you are then faced with the dilemma of perhaps having too much planned for your horse, and having to withdraw from the events you prefer not to run in. Alternatively, a competitor can go to the event and withdraw after the dressage or showjumping. However, in some cases where a horse has been entered for too many events in one period it may turn out that through some misfortune it misses a run, in which case the competitor is then only too glad that the horse is already entered for another event soon after.

KING KONG
Training with Steve Hadley

Conker jumped very well when he went with Basil and William to Stephen Hadley's in the second week of February. He had already been to a showjumping competition, and besides, he has a naturally good technique over a fence which he enjoyed showing off! In the second lesson he jumped even better, having had a chance to settle into his new surroundings and really loosen up after his lesson the day before. Conker's main problem is that he gets over-excited when jumping – he must learn to mind his manners between fences rather than worry too much about improving the way he actually gets over them.

When Conker gets excited and starts to mess around on the approach to a fence, Steve advises Mary to turn him onto a circle and to keep cantering in a circle until he settles down and becomes soft and round. Only then is he allowed to approach the fence again.

Training with Ferdi Eilberg

After Mary had jumped both William and Conker at Steve's, she drove straight to Ferdi Eilberg's home in Worcestershire and both horses were given some dressage work that afternoon. Having had the edge taken off him by a morning's jumping, on this occasion Conker was very good. Mary gave him a chance to loosen up and settle down in the wonderful outdoor arena, and then concentrated on improving his work on the left rein. Conker has always been stiff on the left rein, and this is a sign that he is not driving forwards equally with both hindlegs; as a result he finds it hard to keep his balance on the left rein, and is therefore heavy in Mary's hand.

'When a horse is heavy in your left hand it does not always mean that he is stiff in the left rein – it could be that he is refusing to accept the right rein,' explains Mary. Ferdi told Mary that she must insist on Conker keeping a correct left bend even when he was working in a straight line. As Conker is better balanced in canter than in trot, he suggested she use canter to improve his bend to the left – if the horse can balance himself easily he is more likely to listen and take an equal contact since he will not be fighting to keep his balance as well as trying to bend properly. Improving the left bend in canter would in turn improve his trot work.

To avoid a constant fight with Conker on the left rein, Ferdi advised Mary to ask for a counter bend on the *right* rein (working in counter bend means that the horse is bent away from the direction in which he is going). When cantering on the right rein, Conker tends to bend too much to the right because that is the rein he finds easiest, so Mary made him bend to the left, the opposite bend to the direction he was going; this work progressed to counter canter; counter canter on the right rein means ask-

● *Conker has a good natural technique but needs to learn how to contain his enthusiasm*

41

ing the horse to canter to the right *but* with the left leg leading, and with his body bent to the left; on a circle the horse would therefore be bent to the outside and cantering with the outside leg leading. To encourage Conker to soften the left rein and take up a stronger contact on the right rein, Ferdi made Mary work in counter canter on the left rein but with a counter bend: this meant cantering on the left rein with the right leg leading, but then asking Conker to bend to the *left*. Through this work Conker gradually found it easier to take up an even contact on both reins, and this improvement stayed with him when he returned to trot work.

The following morning, however, after a good night's sleep, Conker was as naughty and excitable as ever, and Ferdi and Mary had to revert to their previous tactics of asking him just to canter round and round in 20-metre circles. This time it did not seem to settle him so Ferdi suggested some medium and extended work to give him an outlet for his endless energy. Such a challenge did help him to settle, and so the lesson progressed to work on 10-metre circles, shoulder-in and half-pass. Conker had not done much work in half-pass, and so the lesson was spent helping him to understand what was required of him in this more advanced movement. In half-pass the horse must move forwards and sideways across the arena, bent in the direction in which he is going; it is performed in either trot or canter, and should give the impression that the horse is almost floating sideways across the arena. Conker tends to shorten his stride and is then unable to produce the 'floating' effect which is required. Ferdi told Mary not to worry too much about the correct position of Conker's hindquarters at first, but to concentrate on encouraging him to keep a clear bend in the direction he was going in, while pulling forwards and sideways enough with his shoulder to allow him to step clearly through during each stride. Once this was achieved Mary could then quietly use her outside leg to ask him to bring his quarters in line.

On returning home from this educational trip, Conker was hacked out quietly the next day to keep him relaxed and to give him time to let all he had learnt sink in. At the weekend another trip to Woodspring was planned: here Conker produced a double clear in the Newcomers class to finish third. In the Grade C he produced a lovely clear round – he was very sharp and careful, and basculing well over the fences. However, in the jump-off Mary cut a

corner to save time, and this was all it took to get Conker excited again – on the approach to the last fence he started to rush and throw his head around, so Mary followed Stephen Hadley's advice and turned him away in a circle before allowing him to approach the fence again. Although this cost her a place in that particular class, Mary hoped that reminding Conker of how he *should* behave in the ring would persuade him to behave properly in future competitions.

Training with Captain Mark Phillips

More intensive training had been arranged for Conker the following week, this time with Captain Mark Phillips. As usual, Conker was very full of himself, and the Captain advised Mary to spend as much time as it took to develop a good canter before she even thought about jumping a fence. The Captain likes horses to be very light in front when jumping, their hocks well engaged and underneath the body, the horse almost above the bit; only then can the front end remain light and manoeuvrable. Conker was cantered on 10-metre circles to keep him supple and light in the hand.

Jumping was introduced to the lesson by asking Conker to trot to a fence with a placing pole in front; progressively he was made to jump quite high from trot. The Captain concentrates on the rider's position as much as on the horse's performance: Mary tends to start tipping her body forwards before the horse has actually taken off over the fence, and each time she did this she was corrected. He told her to keep Conker going forwards in balance and in a strong rhythm, and particularly to ride on through the corners and not be tempted, as many riders are, to check the horse on a corner in order to try and see a good stride. It is the Captain's belief that if you check a horse on the way to a fence you flatten the canter, and then you have to re-create more impulsion in order for the horse to jump the fence successfully. If you *do* have to steady the horse, it should be with a give-and-take action so that the canter keeps its spring. So when Conker was tempted to throw his head around and pull, the Captain told Mary to ride him *on* through this and not to pull back at him; by riding him forwards the canter is not spoilt, and the fence itself will in effect back the horse off as he realises it is approaching rather more quickly than he expected.

THE AIMS OF SCHOOLING ON THE FLAT

'The object of dressage is to develop the ability and obedience of the horse. As a result the horse should be calm, willing and confident throughout his work, however difficult it is, and have such a perfect understanding with his rider that he gives the impression of doing what is required of his own accord.

'When I am schooling, one of my aims is to get my horse to remain steadily "on the bit" with his neck arched so that his poll is the highest point. How high the neck is raised depends on the horse's level of training – Basil's head carriage would therefore be much lower than William's. I work towards my horse taking a light, soft, level contact with no resistance, his nose held vertically, or slightly in front of the vertical. He should be completely obedient, responding to any slight aid I give, and doing so confidently and happily. His paces should be free, regular and supple.

'The end result should be that the hindquarters become more and more engaged and active, allowing the forehand to be light so that the horse learns to carry himself by taking the majority of his weight on the hindquarters; he must learn that he cannot use the rider's hand to support his forehand.'

THE PACES

'**The halt**: the horse should remain still and straight, and should be standing square. I aim for my horse to come into halt keeping light in my hand and with his hocks active and engaged. He should remain attentive throughout the halt so he is ready to move off at my slightest aid. To achieve this you must not forget to keep using your legs so as to push the horse forwards into halt, and then to keep your legs on his side even when he is immobile so he remains attentive to you and will feel your next leg aid instantly.

'**The walk**: This should be a four-time marching pace. Event horses have to be able to do the following variations in walk:
Medium walk – a free, regular walk where the horse remains on the bit and walks energetically but calmly.
Extended walk – the rider allows the horse to stretch out his head and neck as much as possible, while still keeping a contact. The horse should lengthen his stride and cover as much ground as possible – he is expected to overtrack *ie* the hind feet come forwards and touch the ground in front of the front hoofprints.

'**The trot**: This is a two-time pace when the horse moves on opposite diagonals. I work towards the horse taking long regular steps, the elasticity and rhythm of his stride enhanced by having a supple back and well engaged hindquarters. The

event horse has to be able to show variations in trot, too:
Working trot – the "normal" trot, in which the horse should remain on the bit, show balance, and have active hocks producing plenty of impulsion.
Medium trot – a pace between working and extended trot. The horse should lower his head and neck slightly, and from the impulsion created by the hindquarters, move forward with free and fairly extended steps.
Extended trot – the horse lengthens his steps and his whole frame as much as possible, keeping on the bit and gaining ground by striding forwards with his hocks engaged. The movement should look powerful, balanced and unconstrained.

● *Teaching the horse to maintain a light, level contact is one of the main aims of flatwork schooling*

'**The canter**: This is a three-time pace, in which the horse should show lightness and energy, and have free supple shoulders. As in trot, the event horse must show working, medium and extended canter.

'When schooling my horses at home I insist that they stay consistently straight on straight lines, and bend accordingly on curved lines. I work on getting immediate reactions from my aids so that the transitions to different paces are quick and smooth, but not abrupt. I try to be very strict with myself in correcting any mistake the horse makes, and rewarding him with a pat or with my voice when he goes well. This is so that he understands clearly the difference between right and wrong.'

The following day Conker was quite settled and jumping very well. One of his particular problems is that he finds it hard to approach a fence and jump from a long stride, and so Mary was made to work on opening him up a bit so that the length of his stride increased.

The Captain thought a great deal of Conker; as Mary outlined the schedule of events proposed for the horse, he reminded her that good horses are very hard to find – when you do find one it is your responsibility to look after it and save it for the competitions that really count, rather than risk running it at events which are not a forward step in its education. This comment arose because Mary was planning to do Windsor three-day event with Conker, and Windsor is a 2*CCI, in other words the same level as Osberton which Conker had won the previous season. The going at Windsor can be very hard, however, and this can obviously damage horses. Evidently the Captain's message was this: 'If the going isn't good, don't risk a good horse at an event you already know he is more than capable of doing.'

More training with Ferdi

Dressage is now a highly influential part of eventing, and a good dressage mark is essential to be in contention at any level of competition these days. It is a strong point in all of Mary's horses, but this is only because she works hard with them and is prepared to listen to the advice of other people. For the last week in February she had planned another trip to Ferdi Eilberg. In the stable Conker appeared to be very relaxed and peaceful, but all this changed as soon as he was asked to work in the outdoor arena – once again he became all too skittish and easily distracted. So it was back to simple exercises to try to settle him, cantering in a figure-of-eight with a simple transition through trot in the middle; but even in this Conker was determined to show that he knew best, and kept anticipating the transition to trot. Darkness had fallen before Conker finally decided that he would allow Mary to tell him what to do.

'It's very frustrating when you have the opportunity to learn from a top class trainer, and all you are able to do is figures-of-eight!' laughed Mary good naturedly.

Nevertheless things did begin to improve the next morning. 'Conker was much more settled,' said Mary. 'He was probably more submissive having got to the bottom of his naughtiness the night before.' Once he had loosened up, Ferdi suggested that Mary introduce frequent transitions into her work, being particularly careful to insist that Conker waited for the aids and did not anticipate them. 'Transitions also help the horse warm himself through his whole body,' explained Ferdi, 'as he has to keep bringing himself back and up together, and then open up and go forward again. Transitions can be used between different paces or within the same pace, and they are the most important work for any horse.

'A dressage test is full of transitions, so if your horse will stay soft and round through these, then you have half the test organised already,' he said.

Ferdi normally starts a session with the horse performing simple transitions such as from trot to walk and back to trot again; he will then move on to the more demanding ones, where the horse must lower his quarters and carry more weight behind, such as from canter to walk. He soon had Mary and Conker working in counter canter. 'Conker finds everything very easy, and he always uses this ability to try and do his own thing. His training needs to concentrate on obedience in the basic movements as he likes to be more fancy than he needs to be!' said Ferdi with a wry laugh, as Conker executed a superb flying change instead of staying in counter canter. So Mary worked on going from counter canter to inside canter (normal canter) and back to counter canter. Once Conker is in counter canter he holds it very well, but the vulnerable moment is in the first few strides when he is likely to slip in a flying change. 'He needs to be reminded of the compulsory movements all the time,' continued Ferdi. 'If it was left to him he would produce his own freestyle test on every occasion!'

It does not take much to distract Conker, and when he decides to look at something or goes a little tense, he loses his balance, and this is when he throws in another movement that was not asked for. Mary has to be very patient with him – if something has to be repeated fifty times before Conker obeys what he has been asked to do, then so be it. He is also a very powerful, compact horse and he tends to overpower himself – the drive from his hindquarters is almost too much for his front end to cope with, and when this happens he falls onto his forehand and needs too much support from Mary's hand.

Mary then moved on to do some work in half-pass. Half-pass in trot is more difficult to estab-

44

lish than in canter, as it is harder to keep an even rhythm; Ferdi told Mary to make sure she had established the correct bend before she asked for half-pass. He suggested she turn a small circle first and then go from shoulder-in to half-pass. Ferdi explained that in half-pass the rider must keep a firm contact on the outside rein as the horse pulls away from this rein to achieve the sideways movement. In fact Conker produced some very pleasing work, so he was then allowed to rest: the session was over.

Ferdi Eilberg summed up Conker perfectly when he said: 'Discipline is what Conker finds difficult, not the actual movements. He is an exceptionally talented horse, but he does not always use his talent in the most honourable way!'

KING WILLIAM
Training with Steve Hadley

William was a bit rusty for his first jump training with Steve Hadley; he was also a little on edge, which made him tense over his fences. Stephen Hadley does not do too much work over grids because, as he points out, you never jump a grid in a competition. Mary and Steve therefore worked William in canter over medium-sized fences, about 3ft 6in to 3ft 9in; cantering to a single fence helped William to relax and loosen up. William's tendency is to draw his head and neck up and back, and then to launch himself at the fence. Tension also causes him to clamp up his hindlegs with the result that he drags them through the fence, instead of lifting them up to clear it.

Mary encouraged him to canter in a very round outline with his neck bent more than usual and his whole body bent around her inside leg. This made him really soft and round through his back and neck, and helped him to lift his shoulders and put some elevation into the canter.

The next day he was jumping much more freely and easily and so he was asked to jump a few fences together, including a combination and a related distance. However, in spite of being more relaxed, his tendency to jump to the left was still there. Steve made Mary approach the fences at a slight angle from left to right so that his tendency to jump to the left actually straightened him up over the fence. He also put a pole diagonally across the fence, with one end on the top of the left upright and the other on the ground; this also encouraged William to jump in the middle of the fence. Horses often jump to one side or the other to make more room for themselves as they approach the fence – it means they can avoid having to really snap up their front legs and use themselves properly; it also means they are less likely to clear a fence, particularly one of any width. The more relaxed William became the less he tried to do this.

As had been the case with Conker, jumping William in the morning meant that he was relaxed and settled when he arrived at Ferdi Eilberg's for his lesson that afternoon.

Training with Ferdi Eilberg

Ferdi knew William already, and assessed him thus: 'William is quite an experienced horse, and experienced horses do not forget the dressage movements that they have been taught – after a long break it is often just a question of getting the horse's general way of going back up to scratch. This means working on obedience, engagement, suppleness and willingness to go forwards.'

One problem associated with bringing a horse back into work after a long break is that it will very often revert to the bad habits it had as a youngster. William used to be very stiff on the right rein and would take an extremely strong hold of it, refusing to bend or soften at all to the right. During the lesson it was evident that William was slightly stiff to the right again. Ferdi therefore insisted that when riding on the right rein, Mary kept William slightly bent to the right the whole time, even when he was not on a circle or turn. They went on to working on transitions to improve his engagement and obedience. The next day his work progressed to shoulder-in and half-pass – and as Ferdi had predicted, William performed this work well straightaway.

'William is a very impetuous horse, always wanting to rush forwards,' explained Ferdi, 'and with a strong, keen horse it is easy to keep steadying with the hand but *forgetting to use your legs*; this means the horse slows down, but falls on to his forehand. You *must* keep using your legs so that the horse steps under and begins to carry himself.'

To Woodspring Equestrian Centre

William joined Conker the following day for a quiet hack, and then he too made the trip to Woodspring to put into practice all he had learnt. This was William's first competition

---

CUTS AND WOUNDS

Superficial wounds such as cuts and abrasions are treated by trimming away the hair around the cut and cleaning with a surgical scrub. A warm Animalintex poultice is applied, with a bandage to hold it in place. The next morning it is cleaned again and sprayed with antiseptic spray which helps seal the wound against dirt. If the cut is still weepy later in the day another poultice will be applied; after that, Dermobion cream is used, as it helps to prevent proud flesh forming and stimulates the healing process.

● *Steve Hadley's advice pays off as William produces a double clear at Woodspring*

since Punchestown and he was a little tense and excitable when warming up. His tendency to jump to the left returned, so Mary, remembering Steve's advice, approached each fence at a slight angle from left to right so that William was obliged to jump straight when he actually reached the fence. He produced a double clear in the Newcomers to finish 5th; but in the next class, the Grade C, his enthusiasm overcame him – he started to bowl on into his fences and had one down.

Training with Captain Mark Phillips

Towards the end of February William started his fast work; he also made the trip to Captain Mark Phillips for more work on his showjumping. It was Mary's first lesson on William with the Captain, and to add to the pressure there was also a TV camera crew on site, taking shots of Mary for future use. William found all this a bit distracting, and the lesson did not get off to a good start; when a rider and trainer team up for the first time it takes a while for each to get to know what the other expects, and also what best suits the horse. To start with the Captain was asking Mary to approach the fences in a

certain way, but she could not quite see what he meant – each became increasingly confused until Mary suggested that she just jumped the fence in her normal style and the Captain could then correct what he saw. This she did and as it turned out, produced exactly the sort of approach and jump that he had been looking for – which certainly shows that teaching is a two-way communication.

The next day, without the camera crew, things went much more smoothly. They worked first on William's canter and transitions, the Captain stressing how important it was that the horse stayed soft in the canter, and also in the transition down to walk. To avoid tension and to stop the horse leaning on the hand, he suggested the rider should always be thinking 'Balance and carry yourself, steady and *then* soften.'

They started jump schooling by trotting to a cross-pole with a placing pole in front, and the Captain had to remind Mary not to tip forwards as she went over the placing pole, as this will unbalance the horse. He expected the trot to be energetic, and explained that the more energy there is in the trot, the sharper the horse will be over the fence and the less the rider will feel he has to help the horse.

William still had his tendency to jump to the left, but the Captain observed that this only happened when he became tense going into a fence. He also continued to bring his head and neck up and back as he approached, but the Captain advised Mary to ignore this and to do no more than stay soft with her hands; when she did so, William jumped straight and smoothly. Soft hands means that he does not become tight in his back and neck, and this enables him to produce a straight jump.

When riding a corner to a fence the Captain reminded Mary not to restrict William's forward movement by holding onto the inside rein. 'You should turn the horse using your outside leg and outside hand – and you can even bring your outside hand across over the wither a little to keep the outside shoulder in, which will help the horse to turn smoothly. You should be able almost to give the inside rein away so that the horse feels no restriction or interruption to his forward movement.'

When Mary needed to lengthen William's stride into a fence the Captain observed that 'your first reaction is to drive forwards with your *shoulders* rather than with your heels. Sit up and *kick* the horse forwards to make him lengthen his stride and move up to the fence.'

'When you ride a horse every day,' said the Captain, 'it is easy to get preconceived ideas about what the horse will or won't do, and your anticipation of these problems shows in the way you ride the horse – and of course this can aggravate the problem. When someone new looks at the horse, they have no idea about his capabilities or problems and they can only see what is actually happening then and there.'

The Captain summarised the correct approach to jumping with three questions:

- Did I keep the horse going forwards?
- Did I keep the horse balanced?
- Did I wait for the fence to come to me, rather than looking for a stride?

'Whenever I jump a horse I ask myself those three things, and hope that the answer is always yes,' he said.

More training with Ferdi

At the end of February William went with Conker for a couple of days to Ferdi Eilberg, to concentrate on the all-important dressage training.

As Mary quietly warmed up in the outdoor

● *William was more interested in the resident camera crew than in Mark Phillips' advice!*

school, Ferdi recollected that at first the horse had been very tall and gangly, and did not really know how to hold himself together or what to do with his hindquarters. 'Now William has become a bit of a star,' said Ferdi. 'I will never forget him storming round Punchestown with such open confidence, and then the look on his face when he and Mary parted company in the water.'

Mary had warmed up William by quietly trotting and cantering large circles, staying up off the saddle as much as possible to encourage him to be relaxed and free through his back. Ferdi then worked on William's transitions to help settle his hindquarters. He reminded Mary to keep the right bend as William prefers to bend left.

'Whatever Nature has given the horse, it will always stay with him, so you have to keep reminding him to do what you require,' said Ferdi.

In canter they worked on transitions within the pace, creating energy by sending William strongly forwards, and then containing that energy by collecting him up – this exercise puts more life into the canter as all the impulsion generated in the strong forward canter is then contained in the slower collected canter.

'Always think of influencing the hindquarters first,' said Ferdi, 'before you try to influence the horse with your hands.' When working from extended into collected canter William tended to bend out to the left and would not hold the right bend; to get over this problem, Ferdi told Mary to turn him in a 10-metre circle as soon as she brought him back to collected canter. They then worked in trot, keeping a very pronounced bend to the right. As Ferdi pointed out, William was quite capable of doing whatever was asked of him, but he needed to keep practising it so that it became easier for him. 'When he is excited or tense that natural deficiency will always come to the fore,' said Ferdi. 'However, day-to-day work will keep any horse's deficiencies at an acceptable level.'

Ferdi explained that in Germany there are two different words to describe the bend in the neck and the bend in the body: but although they are treated as two different things, they are nonetheless connected because one bend follows through into the other bend; however, the rider should be able to separate the two bends if necessary. In William's case he was able to maintain the right bend in the body but found it hard to hold the right bend through the neck.

After a rest, William returned to some trot work, with Mary using shoulder-in to activate his hindquarters. William has to be constantly reminded to contain the energy that is created, and not to burst forward with it by going faster. The main aim when training the horse in gymnastic exercises such as shoulder-in and half-pass is to keep his body in the best athletic shape possible – being athletic enables the horse to improve his dressage and his jumping.

A few minutes were then spent in trying to improve William's halt and rein-back. To make William halt squarely, Ferdi advised Mary that she must halt from an active trot: it is always easy to lose the activity of the paces when you are preparing for a downward transition, and particularly to halt. The day ended with some more work on canter-to-walk-to-canter transitions. With William, Mary had to collect the canter and keep it very round before trying the downward transition to walk, when the hindquarters need to take more of the horse's weight so that the front stays very light and is held up and back a bit. Ferdi was quick to notice that as Mary collected the canter, William felt that more effort was required, and tended to hollow his back to evade Mary's commands. So Mary has to create a rounder outline before collecting the canter, and must keep asking William to 'come back, but stay round'.

William has a very good attitude to his work, and according to Mary is a most rewarding horse to work with as he responds quickly to new instructions; his work therefore improves quite rapidly. With his first event of the 1992 season only a little while away, the last few weeks of intensive training and preparation had been very encouraging.

By the end of February the FEI had decided that all horses being considered for the Olympics in Barcelona had to be vaccinated against rhinopneumonitis. This involves two injections which are given twenty-one days apart. It was also decided that potential Olympic horses must be given an additional flu injection. Mary had hoped that these injections could wait until after Badminton when William would be having a short rest anyway, but the vets felt there was less chance of a reaction if the injections were given to a fit and well horse, rather than one that was tired and perhaps a little run down, as well he might be after a major three-day event. So William had his injections at the end of February; and since horses must not be put under any great stress for the first fortnight after a vaccination, he could look forward to two weeks of quiet, easy work.

MARCH

March brought the start of the long-awaited event season. The horses' build-up had gone smoothly, but now it was time to put them to the test – and they all fulfilled my hopes. Once they had managed to get rid of their initial freshness they settled down and showed their potential by achieving regular placings – the wins, I hoped, would come later. It was wonderful to get going again, especially as the horses seemed to share my enthusiasm.

William's competition programme was obviously the most important, and the others had to fit in around him. He was feeling as good as ever this year, which was exciting, but nonetheless, I was thankful to get the first of his three preparatory events for Badminton safely under his belt. Conker's March events confirmed that discipline was still his greatest problem, poor chap; he just can't help enjoying himself rather too much! I thoroughly enjoyed introducing Basil to his first proper competitions; watching and feeling his confidence grow from one event to the next was fascinating and rewarding, and long may it continue.

Boris, Sammy, Apple and Mars also started the season well. It was a great relief to find that Boris loved competing as much as he ever did, after his injury at Badminton last year. All the horses except Boris, Mars and Basil are being aimed at a three-day event later on in the spring, so their one-day events are very much outings to prepare them for these goals.

In March, all the pre-longlisted Olympic riders, myself included, were invited to a three-day training course at Stoneleigh with instruction available from Ferdi Eilberg and Captain Mark Phillips. Obviously this was a great help to me, since I usually go to them for training anyway. It was great fun to meet up with the other riders again, many of whom I had not seen for over six months. William and Apple were my rides for the course, and Ferdi introduced me to a fascinating 'aid' to help Apple, who has always found it difficult to lengthen his stride and produce medium and extended work: he put some weighted 'sausage' boots, each about 2lb (1kg), on his front legs. At first Apple was quite bemused, but once he went forward into trot, the weights on his legs made him really lift his shoulders and stride out. They

also seemed to hold him in a good, even rhythm and he felt a completely different horse. When we took them off, he was able to produce a greatly improved medium and extended trot. Ferdi explained that when he is buying a horse he is never too worried about the quality of its trot as there is so much you can do to improve it, as this exercise showed. He would select a horse more on the quality of its canter, as this is a harder pace to influence.

In the course of each year I have quite a few school and college students who come for one or two weeks' work experience, and March was no exception, with a different person each week. This scheme is, I think, an excellent idea, giving students the chance of an insight into the real work involved in looking after competition horses. It's a sport which looks very glamorous from the outside, but there is an awful lot of work behind the scenes.

● *Basil produces a green but careful jump at Stilemans. He rapidly
gained confidence as he progressed
around the course*

King Basil

The beginning of March saw the final preparations for Basil's first BHS one-day event:
he was entered for the Pre-Novice class at
Stilemans horse trials, held in Surrey. Mary
used this time to build on all that Basil had been
learning over the last few months and to put the
final polish on his performance.

Basil was schooled three times in the 'outdoor arena' marked out in the field; this was to
help him learn how to maintain his rhythm and
balance whilst working within the 20 x 40m
confines of a dressage arena, and without the
'support' of the rails round Mary's school. It is
also good discipline for the rider to ride to
markers, to practise making transitions in the
right place, and to be accurate with the turns
and circles that are required in a dressage test.

To keep his work varied Basil was also taken
water schooling again, something he thoroughly enjoys – by this time he was happy and confident to jump off the river bank straight into
the water. Even though the water is never very
deep in Pre-Novice and Novice events, it is
important always to help the horse keep his balance and maintain impulsion through it, otherwise he may well come unstuck as the fences
become more demanding. When jumping into
water the rider must give the horse the freedom
of his head and neck as he jumps, but then
immediately pick up the reins to steady and balance him as he splashes across. To get out there
is often a jump up a step, and the horse must be
balanced in order to tackle this successfully.

Three days before Stilemans, Basil did his
fastwork. The amount of cantering he does has
been increased, so he now goes twice up the
middle of the 'gallop field'.

With only one day left, Mary put up a course
of 'spooky' jumps at home and schooled Basil
over these in the hope that whatever he was
presented with the next day would not surprise
him too much. Basil jumped a smooth, confident round; so now it was all down to what happened on the day.

Stilemans one-day event

'The main aim of Basil's first event,' explains
Mary, 'was that he should enjoy himself.'
Knowing that he is quite a calm horse, Mary got
on him about half an hour before the start of his
dressage test. She let him just wander around
and get used to the atmosphere. 'It is very

FEEDING

On the advice of the Spillers nutritionist, the horses' feed ration was now based on a 70:30 ratio of competition cubes and breeding mix. The competition cubes provide the horse with extra energy now that the competition season has started, and the breeding mix provides the nutrients required for muscle, bone and tissue development. Mary sometimes supplements the diet with stud nuts as they are low in energy but again provide nutrients for growth and development. Once the horses are competing, she adds salt to their morning and evening feeds.

WILLIAM

William was still very full of himself, so his concentrate ration was kept quite low although he was allowed plenty of hay.

Morning feed: 2lb (1 scoop) breeding mix; a handful of Provider Plus (chaff); salt
Lunch: 3lb (1 scoop) competition cubes
Evening: 1lb ($^1/_2$ scoop) breeding mix; 1$^1/_2$lb ($^1/_2$ scoop) stub cubes; a handful of Provider Plus; salt
Haynet: Large (5lb) morning and evening

CONKER

Conker, in spite of being very lively and naughty, still tends to be a bit of a fatty so he was also on a relatively low concentrate ration; nor was he allowed too much hay! To keep his energy intake down he was fed stud nuts instead of competition cubes.

Morning: 1$^1/_2$lb ($^3/_4$ scoop) breeding mix; Provider Plus; salt
Lunch: 3lb (1 scoop) stud nuts
Evening: 1lb ($^1/_2$ scoop) breeding mix; 1$^1/_2$lb ($^1/_2$ scoop) stud nuts; Provider Plus; salt
Haynet: Medium (3$^1/_2$lb) morning and evening

BASIL

Basil was beginning to put on weight as he was enjoying the new spring grass; he was becoming quite full of himself at events, too! His diet also avoided the energy-giving competition cubes, with stud cubes as a replacement.

Morning: 2lb (1 scoop) breeding mix; Provider Plus; salt
Lunch: 3lb (1 scoop) stud nuts
Evening: 1lb ($^1/_2$ scoop) breeding mix; 3lb (1 scoop) stud nuts; Provider Plus; salt
Haynet: Large (5lb) in morning and extra large (7lb) at night

tempting to warm up by insisting that the horse does everything just so, and to pressurise him too much,' says Mary. She worked Basil in a low round outline at walk, trot and canter so that he stayed soft and relaxed; although the warm-up area was very crowded, this did not seem to worry him at all. She then asked for a bit more from him, riding him up together and working on some transitions and turns to get him listening and accurate. Basil wore brushing boots while he was warming up, but Mary's groom took these off just before he was due to go in, and had hoof oil and a sponge at the ready to give him a final polish.

Dressage arenas at events are marked out with white boards as well as letters – Basil had never worked around such things before and was quite spooky. Mary made him trot around the boards, and also around the judge's car which he was beginning to find quite fascinating. She did a few transitions from trot to halt before the judge sounded her car horn, the signal for them to start. Basil produced a very relaxed test, although he was a bit wobbly up the centre line. He also broke into canter when he was meant to be lengthening his stride in trot, but this was because he hit a bump in the middle of the arena which threw him off balance. As you first trot round the *outside* of the boards, before you actually begin your test, it is always worth taking a quick look across the arena for lumps, bumps and slopes – they are not always perfectly flat or level, and you can then be ready to balance your horse to help him deal with such things. Overall Basil was very calm and obedient and was given 35 penalties; this left him fifth out of fifty.

It was soon time for the showjumping. Basil warmed up very well over the practice fences, but reverted to being quite babyish once he got into the ring – it was as though he felt a little lost in such a wide open space and with so many distractions all around. 'He tried to run out at one fence which had been causing a lot of trouble, but I insisted he stayed straight and kept going forwards. He jumped it awkwardly and had it down, and then we approached the double badly and had both parts of that down, too. He was tending to jump straight up and down rather than boldly forward, so he was coming down on the back rail.' However, although it was disappointing to incur 15 penalties, Mary was pleased that he had tackled the fences in spite of being somewhat in awe of his surroundings, and was comforted by the thought that the faults they had incurred were the result of apprehension which was making him jump awkwardly, rather than sheer carelessness.

With two phases accomplished, they now had the cross-country to tackle. The course was beautifully built and ideal for a first event, but Mary wasn't sure how Basil would react, having felt so green in the showjumping; so she set off very purposefully to try to instil some confidence in him. He was a bit wobbly over the first couple of fences, but then he obviously realised that there was a job to do and started to go more positively. Mary moved him up a gear and he became increasingly fluent as he went on. 'The actual feel he gives me over a fence is lovely,' says Mary 'as he is very sharp and careful.'

All in all, Mary was pleased with Basil's first effort, and was glad that she had entered him for several events in a row; she felt that what he needed now was basically experience, to get out and about and to get to know what was expected of him. Meanwhile Basil himself was enjoying a very well deserved day off in the field.

By this time Mary had acquired a partner for Basil, to travel around with him and compete at the same level: this was Borcombes Masterblend (Mars). At Stilemans, Mars also competed in the Pre-Novice, and finished third in his section.

Basil was hacked out quietly for the first part of the following week, and then activities intensified in preparation for Peper Harow, which would be his first Novice event. Mary knew there was a water jump in the course (there had not been one at Stilemans), so she schooled Basil into water again, to be sure that he would tackle it confidently. Basil performed beautifully, but managed to pull off a hind shoe and cut his pastern, though fortunately this was not too serious.

Peper Harow one-day event

As Basil had been so green in the showjumping at Stilemans, Mary was now worried as to how he would tackle the bigger, Novice fences at Peper Harow. She put up a course of jumps out in the field and used every type of filler she could find – this included hanging day-rugs and bags over the poles! Her apprehension was unfounded, however, as Basil went straight in and jumped everything. So it was with renewed confidence that they set off for Peper Harow on the Saturday. In fact Basil was not competing until the Sunday, so Mary rode him around at the event and then popped him over a course of

WALKING THE COURSES

The showjumping course should be walked with the particular horse you are riding in mind. At a one-day event Mary only walks the course once; first she takes into account what the going is like – 'If it is very deep you may need to ride at a stronger pace to help the horse overcome the "pull" from the ground,' explains Mary. Then she considers distances between fences: 'I always walk the distances between any combinations or related distance fences, and relate the distance to the length of stride of the horse I am riding. Will I need to shorten his stride or ride him forward into a longer stride to make each particular distance?' Remember to check where the start and finish are situated, as well as the order of the fences, and make sure you have included them all!

As with the showjumping course, when walking the cross-country you must consider the particular horse you are riding. Think of the speed with which you should be approaching each fence, and the line you will ride between fences. If rising ground blocks your view of the next fence you must walk on until you can see both fences, and then find a landmark which will allow you to ride the straightest line from one fence to the other. Look out for unlevel ground or rough patches on take-off and landing and help your horse by avoiding these. Walk the distance in any combinations, and no matter how confident you feel, always walk the alternative route so that you know what to do if something does go wrong.

'I don't wear a stopwatch unless it's a three-day event,' explains Mary. 'When you are working to build a horse's confidence and experience you should ride at a speed which allows you to maintain a good rhythm and which helps the horse to jump well. If you are out to try and get placed, certainly you have to ride fast, but only as fast as it is *safe* to do so, and that safe speed will vary from one horse to another.'

jumps at Robert Lemieux's yard, where they were stabled for the night.

On arriving at Peper Harow on the day of the competition, Mary found that Basil was quite different from the horse she had taken to Stilemans the week before. At Stilemans he had been calm and quiet and had done exactly what he was told; today he knew what it was all about and produced quite a disobedient test. In the showjumping he was also a changed character – this time he was very bold, and actually had both parts of a double down through being overkeen and making up too much ground.

Across country he was much more confident, although he did hesitate at the water. Once he saw what was expected of him he jumped in boldly, but not before incurring 20 penalties for taking a step back – in eventing the line between success and failure is sometimes very fine! Nevertheless, with a young horse what is important is whether or not his performance and attitude is improving overall. An inexperienced horse can often finish with a higher num-

RIDING THE SHOWJUMPING COURSE

My main aim when riding a show-jumping course is to keep the rhythm and energy in the canter. The distances between fences in a showjumping course are based on an average stride of 12ft (approximately four paces, each 3ft [0.9m]); every horse has a different "good jumping canter", and you can establish how the stride of any one horse compares to the average by setting up two fences at a measured distance apart and then riding him through it. The distance is measured by walking out your four good-size paces (12ft) per average horse stride, allowing 6ft (two paces) for landing after the first fence, and 6ft (two paces) for take-off before the second. For example, two fences with three average strides between them would be placed sixteen paces (48ft/ 14.5m) apart, so you, the rider, must establish a canter which allows your particular horse to fit three even strides between the two fences. Thus a horse with a relatively short stride will need to be ridden forward in quite a strong canter to make the distance, whereas an onward-bound horse would need to be held in a shorter, bouncier canter to fit in the three strides.

'As a rider you must learn how each horse's "jumping canter" should feel so that you can establish it immediately, almost subconsciously, when showjumping. This leaves part of your mind free to concentrate on where the next fence is, so that you always present the horse at each fence with a straight, clear approach.

'My natural reaction used to be to let my horses get too long and flat into their fences. I am now very conscious of keeping the canter short and bouncy and waiting for the fence to "come to me", rather than rushing the horse into the fence.

'Every horse is different. Conker tends to back off his fences, but he also fights for his head on the approach. However, I still have to ride him forwards into his fences to overcome the effect of his own slight braking – and if I keep him going forwards in a good, strong rhythm it also reduces his tendency to fight for his head, as then he does not feel restricted at all. William, on the other hand, is so onward-bound and powerful that I have to keep his canter as short and active as possible.'

● *Sammy throws a neat, tidy jump over an upright*

ber of penalties than in his previous competition, even though he may actually have put in a better performance overall as far as the rider is concerned.

On this occasion at Peper Harow Mars flew the flag for the Thomson stable by winning his section and his first eventing points.

The following weekend, Basil was to compete at Novice level again, at Aldon, so his programme for the week was just to continue quietly in his routine. He did not do any fast work – Mary considered he was doing enough simply by competing each weekend. He enjoyed some gentle hacking and quiet schooling on the flat and over showjumping fences. He was also treated to a day out: the day before Aldon, he went up to Badminton with William who was taking part in the Badminton Horse Feeds Dressage Championships. Basil was only going for the ride, but he was able to enjoy a hack in Badminton Park – and even had a splash around in the lake, so he should feel quite at home for his Badminton début, when it comes! An outing like this helps teach a novice horse to relax and enjoy himself in a strange environment.

Aldon one-day event

At Aldon Basil was very relaxed and calm: he produced an amazing dressage test for a score of 21 penalties, which put him in the lead. Things continued to go well in the showjumping where he jumped with confidence and care to produce a clear round. At the start of the cross-country, however, he could hardly contain his excitement: 'Basil came out of the start box and then had a bit of a seizure!' said Mary. 'It was as though he was so excited he did not know what to do with himself – he started to run backwards, so I just sat quietly until he stopped. Then a smack with the stick sent him on again, and away we went!' The fourth fence was a coffin; as it was so early on in the course, Mary had decided to take the long route. However, this meant that after jumping the first element the approach to the ditch was from a very awkward angle – Basil did not see it until the last minute, and stopped and had a look before jumping it. But after that his confidence grew, and finally he jumped very boldly into the water towards the end of the course. Mary was delighted with how much he had improved.

After Aldon Basil enjoyed a day off, then he was hacked out quietly to maintain his level of fitness. He had a day of variety, too, acting as

Mary insists upon a high standard of turnout, both for herself and her horses. 'I like my horses to be really well turned out at events – you never know, it may even win you a few extra marks in the dressage.' First impressions count, remember!

A few days before an event the horses will have their manes washed so that when the times comes they are clean, but not too slippery to plait. Annie and the girls keep tails pulled all the time, so these usually just need a quick tidy-up; then the day before the event, they are washed and the ends conditioned with something like Showsheen, and a tail bandage is put on. 'We only ever brush the horses' tails when they *are* clean, otherwise you tend to pull half the hair out and the tail ends up looking thin and wispy,' says Mary.

White markings are washed and towel-dried, and if a horse's coat needs any further tidying-up this is done either with scissors, trimmers or clippers. Ears are trimmed both inside and around the edge with either scissors or small dog trimmers, and then wiped out with a warm, damp cloth. Any cat's hairs are removed from the head and body with the big clippers; these are also used to trim around the heels. Scissors are used to trim the hair around the coronet band into a nice straight line. The mane is trimmed just in front of the withers and also behind the poll, to allow room for the headpiece of the bridle to sit comfortably. In warm weather the horses are often washed all over and then towel-dried the day before an event. The novice horses are usually plaited the night before, but the advanced horses are always plaited on the day so they look really neat and tidy.

The finishing touches on the day of the event itself include putting baby oil around the muzzle and eyes to make them look black and shiny, and brushing in quarter marks on the top and sides of the hindquarters. Hooves are oiled inside and out. Then all you need hope for is a performance as well polished as your horse!

All the horses have leather headcollars, but these are only used for competitions; in the yard, ordinary nylon ones are worn. Depending on the weather, the horses wear either their sponsor's green summer sheets, or woollen day rugs (with a blanket as well if it is very cold). Whatever rug they wear, it is held in place with a matching surcingle, padded at the top to take pressure off the spine, and with a breast girth to stop it slipping backwards. On the way to an event a stocking is put over the horse's tail to keep it clean, as well as a tail bandage. A tail guard is worn over the top. All the horses wear full-length travel boots.

PLAITING

● **1** *Divide the mane into equal-sized bunches. Dampen each section well. This helps to keep all spare hairs under control, making it easier to plait*

2 *Divide the section into three equal parts*

3 *Plait, keeping it tight all the way down*

4 *As you do this, keep your hands close to the neck as this will encourage the plait to lie down*

5 *Fold the end of the plait up, and secure it with an elastic band. This can be done with thread*

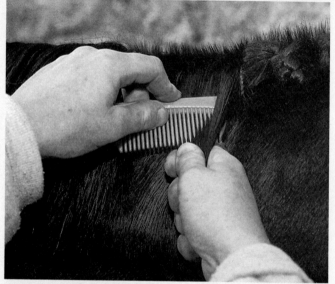

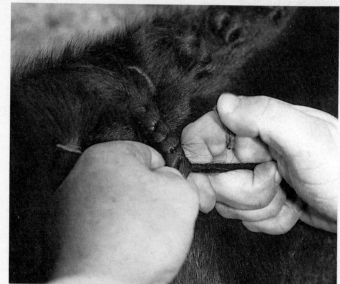

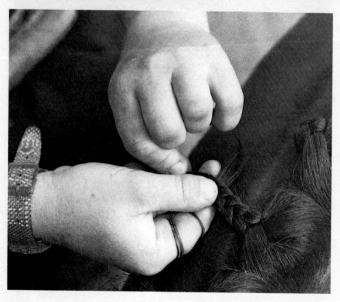

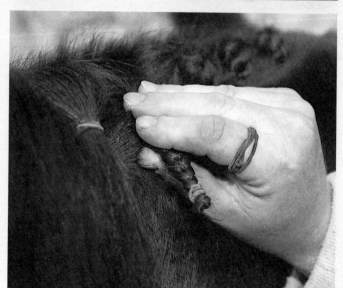

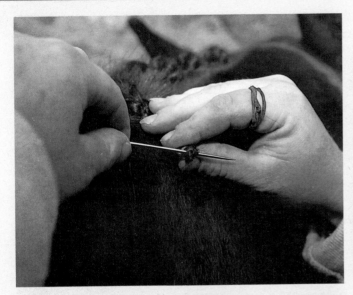

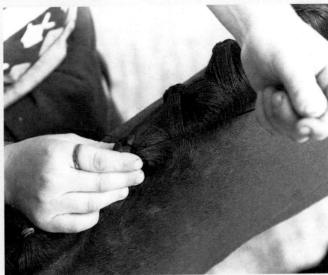

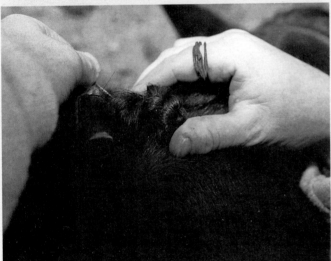

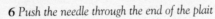

6 *Push the needle through the end of the plait*

7 *Push the needle up through the top of the plait, which will fold it*

8 *Weave the needle in and out back down to the bottom of the plait, then push the needle back through to the top. Secure by sewing firmly through the plait a couple of times, and tie the thread out of sight*

9 *The finished plait should lie neatly against the horse's neck, improving the top line*

10 *The forelock plait can be plaited like a tail, from the very top of the forelock. This should produce a very tidy result*

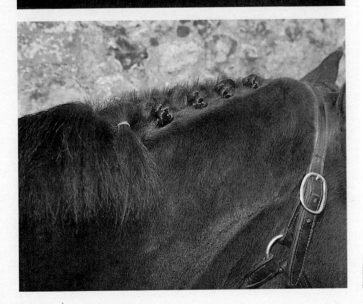

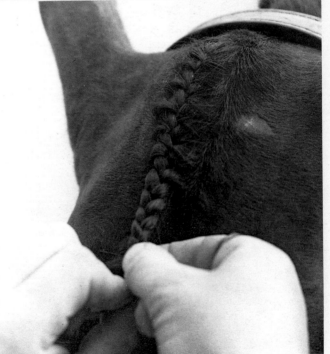

CROSS-COUNTRY EQUIPMENT

For the cross-country phase, all Mary's horses wear very similar gear. 'Firstly, I like to ride my horses in a snaffle bit of some sort,' says Mary, 'but if they are very strong I try them in a vulcanite pelham.' At the moment Conker and Basil wear Magenis snaffles, but William is ridden in a vulcanite pelham.

'I use rubber-covered reins and a breastplate with a martingale attachment. At Novice level I just use a running martingale. *Two* rubber stops are put on each rein, one each side of the martingale rings: one stops the martingale rings getting caught up on the rein buckle by the bit, and the other stops the rings running up and catching on the rubber grip on the reins.'

Mary's particular choice of jumping saddle is a Pandur saddle, similar to the Stübben but a bit longer in the seat. An over-girth is used over the saddle, as a precaution against the girth breaking. Mary has leather loops put on the girth to thread the overgirth through so that it does not slip off the girth and pinch the horse.

To protect their legs, the horses wear Porter boots underneath exercise bandages. The bandage ties are taped over to stop them slipping or coming undone; at a three-day event the bandages are carefully sewn up on the outside, for extra security (see page 104). Mary does use overreach boots, but trims a few centimetres off the bottom of each boot so that the bulb of the heel is still covered but there is less risk of the horse treading on the boot with his hind hoof and tripping over. At Novice level the horses wear Woof Wear brushing boots behind, but at anything higher they wear leather 'speedycut' boots which have extra leather to protect the inside of the hock as well as the front and inside of the fetlock. One stud is used in each shoe, its size and shape depending on the ground conditions.

● *A tubigrip is placed under the Porter boot and folded down over it to prevent any rubbing. At a three-day event the bandage is sewn, otherwise tape is used. Leather speedy cut boots protect the hind legs. (Don't look at Basil's hooves: the farrier was about to arrive!)*

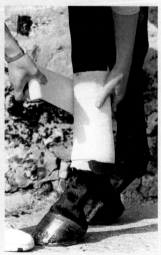

photographer's model for Kit Houghton, jumping across country and in and out of water for the benefit of the camera. To keep his work varied Mary also lunged him in the arena. She had never lunged Basil much as he was always very cold-backed and in his early stages of training used to hunch up and buck and frighten himself on the lunge. However, Mary likes to lunge all her horses; it gives them something different to do, and it also encourages them to find their own balance rather than relying on the rider all the time. In fact she found that Basil was much improved on the lunge.

Ston Easton one-day event

Basil's next challenge was another Novice event at Ston Easton. Mary was riding Mars in an earlier section, and it turned out that she had very little time between Mars' cross country and Basil's dressage test. She set off on Mars and he was going really well; he jumped happily into the water – and then simply fell over! He and Mary were completely submerged, and this gave Mars quite a fright. Mary retired him, deciding to save him for Hilmarton Horse Trials which were the following Wednesday. By the time Mary had changed out of her soaking clothes she had little time left for Basil so she decided not to run him at all. The going had become very deep and as he had already completed three events in a row, she decided it would not hurt to save him for another day.

KING KONG

Conker's first event of the season was to be Aldon, towards the end of the month, so Mary spent the first fortnight putting the final touches on his fitness and schooling. He was doing his fast work every four days, and in between would be hacked out, and schooled on the flat or over showjumps. The distance that he covered in his fast work was gradually increased over this fortnight: he started by going once up the short side and once up the long side, increasing to once up the middle and twice up the long side.

Conker is *always* extremely full of himself so the emphasis was on discipline – Mary did not want to risk getting to Aldon and having him be thoroughly naughty. In fact with Conker she discovered that it often helped either to lunge or hack him out before a schooling session, as this would settle him and meant he had less excuse to misbehave.

With just a week to go, Mary was still concentrating on obedience: 'He can be quite wicked sometimes, but you just have to keep on with him until he gives in and does it, as he is perfectly capable,' says Mary. She also schooled him round the showjumping course in the field; after jumping on artificial surfaces it takes a while for a horse to adjust to jumping off grass again, particularly in deep, muddy conditions as so often prevail at the spring events.

● *Conker demonstrates his super technique in a schooling session at home – even though his eyes are half-closed!*

STUDS

Once a horse is shod with metal shoes he gains protection of the hoof, but he loses the natural grip which it affords. During an event the horse is asked to jump and turn at speed, and it is important that he has the confidence to do this without fear of slipping. As events are run over all kinds of terrain and in varying weather and ground conditions, most horses are fitted with shoes which have stud holes. This allows the rider to screw in metal studs of various shapes and sizes which enable the foot to grip.

'I always use studs of some sort for jumping,' says Mary, 'and although I do not like big studs because I think they unbalance the horse's foot, there are occasions when this disadvantage is outweighed by the need to have some grip in very wet conditions.

'As a general rule I use the square, chunky studs early on in the season, but as the ground gets harder I use more pointed ones which have some chance of digging into the hard surface. In very wet, boggy conditions larger studs are called for, and these I would put in the hind shoes; only in exceptionally bad conditions would I use them in front as well.'

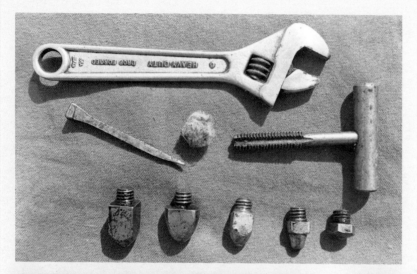

● *The stud hole is cleaned out using an old horseshoe nail and plugged with oiled cotton wool until the stud is put in. The tool on the right (the tap) re-threads the hole. The stud is screwed in using a spanner. It is important to support the horse's leg so that it is not wrenched or twisted as the stud is tightened*

Aldon one-day event

The Open Intermediate class at Aldon was the day after the Novice classes, but Conker went up with Basil so he could get used to the atmosphere of a competition again. He was very excited and needed to be ridden around for nearly an hour before he settled. Then Mary lunged him before starting on some quiet schooling.

Aldon was Conker's first Open Intermediate event; although an OI competition is no different from an ordinary Intermediate event in severity, advanced horses are able to take part and so the standard is usually higher. 'Conker earned a good mark in the dressage, although it must have looked better than it felt,' said Mary. 'He was very strong, and was relying on my hand to keep his balance instead of carrying himself. But it was an obedient test, and left him in third place after the dressage.

'He performed well in the showjumping although we did have one down, mainly due to his over-enthusiasm which means he sometimes comes into his fences in a bit of a rush.

'At the start of the cross-country I did suddenly think that perhaps I should have given him some cross-country schooling before doing an event, but we set off at a medium pace and he gave me a fabulous round. He finished seventh.'

After a day off and then a quiet hack, Conker was also required for the photography session with Kit Houghton. Then it was back to more serious work in preparation for his next event, Ston Easton.

As part of his schooling Mary worked him in the field, and concentrated on increasing and decreasing the pace at canter. As Conker is quite easily excited it does not take much for him to become a bit unruly during canter work. 'At first he kept trying to run on and pull at my hand when I asked him to increase the pace, but I kept on and on, insisting that he carried himself and stayed soft and light within the pace and throughout the transitions.'

Ston Easton one-day event

Right from the start, Mary was in two minds as to whether or not she would run Conker across country – she does not like to compete any of her horses on consecutive weekends at this level. 'Having walked the course, which was very undulating and included a lot of drops, I decided definitely not to run him,' said Mary.

● *Conker shows some resistance by coming above the bit during his medium trot, in the dressage test at Aldon*

The journey was not completely wasted for Conker, however, as he could still do the dressage and showjumping which would all add to his experience. And indeed, Mary was pleased with his dressage, even though it did not earn him as a good a mark as the week before: 'He was very calm and worked with much more self-carriage. Because he was much lighter in my hand he was a bit wobbly in parts of the test as he was learning to carry himself and not to rely on my hand for support. You have to go through this stage with a horse to achieve the long-term goal of having the horse working in self-carriage. He did make other odd mistakes such as striking off on the wrong leg because there were some flowers to spook at and so I could not keep

● *So far so good; but Conker went on to dislodge the very last pole in the showjumping phase at Ston Easton. In this picture Mary is reverting to her old bad habit of throwing her weight too far forward*

● *A week after his injection, William was able to resume his fastwork*

For the first few days in March William was still only being walked out because of the Pneumobort K injections he had had. However, later in the week he did some work on the lunge to get him back in the swing of things again, and at the end of the week Mary gave him a school round a showjumping course at home. Fit and well, he was then able to start his fast-work again, galloping every four days.

Mary had been invited by the Olympic team selectors to spend three days at Stoneleigh on a training course for potentially long-listed Olympic riders. She was allowed to take two horses, and so William and Star Appeal (Apple) made the trip to receive instruction from Ferdi Eilberg and Captain Mark Phillips.

William did dressage on the first day; this was outside, and William was very strong and onward bound, back to his old habit of just pow-ering on. Ferdi made Mary work on half-halts, transitions and rein-back, all movements which they hoped would persuade William to listen to and wait for his rider. For the rest of the course Mary concentrated on showjumping; this was meant to be with Captain Mark Phillips, but Stephen Hadley had come over to

him bent around my inside leg, but over all he felt much more engaged.'

Again Conker produced a good showjumping round, just dislodging the last pole in a tight combination at the very end. The overall improvement in his performance made up for the inevitably disappointing, but wise decision to withdraw from the cross-country. As Captain Mark Phillips had pointed out – no harm can be done by keeping a good horse for another day.

watch, and before the end of the first session Mary had both the Captain and Steve helping her. For Mary this proved especially useful as she was able to consider different ideas from both trainers and come up with an approach that suited her and William. Whether the two trainers enjoyed sharing their task was another matter! In fact William jumped very well which was most encouraging, especially as on the final day the Olympic selectors came for a look at everyone.

Once back at home, William's fast work was increased. With a week to go before Aldon, he shared much the same programme as Conker: fast work every four days, hacking, lungeing and schooling in between. Mary also jumped him out in the field to help him get used to jumping off grass again.

The Badminton Horse Feeds Dressage Championships

Mary and William had been invited to ride in an international team competition at Badminton as part of the Badminton Horse Feeds Dressage Championships. Those taking part rode a warm-up test in an outdoor arena in Badminton Park, then performed the Championship test in the Riding Hall at Badminton. As well as a competition for individual honours, there was also a team competition between the event riders and the pure dressage riders.

William was very obedient and calm; he was second in the warm-up class, and finished third overall in the Championship class in which he had to perform the FEI test. And for the first time ever, the event team beat the pure dressage team!

Aldon one-day event

The day before the Open Intermediate class at Aldon, William was able just to hack around quietly and soak up the atmosphere of the event while Basil and Mars were competing and doing the real work.

With all the excitement and anticipation which goes with the first events of the season, Mary was really looking forward to riding the 'big boys' at Aldon. Although William is an advanced event horse, he is allowed to compete in Open Intermediate classes which are of intermediate standard but open to all grades of horses – they are a good way of getting an advanced horse back into the swing of things after a long break.

● *Showjumping is not always William's strongest point. This sequence shows how William tends to draw his head and neck up and back on the approach, especially when he is being strong, so tending to throw a hollow jump*

● *William gives Mary that Rolls-Royce feeling at Aldon*

William produced a good dressage test although he was very strong, and Mary felt he could have done better. But never mind, the judge loved him and gave him a score of 26 which put him in the lead.

In the showjumping he was again very strong. 'I tried to remember everything I'd been told,' said Mary, 'to keep his canter short and bouncy and to be soft with my seat and hands. But it's very hard when they're pulling like mad!' He ended up having one down, just to let Mary know there was still room for improvement!

'On the cross-country we had a magic round,' said Mary. 'I kept him at medium speed and he set off with his ears pricked. He always gives me a wonderful ride – really eats up the fences and just loves it. He did not get too strong and was very manoeuvrable. At the water he just leapt straight in, and that was a great relief as it was the first water he had done since our catastrophe at Punchestown.'

William was placed fourth, a good start to his Olympic season. At the end of March he had to have his second Pneumobort K injection, so his work programme was once again reduced to gentle hacking. He will probably be as relieved as Mary to really get back into action in April!

CARE AFTER THE CROSS-COUNTRY

On return from tackling the cross-country course, all the horse's tack is removed immediately and a headcollar put on. If the horse is still blowing he is walked round quietly until his breathing returns to normal, when he is offered a mouthful of water. He is offered small amounts of water regularly while he was being washed down until he has had enough. He is then tied up on the outside of the lorry and allowed to nibble at a dampened haynet while he is being washed down. A sweat-scraper and towel is used to help dry him off, and either a sweatsheet or thermatex rug is put on to stop him getting cold; he then has another walk round before his boots and bandages are removed and his legs thoroughly washed and dried.

He is carefully checked over for any cuts or bumps; these are treated immediately with either antiseptic cream, spray, or a warm Animalintex poultice. His studs are taken out before he is put in the lorry. If a horse is excitable after the cross-country it is a good idea to take the studs out first in case he treads on anyone's feet or kicks out while being washed off. If there is time he will be led out for a graze before going back in the lorry for his haynet and normal 'lunch' – and is left in peace to enjoy it. Lunch is given no sooner than an hour after his cross-country. He has another walk round outside to stretch his legs before his travelling gear is put on and the journey home begins.

APRIL

*T*he spring event season is now well under way, and my whole team of horses have been performing very well. This month was extra special as Basil had his first-ever win – this was very satisfying, particularly when I think back to how green he was at his first event; he has improved in leaps and bounds through the month and has accumulated 13 BHS points.

Conker has carried on throughout April emphasising the fact that he thinks discipline is not worth bothering about. At home I could feel the beginnings of an overall improvement as his balance, rhythm and engagement were getting better – though he was not prepared to admit to this when he got to an event!

William completed his pre-Badminton competition programme in one piece, which was an enormous relief. We won the International Event Riders' Dressage competition at the end of the month, with a convincing lead over Ginny Leng and Master Craftsman. This gave our confidence a great boost. In most of his tests this year William has been quite tense, and so on this occasion it was wonderful to feel he was starting to relax.

I knew that in May I would be too busy with the horses to involve myself in anything else, so I devoted some of my time now to raising both awareness and money for the orphans of

Romania in preparation for our Riders for Romania trip in October. Our main aim this year is to help fund a new Craft and Skills Centre which is being built at one of the orphanages we supported previously.

The centre will be used to teach the orphans a trade or profession in the hope it may be easier for them to to support themselves when it is time to leave the orphanage. We also intend to take out general supplies such as educational toys, school equipment, food, clothing, disinfectant and medical supplies.

In my spare time in April I gave a series of evening lectures, including a video of the previous year's trip, with the aim of persuading more and more people to help raise funds and collect supplies. If I don't get organised now there certainly won't be time in May!

KING BASIL

So far this season Mary had felt that Basil was not quite ready to attempt the direct routes at some of the trickier cross-country fences, but she was keen to remedy this situation. Nearly every Novice cross-country course includes a coffin fence, usually a rail followed by one stride to a ditch, then a further stride to another rail. Generally an easier alternative is provided at this type of fence, but in order to progress the horse must eventually face the challenge.

With Hilmarton one-day event only a few days away, Mary concocted her own coffin fence at home (see below). She used showjumps for the rails, and empty feed bags, weighted down with showjump poles, to represent the ditch.

As an easy introduction to this new obstacle, Mary asked Basil to jump it first as a half-coffin, which involved jumping just the ditch and then a stride to the rail. Once he was jumping this happily in both directions, she put up the second set of rails and jumped it as a proper coffin. As Basil's confidence increased, Mary made the combination more difficult by reducing the distance between the rails and the ditch so there was no jumping stride between the elements and Basil had to bounce through the combination.

Hilmarton one-day event

Torrential rain on the morning of Hilmarton horse trials left Mary wondering whether she should run the horses. She decided to see how they coped with the dressage and showjumping.

Despite the deep, muddy going Basil performed a very relaxed and obedient test to take the lead with 26 penalties. The ground had deteriorated further by the time Basil was warming up for the showjumping, and this phase was causing plenty of problems for the competitors. It took Basil a while to work out how to cope with the conditions; his first few practice jumps were awkward, but once he had realised that the heavy going simply required more effort and push from him, he rose to the occasion and produced a clear round. Mary decided it would be good experience for him to run across country, and set off in a steady but strong rhythm so that they would have enough impulsion to jump out of the mud.

The course itself was not too difficult; it included a half-coffin which Basil jumped a little spookily, but happily enough. To Mary's delight, he won his section – and to cheer up a damp, dull day still further, Mars also took first place in his section! Although Mary still felt that Mars had a rather strange jumping technique, his performance impressed several observant riders who were keen to know more about this latest addition to Mary's team.

As Basil had performed so well, Mary allowed him a few relaxing days of quiet hacking.

Ferney Hall one-day event

Ferney Hall was the next event on Basil's itinerary, and in preparation Mary spent sever-

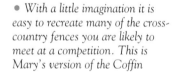

● *With a little imagination it is easy to recreate many of the cross-country fences you are likely to meet at a competition. This is Mary's version of the Coffin*

al days concentrating on his flatwork. The main aim was just to improve his general way of going rather than to teach him anything new; a few lungeing sessions, as well as schooling in the field, all helped in achieving this.

To keep Basil's jump training up to scratch Mary gave him another school through the home-made coffin, and hacked down to the river for some last-minute water schooling.

Basil arrived at Ferney Hall feeling very bright and lively; this was a change from his last outing when he had been quite lethargic, and Mary expected him to be naughty in the dressage. 'Fortunately the more I worked him outside, the quieter he became, and he calmed down even more when he entered the arena,' said Mary. 'He produced a lovely calm test, and earned just 24 penalties which took the lead again.'

The showjumping was quite spooky, the bright sunshine making the fences look very stary. This often makes horses jump higher and more carefully than usual, and unfortunately it had this effect on Basil who jumped awkwardly and knocked down two fences with his hindlegs. It was back to his previous problem of being too careful and dwelling in the air when tense, rather than jumping boldly forward over his fences. However, Mary felt that basically all he needed was a little more experience to help him handle the more exciting circumstances of a competition.

The cross-country course was big but beautifully built, with a great variety of fences; it therefore promised to be quite an educational course for Basil. 'We set off very purposefully, though did opt to take the long route at the sunken road and the coffin as they were quite complicated combinations. All the same, for the first time Basil felt as if he was really enjoying the challenge and not just doing it because he was asked,' said Mary. 'I felt he was now ready to tackle the bigger, more complicated questions that may face him in future events.'

Schooling at home

After a few days of quiet hacking, Basil resumed his schooling in the field, in the continual attempt to improve even further his basic way of going. It is so important to establish thoroughly the basic essentials of straightness, impulsion and suppleness – then as the horse is required to perform at a higher level he is well prepared. The long-term aim is for the horse to work in self-carriage, so each time Mary schools Basil she asks him to work with a little more engagement of the hindquarters so that he can gradually adjust his balance, strengthen the correct muscles and move a little further towards this ultimate goal.

Later, the weather turned cold and windy and Basil became rather exuberant, so Mary resorted to lungeing. 'He went quite wild on the lunge, bucking and squealing and I was glad he had a chance to get it all out of his system before I asked him to concentrate on some proper work', said Mary. Once he was settled Mary got on him and did some jump schooling..

INTRODUCING LATERAL WORK

Mary introduces the full pass very early in a horse's training programme, to teach him to move away from the leg. As it sounds, in full pass the horse moves fully sideways. She taught Basil this movement within the first few months of buying him, because at five years old, he already had a good understanding of free forward movement and straightness, the basics which must be established first of all.

To teach a horse the full pass, Mary first halts him at right-angles to a fence or wall. 'To perform a full pass to the left, I would first create a slight bend to the left through the horse's head and neck…then I would ask him, with my voice and leg, to "move over", using my outside leg behind the girth to ask him to move sideways. It often helps to have someone on the ground who can give the horse a gentle push in the right direction as you ask him to move over. As soon as a few steps sideways are achieved, I halt and make a big fuss of him. I then turn the horse away

● *Mary turns him to the right, rewarding him with a pat*

to the *right*, that is, in the *opposite* direction so that he does not learn to fall away to the left after the full pass.'

This exercise should be repeated until the horse can perform a full pass on both reins. Most horses are less co-operative

on one particular rein – even though they understand and obey the aids on, say, the right rein, they refuse to oblige to the left. The rider must be patient but insistent until the horse understands that it is possible to go on both reins.

For Mary, the next step in lateral work training after full pass would be the shoulder-in, as she does not use leg-yielding as a schooling exercise. The shoulder-in is a gymnastic exercise in which the horse works on three tracks: the outside hindleg forms one track, the inside hind and outside form the second track, and the inside foreleg the third track. The horse maintains a bend through the length of his body, and he is bent away from the direction in which he is moving. The purpose of riding shoulder-in is to activate the inside hindleg by displacing the horse's shoulder on an inner track. The inside hindleg is well under the horse and carries the weight of both horse and rider; it is therefore an early introduction to the ultimate aim of self-carriage.

'I always introduce shoulder-in by riding a 10-metre circle at walk, because this establishes the degree of bend the horse

● *Basil halts facing towards the hedge. Mary asks for left bend and puts her right leg back as for the aid to ask him to step sideways*

● *Basil moves forwards and sideways, moving away from Mary's outside leg*

• *Here Basil is resisting: he does not understand Mary's aid, and is moving into her right leg rather than away from it. This is a typical reaction during the learning process, and this is when assistance from the ground can help*

my outside hand slightly to encourage the horse to come off the 10-metre circle and down the long side of the arena, although my inside hand would stay in position to control the degree of bend.

'A very common fault is for a rider to lean in the direction he wants the horse to move, crossing the inside hand over in an attempt to create the bend and hold the horse in position. However, by crossing the hand, the bend through the horse's body is dissected, with the result that he only bends from the shoulder and not right through his shoulder and back as well. Some riders put the horse into shoulder-in by allowing him to swing his quarters out; but the horse must learn to perform this movement by moving his shoulders in, and then holding this position. Otherwise he will find it difficult to understand what is required when you try to teach him the half-pass.

'As soon as possible you should ride this movement with both hands in the correct position. As Ferdi is always saying, "You should ride the horse in the position you are *meant* to be in, *not* in the position

the horse tries to make you ride in." At this stage in his training the horse will quite often start tilting his head, which constitutes a resistance. You can – and must – correct this by raising your hand slightly to straighten his head; however, only do this to correct the fault, and do *not* continue to ride in this position.'

Once shoulder-in is established at walk on both reins, Mary introduces the movement at trot: 'When you do this, do not let the trot be too free or the horse will find it difficult to keep his balance. Ride in a slightly slower working trot than you would normally, and then build up to a strong, flowing working trot. Reward the horse when he is right, but be strict with yourself and correct anything that you can feel is wrong. Do not ask for too much at once; just make your point and then leave it.

'I would normally work on a new movement over two days, though as soon as the horse understands what is required and the aim of the lesson is established, I would give him a break from schooling for a couple of days.'

needs to hold throughout the shoulder-in. The bend must be correct, with the weight of the contact taken in the outside hand, and off the inside rein and shoulder. On completing the 10-metre circle, I would let the horse step off the track as if he were going to ride another circle, but I would then hold this position and ask the horse to progress up the long side of the arena, with his hindquarters on the track and his shoulders displaced on the inner track. The aids for this movement require the rider to sit with most of the weight on the inside seat-bone, the hips in line with the horse's hindquarters but the shoulders turned so as to be in line with the horse's shoulders; and all the while looking straight ahead in the direction the horse is required to move. The inside leg stays on, or just behind the girth, and is used to create forward movement by activating the inside hindleg; the outside leg controls the position of the hindquarters. When first teaching this movement I would open

• *A common mistake in shoulder-in is for the horse to bend from the shoulder and not through the whole body*

• *Basil is now bent through his body and working correctly on three tracks*

FEEDING

During April the feed rations for William and Conker were altered, as they neared their target three-day event, to include a higher ratio of competition cubes, and were maintained at this level right up until both horses had completed their competition. William loses weight very quickly, especially when he is competing, so he was allowed as much hay as he could comfortably eat, even at Badminton. Basil's ration for April and May remained the same as it had been in March.

WILLIAM

Morning: $1^1/2$lb ($^1/2$ scoop) stud cubes; 2lb (1 scoop) breeding mix; Provider Plus; salt
Lunch: 3lb (1 scoop) competition cubes
Evening: 1lb ($^1/2$ scoop) breeding mix; 3lb (1 scoop) competition cubes; Provider Plus; salt
Haynet: Large (5lb) morning and evening

CONKER

Morning: 2lb (1 scoop) breeding mix; Provider Plus; salt
Lunch: 3lb (1 scoop) competition cubes
Evening: 1lb ($^1/2$ scoop) breeding mix; 3lb (1 scoop) competition cubes; Provider Plus; salt
Haynet: Medium ($3^1/2$lb) morning and evening; reduced to small (2lb) in morning just before, and during the Windsor three-day event.

Basil's problem seems to be that when he is faced with spooky fences he loses his concentration and his normally good jumping technique – he tends to jump high to clear the obstacle, but is too tense to open out over the fence and so comes down on the back rail. Mary worked him through a grid of an upright to a parallel to an upright, with one stride in between each of the elements. She put barrels under the poles to make the fences quite spooky, giving Basil something unexpected to look at. Also, a grid like this teaches the horse to open out and then to shorten his stride quickly, depending on which fence he is faced with. He must approach the upright at the start of the grid in a short, bouncy canter, but then he must open up his stride and his jump to clear the parallel; then quickly shorten his stride, as he will have made up ground by jumping the spread, to jump neatly out over the final upright. It was important to make the fences spooky so that the conditions were as close as possible to those the horse faces at a competition. It gives him two things to think about : the way the fence looks, and the way he needs to jump it.

Portman one-day event

Basil's dressage was proving to be very consistent, and he produced another calm, obedient test which scored 25 penalties.

In the showjumping it was obvious that the work at home had been to good effect as he produced a very nice clear round. 'He was almost *too* quiet and soft!' said Mary. 'At this stage the main aim is to keep him steady, balanced and straight, but I will soon need to get his canter shorter and sharper in readiness for jumping the larger Intermediate tracks.'

As Basil was being so co-operative Mary decided to try all the direct ways on the cross-country course. This decision was partly influenced by the fact that there was no alternative at the coffin fence, and also because the course was fair and well built – all in all, perfectly suited to asking that little bit more from Basil.

He rose to the occasion and jumped very boldly; Mary recollected that the third to last fence was a ditch and palisade onto higher ground, and then a bounce over a log: 'I rode a strong approach thinking that Basil would spook and back off the ditch, but he didn't – and on take-off I could feel he was contemplating leaping the whole lot in one!' she said. Luckily he put his front feet down, and although he was quite close to the log, he was able to jump out safely. The course had included his first bullfinch and some big steps up, and Mary was more than pleased with his effort.

The importance of relaxation

Now that Basil seemed to know what was expected of him and seemed to be really enjoying his work, and particularly as he was showing so much improvement, Mary did not want to put too much pressure on him. Although perfection is worth striving for, it is all too easy to keep up the pressure too much, and forget to allow the horse any let-up – as with people, they can be pushed that bit too far and can become resentful and unco-operative. An event horse must *want* to do the job, and it is vital that his enjoyment and enthusiasm are not compromised. Basil was therefore hacked out quietly for several days running, and was only schooled in the last few days before Milton Keynes, his next Novice event.

Mary was now looking for a bit more engagement, and lightness of the forehand from Basil, and was doing more lateral work with him. An exercise such as shoulder-in really makes a horse use his hindlegs and carry himself better, and the hope is that by doing so gradually it becomes his customary way of going – he will prefer to stay off his forehand and carry more weight on his hindquarters. As far as Basil was concerned, to improve his balance and, again, to encourage him to use his hindquarters more actively, he was asked to canter on much smaller circles than the usual 20m ones – 15m and 10m circles really make the inside hindleg come under the horse and carry his weight. Mary also asked him for transitions within canter, from working to medium canter and back to working canter – this also encourages greater use of the horse's back end as he has to keep coming back onto his hindquarters when he is asked to slow down to collect the canter before having to push forward with the hindlegs into medium canter.

Milton Keynes one-day event

The day before Milton Keynes Mary gave Basil some more water schooling in the river as she knew from past experience that there was quite a complicated water jump on the cross-country course there.

'During the warm-up for the dressage Basil was quite strong and heavy in my hand. He is just starting to get a bit bossy, and is discovering his own strength.' Fortunately he is the sort of horse who calms down the more he is worked, besides which he seems to find the atmosphere of the dressage arena relaxing and becomes calmer still; this was well demonstrated when he produced a score of 25 and took the lead.

● An excitable horse will often settle into his ridden work more quickly if he is lunged first

● Mary keeps her weight back and allows enough length of rein to give Sammy sufficient freedom of movement as he jumps down the step at Milton Keynes

HALF-HALTS AND COLLECTION

The half-halt is a signal given by the rider to the horse which warns him to expect an immediate instruction; it also serves to rebalance him within a pace. It is a very subtle integration of the seat, leg and hand so that the horse's hindquarters are driven further under him and lowered, and his forehand is slightly elevated; it is an aid which is used throughout a horse's training. Every horse will require a varying degree of leg, seat and hand to achieve the aim of the half-halt, and a rider can establish the precise aids required by using the following exercise. Ride the horse forward in trot on a circle, then close the legs and hands as if asking him to walk; however, just before he breaks into walk, send him forward into trot again, though *without* throwing away the contact. Dr Reiner Klimke, the much respected dressage rider and trainer, has such a perfect understanding with his horses that they carry out the half-halt on a word of command, without him needing to use any other aid! A series of half-halts can be used in quick succession to collect and balance the horse within a pace, or the half-halt can be used to prepare the horse for a change of direction or a transition.

To help her horses become more collected in their work, Mary uses an exaggerated form of the half-halt to ride transitions within the pace. When a horse changes from collected trot to extended trot, and back to collected trot, his hindlegs are driven further beneath him in the downward transitions. The energy that is stored up by reducing the pace with the rider still keeping the legs on to maintain the impulsion, is then released to produce the medium or extended pace. Then all the power and energy created in the extended work is 'compressed' as the horse returns to a more collected pace – and the result is a more elevated movement. Instead of the energy in the hindquarters being used to lengthen the steps, it is used to lift the forehand and elevate the stride.

● *Mary sits up and keeps her leg on during the transition from medium canter back to working canter, to keep Basil's hind legs engaged, and to prevent him throwing his weight onto his forehand*

The going in the showjumping was very deep, but having experienced such conditions already at Hilmarton, Basil was confident enough to cope and produced a clear round.

The cross-country was more difficult than anything he had tackled before and included some quite tricky combinations – the water, the coffin and the uphill steps. 'I did not want to hassle him too much in case he became tense and worried about what was to come,' said Mary ' so I kept him in a strong rhythm and then tried not to interfere with him. We did take the long way at the water as he still feels a bit babyish occasionally and the coffin was the very next jump – two difficult jumps in a row could have shaken his newly found confidence, and so we played safe at the water and were rewarded with a good jump directly through the coffin and over the rest of the course.' Basil and another horse finished in the lead with an equal score, but Basil was relegated to second place as the other competitor was nearer the cross-country optimum time. Basil is now over halfway to intermediate, having won a total of 12 points.

Bicton one-day event

Another quiet week of hacking followed in preparation for Bicton which is Mary's most local event. Basil did not do any fastwork as he had run across country the weekend before; a quiet schooling session on the flat and over some showjumps the day before the event was his only serious workout.

'Basil went really well at Bicton,' said Mary. 'He did his best dressage test so far and went on to jump clear in the showjumping – and the showjumping arena at Bicton is always very stary and spooky, and generally causes a lot of trouble, so it was no easy task. Then we set off confidently across country, having led from the start of the event. I thought we were making good time, but finished to find that most people had gone a lot faster and so we dropped to 7th place. In fact I do not wear a stopwatch at a one-day event as I think it is more important to establish a rhythm which suits the horse and the conditions, particularly early on in a horse's career. A watch is most useful when the time is *easy* to achieve, when you use it to see if you can afford to slow down a little and save the horse for another day. I wasn't a bit worried about slipping down the placings as Basil is already gaining points quite rapidly – but he is not quite ready to tackle an Intermediate event.'

KING KONG

Conker's next event was in the middle of April, so the first two weeks were worked out to include fastwork every four days, and schooling and hacking in between. Conker has a naturally good jump and a bold attitude, so for him the emphasis is on improving his discipline and performance on the flat.

As he seems to have boundless energy no matter what he is made to do, Mary will often work him on the lunge before a schooling session. Not only does lungeing often help to settle a horse, it also gives Mary a chance to see what he looks like when he is working, and it is often possible to pick out faults or potential problems which you can't necessarily feel when you are riding. Conker's particular problem at the moment shows up both on the lunge and when ridden, namely that he is quite stiff on the left rein because he manages to avoid taking up a contact on the right rein. In effect this means that he does not allow himself to be ridden from the inside leg to the outside rein when on the left rein.

To explain: when you are working a horse on a circle he should be able to maintain the inside bend even if you give away the inside rein to the extent that there is no contact. The bend is created and maintained by making him bend around your inside leg, with a supporting contact only in the outside hand. To overcome a resistance such as Conker's, for example on the left rein when lungeing, it is important to make sure the horse is really bending through his neck and body, and not falling in on the corners when effectively he is bending to the outside. He should be made to go forward in quite a strong rhythm on the lunge, and the lunge whip should be used to keep the forward impulsion: if he falls in on the corners the whip should be pointed at his shoulder; flicked at him so that he *has* to keep his shoulder out, and his body bent to the inside.

In Conker's ridden schooling sessions Mary did a lot of work on the left rein, all the time using her inside leg to push him into a contact on the outside rein, and encouraging him to soften on the left rein. Besides this, when working on the *right* rein she was careful that he did not bend *too much* to the right, as this would result in him hanging onto her left hand, and would further aggravate the stiffness on the left rein.

To keep his work varied, Mary also worked

Conker through the showjumping grid she had set up for Basil. Needless to say he performed this exercise very well! After his last day of fast-work before Goring Heath one-day event, Conker also had a water schooling session, mainly to remind him how much fun the cross-country is!

Goring Heath one-day event

The cross-country track at Goring Heath is big and built on quite undulating ground. It includes a very big corner at the end, and although the going was really good, the course was designed to be quite a challenge.

Conker performed his dressage very quietly and obediently which was pleasing.

'I had lunged him first and then put him back in the lorry for a while,' said Mary 'and when he came back out to work in for the test, he was very relaxed and settled. He lost balance a few times during the test as the arena was on quite a slope, but he tried very hard, which is the most important thing.' His score of 31 put him in the top seven.

The showjumping was causing a lot of prob-lems but Conker produced a fabulous clear round, really springing over the fences. He con-tinued his good effort by going superbly across country. 'The course was a fair test for him and he responded well. I rode fairly strongly into the big corner and he stayed straight and thought of nothing else other than doing what I asked. He finished second.' Mary concluded that Conker's jumping is perfectly good enough for top level eventing but his dressage still needs to improve.

Further training

Conker's next event was the advanced class at Milton Keynes, but Mary was concerned that as he had not done many events to date, he might not be ready for this next step. When horses upgrade quickly, care must be taken that they are not over-faced. If a horse has been getting placed and winning points it obviously has abil-ity, but it also needs experience to ensure it does not lose confidence as it faces new challenges.

Mary continued to work on Conker's dres-sage, and began to bring in some of the move-ments he would have to produce in the

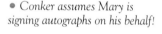

● *Conker assumes Mary is signing autographs on his behalf!*

advanced test. His half-pass needed to flow more, and he would have to be more balanced and disciplined when working in medium and extended trot and canter. Mary had to insist he came back from his extended work without fighting or leaning on her hand – and she had to remember to keep using her legs in the downward transition even when he was being too onward-bound, to help him realise that he must slow himself down by engaging his hindlegs and not just fall onto his forehand and become heavy in her hand.

Towards the end of April Mary took Conker up to Ferdi's for another lesson to help put the polish on his advanced work, and for a change he was very amenable, producing his best work to date. At home, Mary had been having trouble improving Conker's half-pass to the right; he wanted to go sideways too much, rather than *forwards* and sideways across the school, and would then lose his balance and rhythm because of the awkwardness of moving almost directly sideways. Ferdi advised Mary not to ask for so much sideways movement and to ride a very shallow half-pass, so that the emphasis was on pulling forwards. The next day Conker came out and produced a much improved half-pass on each rein. Mary was relieved that Ferdi had helped solve this problem, as at home she and Conker had come to something of an impasse concerning half-pass. This is where expert instruction and help is so important, as the rider can often learn better ways of correcting a certain problem; and he can use this knowledge if in the future the same trouble arises with another horse.

As an advanced event requires greater speed and distance across country, Conker's fastwork was increased over the last fortnight to twice up the middle and twice up the long side of the gallop field.

Milton Keynes one-day event

Conker travelled up to Milton Keynes the day before his class, and Mary gave him quite a workout as he was bursting with energy. Yet on the morning of the event he was as lively as ever, and became very excitable in his test – he refused to concentrate and would not keep a good rhythm. However, he redeemed himself in the showjumping by jumping a clear round over his first advanced track!

Mary had walked the cross-country course the night before and decided it was too much of a test for him so early in the season; she therefore withdrew after the showjumping. Besides, once again Conker had proved that his flatwork – or perhaps rather his attitude to it – needed more improvement.

Mary took Conker to task following his dressage performance at Milton Keynes: she was determined that he should realise that he had to behave himself, and spent a couple of days on serious schooling, insisting on obedience and accuracy the whole time. 'He was tending to hang onto the left rein again, so I rode him in a prickle pad, which had helped correct William's evasion to the left when jumping,' said Mary. 'The prickle pad is basically a leather cheek guard with bristles protruding from it. It is worn like a cheek guard, with the bristles against the horse's cheeks, and it discourages the horse from leaning against it. So if it is placed on the offside bit ring it should stop the horse leaning to he left.'

Mary also used a double bridle for some of Conker's schooling work. He seemed to have considerable respect for this piece of tack and was much quieter in Mary's hand. A double bridle can be used for the dressage at intermediate and advanced level and it often helps just to remind a horse to respect the rider's hand.

Bicton one-day event

Mary took Conker to Bicton with the novices the day before his class to make sure he would settle and work sensibly in the atmosphere of the event. He was very relaxed and well behaved; but his plan had obviously been to lull Mary into a false sense of security, as he was jumping out of his skin next day, the day of his test. Mary decided to ride him in the double bridle as it had worked well at home. However, as Conker started his test he became, as usual, a little tense and excitable and unfortunately did not really accept the double bridle in the way he had at home; and because he was not really accepting the contact and moving forwards into it, his trot became quite stilted, and lacked the swing and rhythm which he is more than capable of producing. But it did teach him to remain obedient, and his score of 39 was not too bad for just his second advanced test. Naturally he made nothing of the jumping phases, and produced a double clear to finish fifth!

For Mary and her supporters the enjoyment of the event was even further increased when her ever-faithful King Boris won his section.

● *William and Apple discuss the day's event – William is obviously convinced that he put up the best performance but Apple disagrees!!*

KING WILLIAM

By April, William's preparation for his first advanced event of the season, at Kings Somborne, was well under way. The interruptions to his training programme caused by his course of injections were well in the past, and he was back to his normal timetable of cantering every four days, and hacking and schooling in between.

Mary had been having particular trouble keeping William round in his outline through the transitions down from extended and medium canter; he was being very strong and holding his head high, and this was hollowing his back. So for one flatwork session Mary rode William in draw-reins, which just helped her to keep him rounder and softer. However, it is important to realise that whilst draw-reins can serve a good purpose, they can also be very severe and should only be used with great care. It is especially important when using them to be strong with your legs to keep the horse working through from behind, otherwise he will become overbent and heavy in the hand. For Mary's purposes with William, the draw-reins helped

her hold him together so that he stayed round through the downward transitions, and could learn what was required of him.

Kings Somborne one-day event

On the morning of Kings Somborne William was very bright and lively, so Mary lunged him first which seemed to relax him. This is her own account of the day:

'William felt very tense and strong in my hand during the test and was a bit too free in his extended trot and canter; he was just taking the opportunity to rush off, rather than containing the energy that is created in these paces. Generally, though, he was very obedient and it must have looked good because he took the lead – but I know there is a lot of improvement needed to produce the winning test at Badminton!

'Captain Mark Phillips helped me warm up for the showjumping. William has got much worse about jumping to the left, and whatever we tried it didn't seem to correct him. In fact the harder we tried the more awkward William became – probably because he was over-excited. Eventually this lack of concentration led to him hitting the practice fence quite hard, and it seemed to surprise him so much that he jumped much more carefully after that. He produced a good round despite knocking the final element of the downhill treble – this was because he made up too much ground and got too close to it. Even though a rider can control his horse's approach into a downhill combination and come in on a short, bouncy stride, once the horse is jumping through the combination there is very little room left in which to correct him if he starts to cover too much ground. If the horse is always schooled at home to jump from a short bouncy stride and is put through combinations set at slightly shorter distances than you would normally get at an event, then hopefully he will remain 'short and sharp' of his own accord. In William's case, his excitement over-ruled his experience!

'As we prepared for the cross-country I was very conscious of the fact that all the Olympic selectors were scattered around the course, watching the potential Olympic horses. William was going quite beautifully as we approached the water complex. This involved a big drop down into the water, very similar to our Punchestown Waterloo last year. As William is so genuine and bold I had decided to bring him right back to a slow trot on the approach, in the hope that he would just drop down off the top rather than launch himself boldly into the middle of the water. In fact at Kings Somborne he was being particularly obedient and attentive, and I obviously did not keep my legs on enough because before I knew it, we were first trotting, and then only walking up to the obstacle – not what I had planned at all! I could hear the gasp from the crowd, who obviously assumed that it was William who had made the decision to walk, and was now going to stop. I had to pull myself together and think "Jump, William!" – which he obligingly did! He was great, particularly having to cope with this pilot error! Strangely enough he jumps completely straight across country, and never reverts to his showjumping style of veering left. I had ridden fairly quietly around the course so we picked up some time faults, but nevertheless finished fourth.'

Run-up to Badminton

After Kings Somborne William's programme returned to three days' quiet hacking and then fastwork on the fourth day. The plan was that he should have one more complete advanced run before Badminton, at Brigstock. In between he would do just the dressage at Belton, to give Mary another chance to try and bring out the improvement she feels can still be made.

The trip to Belton included an extra day for William, at Goring Heath where Conker was performing. Annie rode him quietly around in the morning while Mary was competing and he was very calm and relaxed; but when Mary got on him in the afternoon he was wicked. 'I lunged him in the hope that this would settle him down. He was being very silly and performed some perfect passage with his tail stuck up in the air quite on his own initiative,' said Mary. 'Eventually he did calm down, and after working him quite hard on the lunge I decided there was no need to ride him as well.'

The team then drove straight on to Belton where William was to do just the dressage. In Mary's own words:

'I opted to lunge him first, and again it appeared to work as he was very quiet. But once I was on board and we headed for the dressage arenas he became very excited. There were only 20 minutes left until our test and I had a very tense horse on my hands, so rather than trying to force him to behave, I just let him canter round freely on a large circle and hoped to relieve the pressure in this way. It did help to take the edge off him and he performed a surprisingly obedient test, despite being very strong in my hand.

'Over the last few weeks I had been giving a lot of thought to William's showjumping problem; at home it is quite easy to correct him as you can rest angled poles on a fence to keep him straight, but obviously at a competition you can't do this. I had tried riding him with a prickle pad, fitted to the left-hand side of the bit (a prickle pad is worn like a cheek guard, and the soft bristles which protrude from it lie against the horse's cheek); as I approach a fence I concentrate on keeping him bent to the right, so that if he starts to veer left he then comes up against the bristles which hopefully discourage him. It has worked very well at home, but the test will be whether he still respects it once he is caught up in the excitement of a competition.'

William's last outing before Badminton was fast approaching, and Mary was well aware that there was very little time left now for them to achieve their best possible performance.

'I mostly school William out in the field as my arena is full of showjumps. With so little

● (right) *Ferdi Eilberg helps Mary to perfect her horse's performance on the flat*

time left before Badminton I decided to set up a 60 x 20m arena with my markers in the field. I was surprised at how hard it was to ride him accurately in the confined space; no wonder I find him strong to ride at an event if I can hardly hold him in a field at home!' Mary resolved to do all her schooling before Badminton in the field within these markers.

On the way to Brigstock Mary stopped at Stephen Hadley's for a jumping lesson with William. Steve concentrated on trying to make William jump straight. 'We tried everything,' said Mary, 'angled poles, jumping at an angle from left to right, and we used the prickle pad too, but nothing seemed really to straighten him up. He wasn't as bad as he has been, but he would still 'try to run left until he came up against the prickle pad, which did deter him a little.'

● *Cross-country jumping is all about staying in balance with your horse on the approach and over the fence but getting your weight back behind the movement on landing. William and Mary at Brigstock*

Brigstock one-day event

William was very relaxed for his dressage in the afternoon, having had such a good work-out over Steve Hadley's showjumps that morning.

In fact he did his best test yet, despite being a little tense, earning 31 penalties and going into second place. He produced a clear round in the showjumping which was tremendously encouraging even though he did veer off to the left quite violently a couple of times. Overall he felt calmer and more careful.

Once on the cross-country William was very bold and confident; in fact he seemed to be finding it all a bit too easy and was becoming quite blasé about it – Mary could almost hear him saying 'This is easy, Mum, you just leave everything to me!' But all cross-country fences need treating with respect, and William discovered this to his cost at the coffin: 'He really knocked the first element hard with his front legs and nearly threw me out the front door!' said Mary. 'It was only his leap over the ditch which put me back into the saddle!' After this surprise William gave the task his full attention; he finished the course in good time to take third place. The greatest relief for the rest of the team was that both he and Mary were still in one piece, and that the most serious part of their Badminton preparation was now behind them.

Invitation FEI Dressage

A dressage competition had been arranged at the Haycock Hotel for those riders longlisted for the Olympics and expected to ride at Badminton. It gave them a chance to ride the FEI test that they would be performing at the three-day event, and there was also £2,000 prize money at stake!

Mary took William to Ferdi Eilberg the day before the competition and had a lesson that afternoon, and another the following morning. William was still too strong in the downward transition from extended to working canter, so they concentrated on making it clear to him that after the extended pace, he was expected to come back immediately into a correct, light, working canter. Both at home and at competitions it had been taking too long to get him back to a working canter whilst still maintaining the activity – William just did not seem to realise *how* important it was that he listened to Mary!

'It's very tempting to rely on just your hands to bring the horse back, but if you do he will bear down on your hands, block up in front and

the hindlegs will push the weight of his body onto his forehand. He must learn to take his weight and reduce the pace by lowering his hindquarters and stepping under more with his hindlegs; to achieve this it is important to keep the leg on throughout the movement so that the downward transition results in an active working canter.

'I had to be quite firm, and unusually strong with William to get the message through to him. Normally if you just set your hands against a horse he will simply pull back at you, and being the stronger, will win the "contest". With a less experienced horse you can resort to a give-and-take tactic, but William's education was sufficiently advanced for him to have *known* what was expected of him. So I took a smooth, but very firm, pull and brought him back from extended canter to halt, before going forward into canter again. At the second attempt a less dramatic aid was required to reduce the pace, and at the third attempt we forsook the halt and, by using my legs to push his hindquarters under him and with just a light aid from my hand, he produced an obedient transition from extended canter to a good working canter. At last he seemed to realise that it really *did* matter to me that he performed this task well!

'At the competition William was very calm and settled and he performed his best test this year by far; he was neither too tense nor too strong so I could really ride out the test without worrying that he would go over the top. He made only one mistake, which was to anticipate the transition from medium walk to canter when he became tense and jogged in the walk, he won the competition by a decisive twelve points over Ginny Leng and Master Craftsman.'

Between the FEI dressage competition and Badminton Mary was particularly careful *not* to ride too many walk-to-canter transitions; instead she practised walk to halt to trot to canter, so that William learned to wait for the aid to canter.

Mary also had a lesson to learn concerning her own performance: as she entered the arena, another dressage trainer whispered to her: 'Mary, don't lean forwards!' Mary *felt* she was sitting perfectly upright, but on seeing a video of the test afterwards she was horrified to notice that her upper body did, in fact, tilt forward – something else to practise before Badminton!

Final preparations

There was now only a fortnight to go before William was due to leave for Badminton. With his competition preparation successfully completed the main aim was just to keep him fit and happy and to put the finishing touches to his dressage and showjumping. His fastwork was increased until he was working five times up the gallop field every four days; on the last Thursday and Monday before Badminton this increased to six times up the field.

A final trip to Ferdi's showed Mary that although William had been improving all the time, he could do better still. They worked mainly on his canter; trying to persuade him not to get too strong or to bowl on too much in this pace. They tried to achieve this by doing a lot of transitions from extended canter back to collected canter – emphasising to William the importance of coming back into Mary's hand quietly and calmly when asked.

At home, Mary did their dressage schooling out in the field to try and improve her accuracy and control in the open. She just couldn't wait for Badminton to arrive, but was careful not to communicate this tense anticipation to William – it was important that everyone in the yard kept him quiet and happy in his routine.

He went for some long relaxing hacks, mainly at walk, for up to two hours at a time. He had just one rather unusual schooling session in between: Mary knew from magazine course previews that there was a very narrow arrowhead to be jumped as a bounce out of the lake, so William was put to the test and asked to jump very narrow fences in the arena. Mary even lined up some barrels and played 'barrel elimination', removing one barrel from the line each time they cleared it, until they were jumping just one barrel all on its own (see September diary).

Incredibly William jumped completely straight during this exercise. 'He is *so* genuine,' said Mary '– he knew he was expected to jump it, and that if he veered left he would miss it. So he stayed as straight as a die and jumped it spot on!' This exercise provided William with some light relief and Mary with even more confidence; and soon the waiting would be over.

MAY

My win at Badminton with William was a dream come true. I knew it was possible, but for everything to come right at the right time was absolutely fantastic – I was floating around on cloud nine for quite a few days, hardly believing it really had happened! However, all the press, TV and radio interviews, plus over 400 letters of congratulation, have persuaded me that yes, William and I really did win Badminton, it wasn't a dream, we were there and we did it!

It wasn't long before I was rapidly brought back down to earth. The weekend after Badminton I missed out a cross-country fence with Mars at Weston Park, which meant we were eliminated. Then at Windsor three-day event, I made a mistake in the dressage test; I'm not sure that Conker has forgiven me yet! Despite this rider error, Conker triumphed at Windsor, making it a record five consecutive three-day- event wins for me. I was thrilled with him, as it meant that all the work and patience I had put into him had been more than worthwhile; it was as though he realised what an important occasion it was and stayed amazingly calm and obedient – for him – in the dressage (if his jockey had not been so forgetful he would have led this phase). He then proceeded to go clear in both the cross-country and the showjumping to take the lead. I just hoped I wasn't using up all my luck before the Olympics!

Flying out to Italy the day after Windsor to compete in the Continental Cup Final with King Samuel came as quite a relief. As much as I thoroughly enjoy all the media interest and support, it was great to get away from it all for a few days in a different country; I found myself amongst a very friendly bunch of competitors, and was quite expecting the event to be fairly straightforward. No such luck: it was the biggest three-star course I have ever seen! Despite a hesitation on top of a bank, Sammy coped admirably well; I then fell off just before my showjumping round, and at the end of it all was left feeling that to have taken second place was altogether lucky!

Boris completed a successful spring season by finishing third at the Weston Park Advanced one-day event. He has been placed in all his competitions this year, but I felt his last event came just in time as the ground was starting to get hard. I don't think Basil enjoyed the firmer ground at Weston Park, so I was pleased to let him have a holiday after that event, too. He was turned out in the field with Boris while I was busy at the three-day events.

TRANSITIONS WITHIN THE PACE

At intermediate, and even more so at advanced level, the horse is asked to show transitions within each pace. These variations within a pace are the more accomplished version of the 'few lengthened strides' that the novice horse is asked to demonstrate in his dressage test. Beyond novice level the horse has to produce a definite medium trot across the diagonal from marker to marker. At advanced level a fully extended trot and canter is also required.

● *Sammy proceeds around the short side in an active working trot*

● *Mary half-halts Sammy*

● *Mary then allows Sammy to open up his stride as she proceeds up the long side*

● *Sammy extends his stride*

● *During the transition back to working trot Mary sits up straight, keeping her legs on to keep his hocks engaged and forehand light*

The novice horse will already have learned to open up his stride, but now he must be taught to go straight into medium trot on command, to maintain the rhythm of the trot throughout the movement, and then to produce a good transition back to working trot. A degree of collection is necessary before the horse is able to extend his stride: collecting the horse, usually by means of a series of half-halts, ensures that his hindquarters are placed well underneath him and that he has sufficient energy stored up which can be released to produce the medium or extended trot. It is important that the transitions from working to medium trot, and medium back to working trot are clearly defined otherwise the horse just runs into the movement and falls onto his forehand.

'I make sure I keep using my legs on the horse so that his hindlegs remain active; then he will learn, in the long term, to increase or decrease the pace by using his hindlegs,' explains Mary. 'When schooling, I ride medium trot at different places around the arena, and not just across the diagonal so that the horse does not anticipate the movement – also, by continuing in medium pace around the corners of the school, the horse learns not to back off the corner and fall back into working trot before he is asked.'

The same principle applies in canter. Conker is always looking to his rider's hand to help his balance and so with him, Mary has to make a conscious effort not to let him lean on her. This is achieved by pushing him strongly forwards when he leans so that his hindlegs become more active and take more of his weight. With a strong, onward-bound horse it is easy to forget to use your legs, but in this situation it is even *more* essential to ride the horse from leg to hand. The horse must learn to carry himself so that he remains light in front.

When teaching the horse medium and extended paces it is important not to ask for too much medium work too quickly, otherwise he will be pushed onto his forehand. The trot or canter should be increased stride by stride, so that he has a chance to adjust his balance and maintain it throughout his work.

No sooner had Mary arrived back from Bicton than it was time to start packing for Badminton. She had decided to give Basil a week off, since everyone's energy and concentration would inevitably be directed towards helping William achieve a good result at this prestigious event. So while Mary and her team were immersed in the excitement and drama of Badminton, Basil grazed contentedly in the field, quite oblivious to the challenge facing his stablemate.

KING BASIL

William's success was supreme: his tale is related shortly. For Basil, once the triumphant team had arrived home, it meant a return to work. Weston Park was the aim, the final outing of his spring campaign, and this event was less than a week away. Mary was rather surprised to find that Basil had become much softer and fatter during his week off than she had expected so his roadwork was increased quickly through the week and Mary schooled and jumped him several times in preparation for Weston Park. The day before the event she took Basil for a splash around in the River Sid to remind him that water means fun.

Weston Park one-day event

The break in Basil's routine seemed to have done him good, as he produced a beautiful dressage test and took the lead. The going was the hardest that Basil had ever run on and, although he obviously did not like it as much, he still produced a neat showjumping round and went clear. The cross-country was unfortunately another story.

'Basil never felt really happy,' said Mary. 'His first run on hard ground, plus the fact that he was not as fit and lean as he had been, perhaps combined against him. Even though he wasn't jumping with much enthusiasm, I still decided to take the direct route through the coffin as I did not really want to go back a stage from where he had left off before Badminton, when he was tackling the direct routes quite happily. In fact he put in quite an abrupt stop at the first element; however, I risked trying the direct way once more, because I wanted him to realise that it was something he was more than capable of doing. He jumped it well – but then, only a few fences later, he had another stop at the upright palisade going into the second water-jump.'

83

RIDING THE HALF-PASS

As Conker is now well on his way through intermediate level, he will probably quite soon have to perform an advanced dressage test; it is important to include in his schooling some of the advanced movements which will be new to him and which he will be asked to produce.

The half-pass is one of the movements required at advanced level: in the half-pass the horse moves on two tracks with a very slight bend in the direction in which he is going. The forehand – head, neck and shoulders – is slightly in advance of the quarters. The outside foreleg must cross over and in front of the inside foreleg, and the outside hindleg crosses over and in front of the inside hindleg. The movement activates the shoulder. Mary begins to teach this to her horses once their shoulder-in is well established.

'I come from a 10m circle in the corner of the arena,' explains Mary. 'On the circle I establish the correct bend, making sure that the weight of the contact is in my outside hand and that I am pushing the horse into this contact by using my inside leg. As I come out of the 10m circle and the horse is parallel to the long side of the arena, I move him into half-pass: I hold the shoulder and neck as if he was going to perform shoulder-in, but then use my outside leg to ask him to move his hindquarters across the diagonal; my inside leg is used to maintain the forward movement. In the early stages he will almost certainly not be straight (ie he will not move his quarters over sufficiently to remain parallel with the long side of the arena), but my main aim would be for the horse to stay in a regular rhythm as he moves across the diagonal, and to maintain his outline and rhythm. When riding the half-pass my inside hand creates the bend while my outside leg and outside hand control the degree to which the shoulders lead the quarters as the horse moves across the diagonal. As he learns to balance himself in this position I gradually ask him to bring his quarters into the correct position (parallel to the long side of the arena).

'If he was tending to run on and lose his balance I would bring him back to walk and continue the half-pass in walk before going into trot and trying again.

'If, on the other hand, he was tending to hang back and not really striding forwards and across the arena, I would ride a half-pass with a shallower angle, so that his shoulders were well ahead of his hindquarters. This will help him to increase the strength of the trot as it is easier for him to work at less of an angle, and it teaches him to pull away from the outside hand in the direction in which he is going, and not to hang back on the rider's inside hand.'

● Riding the half-pass with a shallow angle, allowing the shoulders to lead

● The outside leg is used to bring the quarters into the correct position

In hindsight Mary wishes she had let Basil finish his spring season at Bicton where he had gone so well. However, it was now a case of waiting to see how he would react when he was asked to tackle the summer events after the few weeks off which he would now be given. He would obviously be back to his 'working weight' for these as there would be time to prepare him properly; and with any luck the ground would be softer. Nevertheless, it could be that Basil's heart and soul are not completely in eventing: only time will tell.

KING KONG

After his run at Bicton, and while Mary was at Badminton, Conker was just quietly hacked out. He did his fastwork on the Friday of Badminton, and from then on every four days as usual.

After Badminton there was just over a week before Conker headed for his target three-day event: Windsor. On her return, Mary had planned to concentrate on his dressage during this week; though she tried to work in earnest, he did everything *but* what he was told! So Mary just had to keep on insisting, quietly but relentlessly, that he did what he was asked and did it properly. By the end of the first morning she was convinced that they had made some good progress – but when she tried a repeat schooling session the following day, he was as naughty as ever. She had ridden him in a double bridle on both these occasions but although this helped, his exuberance would simply not be overcome that easily!

'Without getting angry, you just have to be really firm with him,' said Mary, 'and keep repeating the exercise until he co-operates.'

A few days before they set off for Windsor, Mary took Conker round her local cross-country schooling course; the fences were very small, but perfect for allowing a horse to have fun and gain confidence. He then did his final fastwork before the three-day event on the Monday.

Conker had another important engagement before Windsor: he went with Mary to the first of the Audi Masterclass lecture demonstrations at Faversham in Kent. He was used during the evening to show off the latest in safety and reflective gear, and was also required to set the example – and Mary just hoped he would be good! – in the jumping phase of the demonstration. In fact he behaved very well, despite the highly charged atmosphere with its loud music, flashing lights and enthusiastic audience.

Windsor three-day event CCI**

After all Faversham's excitement, Conker was remarkably calm once he arrived at Windsor on the Wednesday. After the competitors' briefing Mary hacked him out and schooled him quietly in his double bridle, and he was very relaxed throughout; he also behaved very well for the trot-up that evening.

His dressage test was the following day, and Mary decided to follow the routine that she had adopted at Badminton with William: 'I took him for a hack and steady canter first thing, and then popped him over the practice fences. After a rest in the stable, I schooled him for three-quarters of an hour in the practice arenas; I rode him in his snaffle and he worked in very well. All the same, I was very strict with myself and made sure I corrected even the slightest error. He then went back to the stable for a final smarten-up by Tina while I changed. He performed a very obedient test despite being a little tense. The most pleasing thing was that he managed to control his enthusiasm and that his trot had so much more rhythm and swing, which it had lacked last year.

Conker's dressage score should have been the best over the two days of dressage but two penalties were deducted because of rider error! Mary took a straight line across the long diagonal in the extended walk movement instead of riding a staggered diagonal, and admitted to not having read the test very carefully. Normally

● *Conker settles into a relaxed trot on Phase A – conserving energy for what lies ahead.* (below) *The 10-minute box – damp towels protect Conker from the midday heat*

she would have watched someone else ride through the test first, but on this occasion she didn't, for some reason. This error dropped them to third place – but there is nothing quite like a silly mistake for sharpening the competitive edge!

During the second day of dressage Mary took Conker out for about an hour's hack; she included a short pipe-opener up the hill alongside the Long Walk, one of the broad grass walkways through Windsor Great Park.

On cross-country morning Conker had his normal concentrate feed for breakfast, but was only allowed a handful of hay. 'Many riders do not allow their horses any hay at all on cross-country morning, but I like them to have something as I am sure it helps keep their insides working properly.'

Tina led him around at walk for five minutes in the mid-morning, letting him have a few mouthfuls of grass to keep him happy and relaxed. Walking out like this gets rid of any swelling which may have built up overnight in the horse's legs, and it is important to reduce this completely before bandaging. Conker had the same leg protection as William at Badminton: tubigrips, Porter boots and bandages in front, plus overreach boots, and leather

● *(below) Mary and Conker take off at the start of the cross-country (opposite) Mary slips her reins and leans back to stay in balance as Conker drops into the water*

speedycut boots behind. Mary then had to take her saddle and weightcloth to weigh out while Conker was led up to the start of Phase A. She got on him four minutes before the off; allowing just enough time for the girth to be tightened and the overgirth fastened.

'Conker settled nicely on the roads and tracks, keeping up a steady, relaxed trot – until Kit Houghton, the photographer, leapt out from behind a bush to take a shot of us! We arrived at the steeplechase two minutes ahead of schedule, which is what we had planned to do.

'The going on the steeplechase was very firm, which had been worrying me. Extra soil had been put down on the landings and about halfway round the track but it was still not at all satisfactory. At Osberton, Conker's first three-day event, he had given me a horrific ride around the steeplechase, as he just could not cope with the excitement of being allowed to gallop. So as well as my worries about the ground, I was also concerned about just what he would do. In fact I need not have worried, as he was much more grown up than at Osberton. He remained calm, and I could feel him measuring the distance to each fence and taking it in his stride.

'Although he had apparently galloped and jumped perfectly happily, I could feel his stride was quite stilted once I began to pull him up; which probably meant he was a bit jarred up after galloping on the hard ground. After walking the first kilometre of Phase C, it was rather tentatively that I asked him to go forwards into trot – but thankfully his stride felt free and comfortable again. It was very hot, and so I rode him in the shade wherever I could. He came into the ten-minute box feeling really good; the vets checked him over and were very pleased with his breathing and pulse rate and general well-being.

'Conker gave me a great ride across country. He was honest, bold and positive and kept as straight as a die. I took the alternative route at the first water as you didn't really waste much time doing it, and the direct route involved a bounce into water after a long downhill gallop; I thought it would be difficult to get the horse back on his hocks, and controlled enough, to tackle the bounce. After that, however, I took all the direct ways, even though this had not been my intention when I walked the course. But when a horse is going so much better than you had anticipated, he has earned the right to prove himself over the more difficult options.

We finished just inside the optimum time, although again I had not looked at my watch but had just let him keep going in the rhythm he was happiest with. He recovered extremely quickly and we were all thrilled to bits.

'I watched him trot up that evening and he was supple and level, and still looked happy and relaxed.

'He entered the showjumping phase in the lead, with one fence in hand, and after my Badminton experience – when William had rattled nearly every fence – I was relieved that we had at least that! After a run across country,

● *Conker and Mary head determinedly for home*

● *Conker demonstrates a perfect bascule – lifting his shoulder, lowering his head and neck, and neatly folded in front*

especially on hard ground, there is always the worry that a horse will have lost the natural spring in his jump because he is tired or sore. But dear Conker had not lost any of his – all his naturally good jump was there still, and he produced a clear round to win the Windsor CCI**! In fact he is a much easier horse to show-jump at a three-day event as he is quieter and calmer having had an outlet for his energy the day before.'

When Mary checked Conker over the following morning at home, she could feel just a hint of extra heat in his off-fore. The vet had a look, and even though Conker was sound and the swelling was barely noticeable, he was sufficiently concerned to suggest that the leg should be scanned. This would be done at Newmarket, and until such time as he could be taken there, Conker was just led out at walk each day. Mary used cold therapy to try and minimise the swelling, hosing the leg with cold water three times a day.

KING WILLIAM'S BADMINTON

The Badminton Three-Day Event is one of the greatest challenges an event rider is ever likely to meet; moreover in an Olympic year the challenge is not just a personal one, because the competition offers every partnership of Olympic potential a chance to prove its worth to the selectors.

For Mary and Annie, setting off to Badminton on Tuesday morning was the successful culmination of their aim for the spring season: to produce William fit, sound and superbly prepared for the task ahead. The team arrived at Badminton House in time to let William settle in and have his lunch in his new surroundings. The normal procedure at Badminton is that before a horse is allowed into the stableyard, his passport must be checked at the village hall, to ensure that he is, without any doubt, the horse that is entered. He is inspected by a vet to make sure that he had no

---

PACKING FOR BADMINTON

Annie is responsible for making sure that all the gear and equipment that might possibly be needed for Badminton is packed in the lorry.

'I take just about everything I can think of,' says Annie. 'You have to be prepared for all weather conditions and need appropriate clothing for both horses and humans. As well as all the rugs and usual competition tack we take plenty of spares so we are prepared for anything. A well-stocked first-aid kit is also essential. Once we are there, the night before the cross-country I pack a trunk full of equipment to take to the 10-minute box, as well as a rucksack to take with me to the steeplechase phase.'

Steeplechase rucksack:

Spare set of horseshoes complete with studs	Pressure bandage
Hammer	Woof boots in case a bandage has come off
Spare bridle	A drink for Mary
Hole punch	Spare gloves, whip, stirrup and stirrup leather
Stud kit	

Trunk for 10-minute halt box:

Contents of steeplechase rucksack plus:	Spare martingale and breastplate
Buckets of water, sweatscraper and sponges	Spare set of numbers (in case Mary's number holder had broken)
Lots of towels	Assortment of rugs including sweatrug, thermatex rug, woollen day rug and rain-sheet
Cross-country grease	

Spare reins	Full first-aid kit
Ice	Scissors and elastic bands
Spare stopwatch	Spare saddle and girth
Drink and seat for Mary	Spare bandages and boots
Pen and paper	
Equiboot	

contagious skin infections, for example ring-worm, and no sign of a virus such as 'flu. He then receives a ticket which allows him into the stableyard. In the afternoon Mary took William for a long hack around the park, giving him the chance to take in his new surroundings. They had a long steady canter along Worcester Avenue, the beautiful grass ride which runs from Badminton House to Worcester Lodge, one of the ornate gates to the park.

Official preliminaries

There is always a social whirl at Badminton, and it started that first evening with a party hosted by Spillers Horse Feeds in a local village – Littleton Drew – wonderful food and a chance to meet everybody. Officially the three-day event starts with the competitors' briefing at ten o'clock on the Wednesday; Mary took William for a quiet half-hour hack early in the morning so she could concentrate her mind on remembering all the vital information given out then. First there are introductions to all the officials and the Ground Jury. The rules apper-taining to Badminton Park are explained, and full information given concerning the facilities

available for horses and riders. Points of partic-ular note concerning the course are explained – for example where penalty zones overlap between two different fences. After the brief-ing, competitors are taken on an official tour of the roads and tracks and steeplechase – every-one piles into four-wheel-drive vehicles and traditionally there is a mad race to the start of Phase A; Hugh Thomas, director of Badminton, is meant to lead the convoy but the likes of David Green or Mark Todd have usu-ally given him a good run for his money!

The cross-country course is officially opened at 12 o'clock on Wednesday, and everyone sets off for their first real look at what is to come.

'The first course-walk just gives you a general feel for the track,' explains Mary. 'You usually get caught up amongst a group of riders so it is not the ideal time for taking in all the detail. This year I thought the course looked very jumpable, and it was similar to last year's, when William had gone so well which made me feel quietly confident; though you daren't hope for too much, as you can never tell what may happen!'

Annie spent the afternoon beautifying William for the first horse inspection; this is conducted in front of Badminton House in the

● *The rider is meant to keep in step with the horse – difficult when William goes into overdrive!*

● *A relaxed moment before the pressure begins*

evening. It is a wonderfully traditional and dignified affair: as each horse is called and led up by his rider, the stewards remove their bowlers and salute the combination, and the Ground Jury watches carefully as the horse is walked up to them. He is halted so they can inspect him more closely, then trotted away and back past them. At the end of the trot-up the competitor waits for those crucial words: 'Number X, passed!'

William had been drawn number 38, and he trotted out beautifully for the inspection. Mary always maintains that if William were human he would be a real ladykiller, his proud, aloof manner, his great presence and impressive appearance had obviously won him a tremendous crowd of admirers.

With the first stage of the three-day event happily passed, Mary took William away from the large crowds who always gather to watch the inspection, and a little later took him for a school in the practice arenas. Ferdi was there to help, and they worked through the main movements required in the dressage test. William went very well; he was settled and not too strong, so there was no need to work him for too long.

AHEAD FROM START TO FINISH

During Badminton this year (1992) much was made of the fact that only one other competitor who led after the dressage had then gone on to win the overall competition, staying ahead from that start to the finish. No doubt this all added to the suspense and excitement for Mary, particularly as – ironically – this rider was Mary's eventing mentor, Sheila Willcox. Sheila won Badminton three times, each time leading after the dressage: in 1957 and 1958 she achieved this with High and Mighty, and in 1959 with Airs and Graces, and this was particularly remarkable in that her victories came at a time when ladies were not allowed to ride at international level, a situation which seems almost unbelievable in a sport which is nowadays dominated by women. For Mary, her win put her and William indisputably on the shortlist Olympic team.

Dressage day

William's dressage test was on Thursday afternoon, and Mary's concern was that he might be too strong, despite his apparently co-operative mood. At the European Championships in Punchestown the previous year he had appeared to be really relaxed, but had then brightened up rather too much just before entering the dressage arena. Mary knew that when working him in, she had to find the right balance, so that he was sufficiently contained for the dressage, but without wearing him out before the speed and endurance phase which followed.

'A horse always performs its best and most impressive dressage test when it is on the borderline of really wanting to explode, but just being able to contain itself. On the Thursday I decided to ride William early in the morning in his pelham and my jumping saddle – we enjoyed a long steady canter and then popped over the showjump and cross-country practice fences; he was very bright and happy, and really sprang over them. My aim was to give him a good workout but without putting any particular pressure on him,' explained Mary. Annie then led him out for some grass to keep him relaxed.

Later on in the morning Mary had arranged another schooling session with Ferdi, just to put the finishing touches to their work. 'William worked quite beautifully and I really felt we were getting somewhere with him,' said Mary. Afterwards they stood near the dressage collecting ring so he could see the crowds and get used to the sounds of applause and the general bustle. He was then taken back to the stables and left to enjoy his lunch, while Mary changed into her top hat and tails. She planned to get on William forty minutes before his test; it was about a ten-minute hack from the stables to the dressage practice arenas, and she wanted to leave half an hour to work him in.

'...William felt wonderful – he was calm, smooth and relaxed, just like a proper dressage horse.' Ten minutes before his test, Mary rode

● *Last-minute advice from Ferdi*

up to the collecting ring. William became a little bit brighter there so Mary carried on working him quietly around the collecting ring.

'I purposely kept William well back from the entrance to the main ring when the competitor before us came out, and did not ask him to enter the arena until the applause had died down,' said Mary. 'He perked up again in the arena but contained himself to perform a very obedient and active test. His brightness showed a little in his lateral work as he was trying to tilt his head which meant there was a bit of resistance – he also had a subtle spook at the flower arrangement! I didn't dare ride out his medium and extended work as much as I would have liked, because by then I felt he was on the verge of going over the top.'

The applause as William and Mary left the arena was tremendous. It was followed by a tense hush as the people watching waited for her score to be announced – then sheer delight when it was obvious that she had taken a good lead.

They retained this lead all through that first day; the second day of dressage, however, would see some very good combinations determined to challenge the situation. Captain Mark Phillips had stated his conviction that Badminton 1992 was going to be a contest between the two 'great-

● *Relaxed and happy. Mary, Lucinda Green and the Captain share a joke*

est technicians in the world: Mary Thomson and Ginny Leng', as Ginny was staging a comeback on Master Craftsman, her World and European Championship horse. Ginny and Crafty had been in the Olympic silver medal team at the Seoul Olympics; after a long lay-off due to injury, they were a combination determined to prove to the selectors that they were as good as ever.

Blissfully unaware of the battle to defeat him, William enjoyed nothing more than a hack on

the Friday. Mary gave him a good pipe-opener along Worcester Avenue, working at three-quarter speed until she could feel him puffing and really using his lungs; she then walked him back to the yard where he could relax. Mary herself had to wait until she knew if anyone had been able to beat their score: nobody had! She and William had scored the first victory – but there was still a long way to go! That afternoon Mary hosted an official course-walk for the British Equestrian Olympic Fund, as well as walking the course on her own.

Badminton 1992 will be remembered for the atrocious weather conditions and consequently very difficult going on cross-country day. By Friday evening the weather had already begun to change for the worst: dark clouds had gathered and it had started to rain – Mary woke several times that night to hear it falling in torrents, and in the morning it was still raining.

● *William was sufficiently relaxed to allow Mary to ride out the extended trot*

THE BADMINTON COURSE WALK

In addition to her many other duties and preparations at Badminton, Mary was asked to host a course walk in aid of the British Equestrian Olympic Fund. Ian Stark joined her on this occasion and together their comments and ideas gave a unique insight into how to tackle the challenging Badminton course.

The Shogun Seat: 'The first fence this year was bigger than it has been in the past. I thought this was a good idea as it helps to have something substantial to get the horse back up in the air over his fences – the effect of the steeplechase is always to flatten him out and can make him a little careless. One look at a fence of this size should be enough to remind him that he is tackling solid fences now. Ian, on the other hand, was not so keen. His horses are very bright and strong when they come out of the start box, and he did not feel that they would be concentrating sufficiently to tackle a big fence well. And as it happened he *didn't* have a very good jump over the first fence. The main aim as you leave the start box and head for the first fence is to get into a good rhythm as quickly as possible.'

● *The Quarry looks deceptively easy, but is one of the first big questions on the course*

The Lamb Creep: 'This year the course took you round a sweeping corner to the Lamb Creep, and most riders would have aimed to hug the right-hand, inner side of the track so as to save precious seconds. This fence had been moved on slightly from the previous year so it was well clear of the road-crossing just before; this meant that the horses had a more balanced approach to the fence, and this should have helped them all achieve a comfortable, confidence-giving jump. But although the fence is straightforward it is still big, so horse and rider must be concentrating.'

Pheasant Feeder: 'There was quite a long galloping stretch to Huntsman's Close where the Pheasant Feeder is sited, and you then had to choose your line into the wood: either you cut the corner, in which case the fence came up on you quite quickly; or you went wide and gave yourself a better approach. I had decided to cut the corner, but knew I would then really have to attack the fence – the horse is quite likely to back off as he enters the dark wood, and it is easy for the rider to think he is going faster than he really is, because the trees whizz by quickly. So you had to make a conscious effort to ride positively forwards to the fence.'

KEY

Mary's route

Slightly easier direct route

Long route

The Cross Question: 'This was a new fence, of maximum height criss-cross rails set over a deep, wide ditch. From Huntsman's Close the track takes a fairly sharp turn to this fence, and it was on this corner that William had slipped up the year before; so as I walked my line I was well aware of needing to keep the horse steady and balanced. The Cross Question looks huge on first sight as it draws your eye into the bottom of the big ditch, but William doesn't mind ditches so my intention was to jump it straight through the middle with the ditch providing the ground-line and keeping the horse off the rails. There was a long route which involved trotting along, through the ditch under the crossed rails, but this was only for the really faint-hearted As it was, once William was clear of the corner I rode him on strongly to the fence and he jumped it beautifully.'

BEOF Olympic Horseshoes: 'There was a long, long gallop to this new fence. Again you could choose exactly where to jump it, and my choice was to jump where there were flowerbeds as a ground-line which would help to keep the horse off the very upright rails which formed the horseshoes. Although it was a relatively straightforward fence it was very upright and brightly coloured, and so would probably look quite strange to the horses.'

The Quarry: 'This was the same as last year, with a choice of two walls to jump into the quarry and the large log-pile to tackle on the way out. Last year I had jumped in over the right-hand wall which has a sloping top and is followed by quite a steep drop into the quarry. We had then met the log-pile on a rather awkward stride, but William had coped well and it had been my intention to do the same this year, Ian, however, planned to jump the bigger left-hand wall, which had a flat top and was on a more direct line. I thought that the sloping wall on the right was more inviting, but Ian pointed out that when horses suddenly see a drop on the landing side of a fence their reaction is to drop their hindlegs so that they sometimes bank the fence they are jumping. If they were to do this over the right-hand wall their hindlegs could quite likely slide back down the slope of the wall and get caught up on the fence; whereas on the flat-topped wall they would be likely to get away with it.

'The log-pile looks enormous from the bottom of the slope, but horses seem to find jumping uphill very easy and it is just a matter of riding then forwards and keeping then straight. On cross-country day I did in fact opt for Ian's route through the Quarry complex and jumped over the left-hand wall, which actually gave us a better stride to the log-pile. The wall into the quarry is one of the first real questions on the course, and so the horse needs to be set up a bit for the fence and brought in on a strong but sharp stride.'

The Oxer: 'From the Quarry it is another long gallop down to the Oxer. When walking the course it is important to remember the places where the ground is uneven so that when riding it you know where you need to take care and support the horse, and where you can let him bowl on more freely. William is a lovely onward-going horse and just bounds over the big straightforward fences such as the Oxer, so this one held no particular worries for me.'

The Fairbanks Drop: 'After the Oxer the course starts to become more serious; indeed the next fence, the Fairbanks Drop, was a set of very upright rails on a downhill slope with a drop on the landing side. One alternative was to go up onto the bank on the left, and jump off and out over the rails, with a large drop on landing; the other was to go right round the rails and jump a large parallel on the level ground below. I did not consider the second option as I thought it would be very punishing for the horse who would probably launch himself off the bank and then encounter the big drop. The third option was very time-consuming.

'The direct route required a very controlled approach with the horse maintaining a short, bouncy canter to keep him off his forehand. The fence needed to be met on a good stride because if a horse got in too deep he would struggle to get his front legs up and clear of the upright; and if he took off too far away he would probably drop his hindlegs down on the rail, or peck on landing. I wanted to ride the direct route but was prepared to keep my options open. As it was, I thought it best not to decide anything definitely until I was riding the course – I knew William would not have to be too strong and pull me into the fence, and so my finally decision was based on how controllable he was on the day. I checked our brakes at the previous fence, the Oxer, and William responded very well; I was therefore happy to take the direct route, which he tackled perfectly.'

Beaufort Staircase: 'There was another long gallop over quite unlevel ground to the Staircase, which had five elements: a jump over a curved wooden wall, followed by three steps with a bounce distance between them, and then a stride to another wooden wall. It was very important to get a good line into this combination, and this was made more difficult by the fact that the lie of the land and the construction of the fence meant that you could not see your route through the combination until you had jumped the first element. Ian established his by lining up the first element with some trees and a hamburger van – when he saw these markers all in line he knew that if he turned then and rode to them he would get the route he wanted right through the middle of the combination. I have never been very good at using things on the horizon as markers and would have had nightmares that someone might move the van, so I opted to use a burnt patch of grass; to get a good line into the jump I needed to start my turn just before the patch of grass, and then had to ride across the middle of it to give me the line I wanted through the combination.

'With this sort of fence it is important to ride positively to the first element as the horse cannot see what is on the landing side, and may back off when he sees the big steps down. William had jumped this fence well the year before, but I did not intend to be complacent. Another problem was that from the bottom of the last step to the final element it is a very short one-stride distance; a horse tends to make up ground as he descends the steps, so as he comes down the last step the rider must be ready to steady him slightly so that he shortens his stride, thus giving himself room to clear the final element. Ian had had a memorable ride over this combination the previous year on Murphy Himself, who had ignored his rider and bounced from the last step over the final

wall, but whose natural power and exuberance had allowed him to get away with it!

'I did walk the alternative routes, as I do at all the fences, but I had no intention of using them unless something untoward happened.'

The Mitsubishi Pick-Ups: 'This was a very impressive fence, constructed with two pick-ups which were parked back-to-back across the track and filled with flowers. As a jump it was quite a decent size, and it was followed quickly by the jump into the lake. I had decided to take the long route into the lake, so as soon as William cleared the pick-ups I would have to be turning him left to get our line to the rails into the lake. The pick-ups needed to be ridden positively, but not too fast because they were quite upright and square; but as the Lake complex requires tremendous positive riding it is no bad thing to have started your attack at the fence before. Lucinda Green once said that you should ride the Lake at Badminton three times harder than any other fence, and this advice is well worth remembering – many a rider will tell you that you feel as though you are about to launch yourself into the ocean!'

The Lake: 'The direct way into the lake was over a very big fence which needed to be jumped boldly. This was not such a problem in itself, but once in, you only had about three strides in which to turn for the exit, before you were in deep water and swimming. The direct route out of the lake was up a step, then a bounce to a narrow arrowhead. The alternative was to jump up the step, swing left and jump the arm of the arrowhead.

'I could not decide for several days which route to take. William was more than capable, and plenty bold enough to take the direct route but there was so little margin for error, and it was the sort of fence where, as at Punchestown, he might easily be

● *Owen Moore and Locomotion confidently descend the Beaufort Staircase*

punished for his boldness. On the Friday night I suddenly decided to take the long route in and out of the Lake complex, and as the ground conditions this particular year deteriorated, I felt even happier with my decision.

'Walking the route I planned to take, I was particularly aware of the risk of crossing my tracks. At a three-day event, each fence has a penalty zone around it, and at the Lake in 1992 the penalty zone around the fence going in overlapped the zone around the exit fence: crossing your tracks anywhere within the penalty zones incurs 20 penalties. This year, as you turned to tackle the long option into the lake your track was inevitably very close to the track you would take when you came out again; I therefore planned to ride close to the guard rail on the way out to be sure of not crossing my tracks. On the day several riders were caught out here, and despite jumping the fences perfectly they still incurred faults for crossing their tracks. I also walked barefoot along the actual line I intended to take through the water as I think this is the only way properly to test what the bottom is like.'

The Shooting Butt: 'This is another big, straightforward fence which a horse like William will tackle quite happily; it is effectively an easy let-up for the horses after they have tackled the rigours of the Lake combination.'

The Coffin: 'Another long gallop down through the park to the Coffin, which was the same as the previous year. Along this galloping stretch a fallen tree indicates the halfway mark; I rarely look at my watch anywhere else on the course, but it is always helpful to know where halfway is, just to have a quick check on how things are going. On cross-country day it turned out we were a little behind time at this point, but I decided not to alter anything and just kept William in the rhythm he had settled into. The Coffin at Badminton is an awkward fence because the

- (top) *David Green and Duncan boldly tackle the direct route into the Lake*
- (above) *Charlotte Hollingsworth and Solo Performance jump accurately out of the Lake*
- (below) *Becky Warner and Cheeky negotiate the awkward Coffin fence*

KEY

Mary's route ▬▬▬▬▬

Long route ▬ ▪ ▬ ▪ ▬ ▪ ▬

● *The Vicarage Vee. This shows the tremendous accuracy required to jump the rail and ditch in one*

ground slopes steeply down to the ditch, and then rises steeply to the last element so that the horses have to land on rising ground. The fence must be approached in a short sharp canter, and you should aim to ride straight through the middle of the combination to reduce the risk of a run-out. At a fence where you need to get the horse back a bit and keep him in a short bouncy stride, it is then very easy to forget to keep your legs on and to attack the fence. As you walk it, you need to decide at which point you will check the horse, giving yourself time to establish the canter you want and then still enough room to think forwards the last two strides or so into the fence. It is easy to leave it all too late and be still checking when you arrive at the fence – then you get under it and lose impulsion through it, or may even have a refusal.'

The Wiltshire Corner: 'The direct route involves jumping the front of the point of a corner; it requires a bold, accurate horse as you could readily miss your line over the narrow target area and incur penalties. The alternative route was to ride over a foot-bridge, jump a gate and then turn right-handed to a big corner. The previous year I had taken the long route with William, but this time I had intended going the direct way. However, this was

not to be possible, as it was here that, tragically, Mark Todd's horse slipped and fell and broke its leg; the fence was reflagged so that only the long option was allowed. William jumped this combination far more positively than he had previously; he maintained his canter over the bridge without spooking and breaking into trot, and was very neat over the gate and corner.'

The Vicarage Vee: 'Valuable seconds can easily be lost if you swing too far to the right of the track on your way to this fence – I made a point of noting that I needed to keep above the tree and left of the track to achieve the quickest route. The Vicarage Vee itself is basically a corner formed by a wide ditch and rail, but it is vital to have an extremely accurate line to this fence and to know at what angle you need to jump, also at what speed you must approach it. William is very bold and so I do not need to ride him forwards too much. It is important to try and get a good stride to the fence – but equally, not to be so preoccupied with this that you restrict the horse's forward movement. The fence *must* be ridden positively forwards.'

The Vicarage Pond: 'This involved a bounce over silver birch rails into a pond. The year before William had been very strong after he had jumped the Vicarage Vee, and I was worried that if such was the case this year it would be difficult to get a controlled

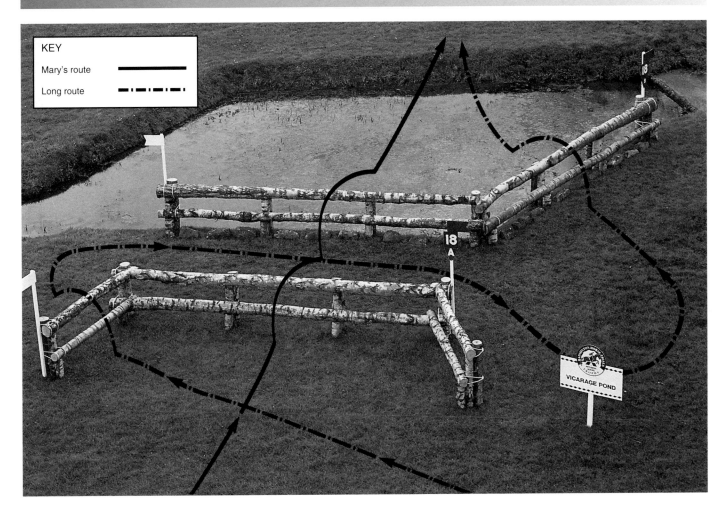

KEY

Mary's route ▬▬▬▬

Long route ▬ ▪ ▬ ▪ ▬ ▪ ▬ ▪ ▬

VICARAGE POND

approach to the bounce. It was quite a long bounce distance so it needed to be jumped from a strong stride so that the horse covered the distance and didn't try and pop in a stride. Water tends to make horses back off and shorten their stride so it is essential to ride the horse sufficiently forwards, to compensate for this. In fact William remained very controllable throughout the whole course, and so I was able to ride him in a controlled but positive canter to the bounce.'

The Luckington Lane Bank: 'You need to ride a good line to this fence so that you meet the bank really square. Very bold horses are tempted to bounce off the bank out and over the rails and drop, but this results in a very punishing landing for them. I planned to check William just a bit as he landed on the bank so that he could fit in a little stride and just pop over the rails and drop into the field the other side.'

The Centre Walk: 'This involves two lovely big brush fences on a related distance. The distance walks as either three long strides or four short ones, but it is worth remembering that by this time the horse may be quite tired and could find the three-stride distance quite long. Last year, however, Ian and Murphy Himself defied belief when they flew through the combination in just *two* strides! And William surprised *me* this year, too – he is a big, long-

● *The Vicarage Pond. A long bounce distance into water necessitates surprisingly positive riding, especially in the holding conditions of 1992*

striding horse and I was confident of his fitness. I planned to go on three strides; but when we came to it he was covering so much ground that the third stride took us very deep into the second fence. It is amazing how much ground a horse can cover once he has been galloping and is really opened up, and before he has started to tire.'

Tom Smith's Walls: 'This involved either jumping the corner formed where two of the walls meet, or finding a path through the farmyard and jumping two elements separately. As you have to wind your way through the farmyard to get to the corner, the horse should be back in a short bouncy canter. Again it is a big, imposing corner, and although the horse must be kept on an accurate line, he must also be ridden positively towards the fence so that he has the scope to clear the spread.'

Second Luckington Lane Crossing: 'The year before it had been easy to cut a corner from the previous fence and get a good line to the long route through the lane crossing without wasting too much time. This year the course had been roped off so that you could not cut across, presumably to encourage more people to tackle the direct route. This involves jumping two large hedges

KEY

Mary's route ————

Long route ▬ ▬ ▬ ▬ ▬

● *The Sigma Trakehner again required bold, accurate riding*

set at a very acute angle, and the obvious problem is that you jump the first hedge and then have a run-out at the second as the horse simply slips out to the right following the line of the hedge down the lane. I decided it was not worth the risk and took the long route. This included a very upright gate which was best ridden in a short showjumping canter to help the horse jump cleanly and sharply over it; at this point he may well be tired and perhaps beginning to flatten out over his fences – he therefore needs a bit of extra help when tackling an upright. The gate was followed by a double of hedges on quite a short distance, so I knew we had to try not to jump in too big over the first hedge or we would end up right in the bottom of the second element.'

Sigma Trakehner: 'This was a big angled rail over a very big ditch, and was probably more off-putting than the previous year when a footbridge had covered much of the gaping chasm. The alternative meant jumping the ditch first and then a stride to a big parallel. The problem here was that it was impossible to know how big a jump the horse might make over the ditch, and this would affect the stride to the parallel. I opted for the direct route, putting my trust in William's boldness. I chose a line which met the rail at not too much of an angle and where there was a little bit of the ditch showing in front of, and behind the rail.'

The Three Diamonds: 'The most direct way through this new combination was to bounce through one diamond, take one stride and then bounce through the next diamond; all the rails were

slightly angled and the distance between the bounces was quite short, so you could not afford to waver from your line. I felt that at this late stage in the competition, with a horse which would, by then, be quite tired, it was too much to ask. The route I chose involved jumping the corner of one diamond and then turning quite sharply left to jump the corner of the next. William jumped it very well, although on my course walk I had not anticipated having another horse and rider in our path to contend with! Although the corners were not very big, some riders incurred penalties for crossing their tracks or for having a run-out because they had not managed to hold their line round the turn to the second corner.'

The Ha-Ha: 'It was then a long uphill stretch to the Ha-Ha, which was in fact a hole in the ground in the approximate shape of a figure-of-eight – to cross it, either you dropped in and hopped out through the wider part at each end, or you jumped straight across the comparatively narrower gap in the middle. I was very keen to jump straight over the middle as I felt that should suit a big, bold horse like William, but I was worried that the gap might present an optical illusion to the horse because of the way the ditch opened up on either side as he galloped towards the narrow middle. Through the alternative, where you dropped down into one end, you could take a short stride before jumping up and out again. Either way the rider needed to be very decisive – either really gallop on at it so the horse would know that he was committed to jumping the thing in one, or get him right back into a slow canter, or even trot, so it was obvious to him that all he needed to do was to drop down into it and out the other side.

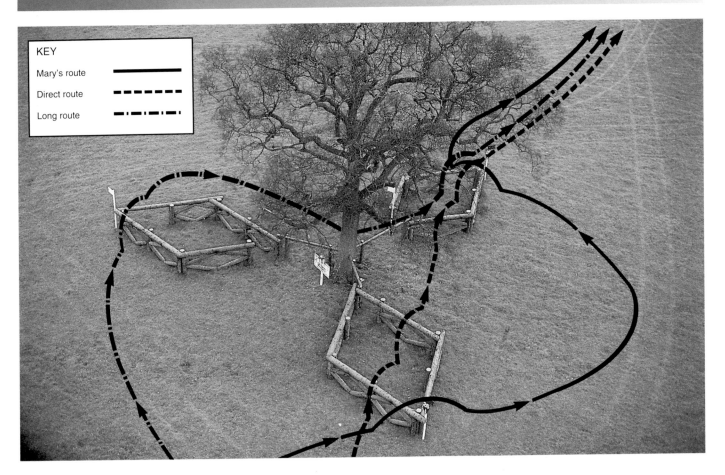

KEY

Mary's route ——————

Direct route ‑ ‑ ‑ ‑ ‑

Long route ‑·‑·‑·‑·‑

• *Various routes could be ridden through the Three Diamonds: as always the rider must keep the red flag on the right and the white on the left*
• *(left) The Ha-Ha: an optical illusion – the gap in the middle was in fact enormous*

'Ian had decided to gallop on and tackle it in one, but on the day the slippery going led to Glenburnie losing his footing on take off, dropping his hindlegs down into the hole and crashing into the far bank. Both were bruised but otherwise unscathed, and finished the course. I had already decided to play safe, as I felt the risk of a mistake outweighed any small saving you might make in time. Only one horse jumped the Ha-Ha in one successfully, and that was Helen Bell on Troubleshooter – a horse which, his rider says, always sticks to his line.'

The Stick Pile: 'This is the highest and widest fence on the course, but it always looks deceptively small because it is straight-

forward and made of such huge timbers. Nevertheless, it is vital that riders give this fence the respect it deserves, no matter how inviting it may look; mistakes have been made here and it is certainly not a fence to underestimate. On William, such fences are a joy to tackle as he has so much scope and power.'

The Mitsubishi Garden: 'The last fence on the course this year was very striking because it was built of bright white rails and full of colourful flowers; nevertheless it was very straightforward. However, again you have to remember that the horse will be tired, he will be aware of the cheering crowds as he approaches the finish and may well be distracted, so you *mustn't* lose your concentration – you are so near and yet so far! – and should ride a good, positive, straight approach to the fence. A tired horse *needs* support from his rider; he must be held firmly between leg and hand so that the impulsion you help him to create is contained, and used to produce a good, sharp jump.

'And so to the finish – but with everything else that is then bound to be going through your mind, you must still be careful to pull up your horse quietly and steadily, and to ride to the steward who will tell you when you can dismount. Then you must weigh in – and only then can you relax and think "I've done it!"'

The evening before the cross-country Annie doublechecks with Mary which studs, boots and bandages she wants to use. While cleaning the tack she thoroughly checks all the stitching and the condition of the leather, to be sure that nothing is likely to break on the day. On cross-country day itself Annie tries to feed William at the usual time if at all possible; he has his usual feed, but only a minute amount of hay in the morning. He is allowed free access to water, although many people like to remove the water buckets; however, Annie and Mary maintain there is no reason why a horse should suddenly want to drink an unusually large amount of water, and it is best to keep everything as normal as possible.

When Annie plaits William she sews an extra piece of thread into the top plait, and this is tied to the headpiece of the bridle to prevent it being pulled off if Mary were to fall off. Mary will put William's front bandages on (which are stitched for a three-day event) about an hour before she is due to start the speed and endurance phase, so William needs to have been walked out for a good 15 minutes beforehand to reduce any filling in his legs.

Once Mary and William have set off on Phase A, Annie rushes to the start of Phase B, the steeplechase. When Mary arrives there, Annie quickly checks that William still has four shoes and studs, and that his boots and bandages are in place.

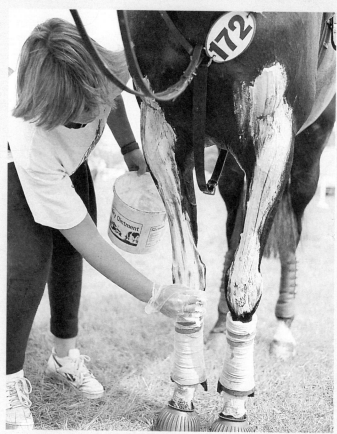

She checks all this again as Mary goes through the finish of the steeplechase to set off on Phase C, the second roads and tracks. Annie then has to get to the 10-minute box at the start of the cross-country course ready for William's arrival there.

'I like to have no more than two or three people to help me in the box. When a horse first comes into the 10-minute box you have to remember not to touch him until the steward says you can. I look quickly to see that he still has all his shoes, bandages and boots, and once we get the go-ahead, I ask someone to hold him. I loosen his noseband and girth one hole and wash out his mouth with clean water. We then give him a really good wash to remove the sweat and dirt from his coat, but trying to keep his tack as dry as possible. He is then dried off with a sweatscraper and towels, and a sweat rug put over him while he is walked around for a few minutes. His studs are checked and changed if necessary.

'Time goes very quickly in the 10-minute box, and one of us is always responsible for keeping an eye on the clock. When we have about four minutes to go, I put cross-country grease on his legs; I usually wear a glove to do this, otherwise you get it all over everything else you touch. With three minutes to go, the girth and noseband are done up ready for Mary to get on. Before she remounts, I towel off the bottom of her boots so there is no risk of her foot slipping in the stirrup. And then she's away, and all you can do is hope they come back in one piece.

'At the end of Phase D, the cross-country, and after Mary has weighed in, the steward will give me the go ahead to take the horse away. Obviously this year there was great excitement, and Mary was dragged off by the press and there were a lot of people around; so I just quickly checked William over, loosened his noseband and led him back to the stables to see to him in peace and quiet. His saddle had already been removed when Mary weighed in. As soon as he had stopped blowing I rinsed out his mouth again, and then gave him a really good wash-off. I took his studs out and walked him around with a sweat rug on; as he cooled off I added more rugs to make sure he didn't get cold. If you don't keep a close eye on him, a horse can suddenly turn really cold, in spite of all his exertions. The amount of water he is allowed is gradually increased until he has all he wants. Once his breathing is back to normal he is allowed to eat his hay. Mary then came and checked his legs, and waited while the vet stitched his cut. Then we put Animalintex on to any other cuts that we can see before applying Ice Tight poultice, which has been refrigerated, to his legs. We then wrap damp brown paper around the legs, and cover this with damp Fibergee held in place with a stable bandage over the top. The damp paper stops the poultice sticking to the Fibergee.

'After an hour, William had a small dampened feed of breeder's mix, competition cubes, chaff and salt. Once we had done all we needed to do, William was left alone as much as possible to recover in his own time. He had a proper feed later in the evening, with a bit more salt than usual to make up for the amount he would have lost in sweat. From then on he was allowed hay ad lib.

'We walked him out late that evening so that the vet could have a look at him, as a cut on his pastern had had to have three stitches. Twice during the evening he was given some laser treatment to reduce the swelling and pain, but in spite of everything was extremely bright and cheerful. This meant that everyone could be pleased with the job they had done!'

Cross-country day

'I got up at 6.30am, although it is always difficult to get up on cross-country day, said Mary. 'You lie there thinking that in eight hours it will all be over, and will I be celebrating, or in hospital?!'

An early start was needed in order to walk the course, one last time, before there were too many other people out and about on it. 'I usually do the final walk on my own, but this time David came with me. It was nice to have the company, and he knows me well enough not to ask too many questions. I had been most concerned about the water because of our mistake at Punchestown last year. This year the Badminton Lake involved a jump in over a very big set of rails, and then you had to be able to turn within three strides, otherwise the water got too deep; the direct route out was a step up and bounce over a very narrow arrowhead. You needed to be able to jump boldly in, but then to turn immediately to jump out accurately. By Friday night I had finally decided to ride the long route both in and out of the lake.

'I knew the Olympic selectors liked William, but we still needed to prove our form by going clear and it was not the sort of course where you could aim for a steady clear – the fences needed attacking. In making the decision about the lake I felt as if a huge weight had been lifted from my shoulders, and I was then far more positive in my mind about the course altogether. The rain had made the conditions quite deep and slippery, and this, too, helped convince me that it was right to play safe and take the long route.

'My other concern was the Fairbanks Drop. My first thought had been to go the direct way, but to do that I knew I would need to meet it on a good stride and with plenty of control. Captain Mark Phillips had said he would be in the 10-minute box watching the TV monitor and would let me know how the course was riding.

'I managed to eat a hearty breakfast, and then the worst thing was waiting until it was time to get ready. I curled up in my sleeping bag and felt extremely ill.

'At last it was time to get William ready. I bandaged his legs and then took my saddle and weightcloth to weigh out. We tacked up near the start of Phase A, and I was on William about five minutes before our start time. As the ground showed no signs of drying out, William wore medium-size square studs in front and

● *Annie tightens the studs in the hind shoes*

● *Cleaning round William's mouth in the 10-minute box*

TIMING YOURSELF ON THE ROADS & TRACKS

I like to have my times for the roads and tracks and steeplechase clearly written down on a piece of card. I slot this into a plastic folder and attach it to my arm with Velcro.

Because I start my stopwatch at the beginning of Phase A, I begin my times from '0'. I keep my watch running all through Phases A, B and C, and just restart it for the cross-country (Phase D). I wear a second watch as a back-up in case my main one conks out!

Usually the times work out so that you can allow 4 minutes for each kilometre. I like to finish Phases A and C with 2 minutes in hand in case something goes wrong.

I leave extra time for the first kilometre of Phase C so I can allow my horse to walk while he recovers after the steeplechase.

For a three-day event with the following time allowances: Phase A: 20 mins; Phase B: 4 mins; Phase C: 39 mins, I would set out my card like this:

1km: 4	2km: 35	A: 20
2km: 8	3km: 39	B: 4
3km: 12	4km: 43	C: 39
4km: 16	5km: 47	
FINISH A: 18	6km: 51	
START B: 20	7km: 55	
HALF-WAY: 22	8km: 59	
START C: 24	FINISH C: 01	
1km: 31	MUST BY: 03	

• The vet pinches William's skin to check for dehydration

behind. It was a great relief to get going, even though all the work was still to be done. The wonderful send-off from the crowd really lifts your spirits and makes you feel that everyone is on your side.

'William settled into a relaxed trot which enabled him to cover the target time of one kilometre every four minutes easily. I could just hear enough of the commentary to know that Mark Todd had had a fall and that the course had been held; so I knew it was something quite serious. (Later, Mary was to discover that Mark's horse, Face the Music, had tragically broken his leg and been put down.) As William was trotting happily along with his ears pricked, feeling so keen and enthusiastic, I was praying that he would not get hurt – you always feel so responsible for your horses, as they are really very vulnerable.

'We had a short canter on Phase A and arrived, as planned, two minutes before we were due to start on the steeplechase; this gave Annie time quickly to check his shoes, studs and bandages. The steeplechase is a wonderful phase to ride on William as he has a great rhythm and just bounds over the fences – it is easy to start seeing a longer and longer stride to each one, but you have to keep thinking, 'Steady!'. About halfway round I checked my watch and saw that we were ahead of time. I slowed William down a little, but then managed to hold him right into the bottom of the next fence – so I left him alone after that. The going was getting stickier, but it did not seem to bother him. Annie was waiting at the end to check that we still had four shoes and all the bandages.

'I let William walk the first kilometre of Phase C while he recovered his breath. We picked up the trot again and I just concentrated on trying to keep him, and me, relaxed. My mind wandered all over the place, even as the cross-country got closer – but then the final part of Phase C takes you along Worcester Avenue, and as you come over the hill you see the crowds and hear the loudspeaker again; and that certainly concentrates your attention.

'The first thing I heard was that Jane Holderness-Roddam had retired at the Vicarage Vee. She is a really experienced rider, besides being the chairman of the selectors, and it made me begin to wonder just what was happening out there. A huntsman (usually from the Duke of Beaufort's, the Berkeley or the Heythrop) escorts each competitor through the last few hundred yards of Phase C to the 10-minute box, and the crowd cheers you in. You then trot past the veterinary panel, and you are asked to halt and dismount while they check the horse over and listen to his respiration and heart-rate. They also ask you how the steeplechase went: if you had a bad time, they will know to double-check the horse.

'Annie, Tina and Mum then took over William while I tried to get as much information as I could about the course. Mark Phillips greet-

THE SPEED AND ENDURANCE TEST

On speed and endurance day at Badminton almost all the spectator attention is focussed on Phase D, the cross-country course, and it is easy to forget just how much the horse has already done before he even starts the cross-country. The endurance test is split into four phases: Phase A, roads and tracks; Phase B, the steeplechase course; Phase C, second roads and tracks; and after a ten-minute compulsory break, Phase D, the cross-country course.

Phase A covers a distance of approximately 4,840 metres and should be completed within an optimum time of 22 minutes. Time penalties are incurred for every second over the optimum time. The main purpose of this phase is to warm the horse up for the steeplechase, and most tackle it at a steady trot to meet the required speed of 220 metres per minute.

Phase B requires the horse to jump eight point-to-point fences at a speed of approximately 25mph. The course is over a distance of 2,760 metres and the optimum time is 4 minutes. The precise speed needed to meet this time is 690 metres per minutes; again, penalties are incurred for being over the set time – 0.8 penalties for every second over.

Phase C is considered a recovery period for the horse after the exertion of the steeplechase; it also keeps his muscles warm and supple so that he is well prepared to tackle the cross-country course. The distance is 10,780 metres, to be completed in 49 minutes, and 1 time penalty is given for every second over the optimum time.

Between Phases C and D horse and rider have a compulsory break of ten minutes in the 10-minutes box, where the horse is checked by the veterinary panel; and then washed down and freshened up; once the go-ahead is given, the now-

familiar cross-country course is waiting to be tackled. Phase D normally consists of 29 fences set over a course of 6,897 metres. The optimum time would be 12.06 minutes, requiring an average speed of 570 metres per minute; for every second over the optimum time, 0.4 time penalties are incurred.

ed me with the news that only one horse had gone clear so far – and I was number 38! He assured me that on the whole the course was riding well but there were just isolated mistakes being made. He told me the direct route through the lake was riding well, too – but I was determined to stick to my plan. Ginny Leng had had a fall at the Fairbanks Drop with Welton Houdini. The Captain's advice was to ride that fence in a short, bouncy canter and not to let William pull me into it otherwise he would not be able to get his front legs clear in time, and like Houdini, would turn a somersault. As some riders had also slipped trying to ride the long route, I finally decided that I would wait and see how William was going; if he was not too strong, my plan was to ride the direct way. The Captain's last words were very good advice: "Go carefully,

but be positive; and make sure you concentrate every step of the way."

'I had an extra ten minutes to wait as the course was being held again, but there were plenty of people to talk to and the time passed quickly. We had changed William's studs to big half-moon ones in front and behind. And then we were being counted down.

'I tried to ride William in a strong rhythm so he had enough impulsion to tackle the jumps out of the mud, but as carefully as I could so that we took no risks on the approaches or turns, and so that he had time to work out what each fence demanded of him. He settled into a good rhythm straightaway. We went very carefully round the corner out of Huntsman's Close where we had slipped up on the flat the previous year, then had to ride on to clear the big

● The Mitsubishi Diamonds: Mary gets in front of the movement – but gets away with it

cross over the ditch. But William was just cruising, and I did not think about the time at all, just kept bowling along in fourth gear, knowing that fifth gear was there if we needed it.

'William was loving it, and just eating up the fences. He would land with his ears pricked, looking for the next challenge. We had a fabulous jump over the oxer before Fairbanks, and I steadied him there to see how easily he would come back into my hand: he had responded immediately, so we took the direct route over the Fairbanks Drop – no trouble.

'Coming down the Beaufort Staircase, William started to drift left slightly, as he was making up ground with each step he descended; I just had to lead him slightly right-handed for the final element to make sure we didn't run out, he was most obliging. Halfway round I looked at my watch and saw that we were a little behind time; but I didn't alter anything. As we approached the Mitsubishi Corners we began to catch up with the horse in front, which suddenly gave us something else to think about – I had to steady up sooner than I had planned before we tackled the combination of two corners. As we cleared the second and passed the other competitor, I remember thinking that we were now over the last of the real "problem" fences, and for the first time I urged William on a bit faster. I steadied up for the Ha-

● William uses his size and scope to advantage through the long bounce distance at the Vicarage Pond

Ha to make sure he realised that I wanted him to drop down into it and not clear it in one, which he obediently did.

'I concentrated hard as we rode to the Stick Pile. Although it looks very inviting, it is the biggest fence on the course, and people have made mistakes there. You are suddenly aware of the crowd as you land over this one; they were shouting "Come on, William!". We managed to restrain ourselves and steadied for the last which he jumped beautifully – and as we landed, I thought "Olympics, here we come!"

'William was still full of running, so I circled him quietly to stop him. Then everyone crowded round us – family, friends, the press, the TV cameras. But the cross-country is not over until you have weighed in and signed your name: then I knew we had done it! Annie led William away from the madding crowd while I was interviewed;' I was so elated that I just jabbered away and probably said quite ridiculous things. I was then asked to go straight to the Press Tent, but I was anxious to see to William as Annie had found a cut on his front leg, just on the side of the pastern – there was quite a large flap of skin hanging and the vet wanted to stitch it up. As this would make him quite sore, we first checked with the British team vet, Paul Faringdon; he agreed that it should be stitched to ensure it healed quickly. William had to have three

stitches, which he did not seem to notice, and the vet used laser treatment to help reduce the pain.

'Once William was happily relaxing in his stable and I had given him a final check-over, I didn't know quite what to do next. Half of me wanted to go out and celebrate; but in the end I felt so exhausted that I had an early night.'

The Showjumping

'When I saw William at 6.30am, Annie had already cleaned his leg up as it had been weeping a bit, and washed the "Ice-Tight" off his other legs. We trotted him up, and he was just slightly unlevel on his injured leg. We put some ice just above the wound to help reduce the heat and swelling, and then left him alone with his breakfast.

'The final horse inspection was at 9am, so William was tacked up at 8.15am and I took him for a quiet hack through the park. He was really bright, and kept looking around for more fences to jump. After a few minutes walking his stride felt free and loose, and I was fairly certain then that he would be all right to finish the event.

'William was most impressive at the trot-up. He was convinced that everyone had come just to see him and stood, proud and aloof, looking

● *Limbering up before the final horse inspection*

out over the crowd, who gave him a huge cheer. He produced a powerful and unrestrained trot for the Ground Jury who duly passed him.'

William was left to relax in his box while Mary attended the Badminton church service. The sun shone, and it did not seem possible that this peaceful place had seen such tragedy the day before. By the end of cross-country day, three horses had suffered critical injuries and had to be put down. There was no common cause or reason: the accidents happened at different fences, and all were experienced horses with talented riders. Every rider who enjoyed a good round that day undoubtedly shared, in equal measure, the grief for those horses. There is always a tremendous partnership between horse and rider in any sport, but in eventing horse and rider do put their lives in each others' hands probably more than in any of the other riding disciplines. Accidents can happen to anyone; sport is a great equaliser, and there can be few riders who have not thought 'There, but for the grace of God, go I'.

The Parade of Competitors was at 2pm and then the top twenty combinations showjumped in reverse order of merit. Mary watched how the course was riding, then once they were down to the top ten horses got on William.

'Stephen Hadley and Captain Mark Phillips were both on hand to help me, and this was reassuring as William was not being particularly generous over the practice fences – he was bold, but not exactly careful. I had been riding him in the prickle pad but decided to take it off as he started to tilt his head, which he had never done before. He produced one really good jump in the practice arena just before going in, and we all decided that it was best to leave him at that.

'I had just one fence in hand, as Ginny had gone clear. The previous year we had had three showjumps down, so I knew that anything could happen. I just kept thinking, if I have four down I will still be fourth, which was better than thinking, if I only have one down I will still win.

'Then it was time to discover our fate. We cantered over to the royal box, having a major spook en route at the fountain by the Mitsubishi feature fence. It is hard to believe that a horse that has just tackled the daunting cross-country course can still find a harmless fountain so startling! I concentrated on establishing a short engaged canter, but we still managed to hit the first fence quite hard. I could feel William's mind was not really on the fences – there were the crowds, the cameras and that fountain! – and we seemed to rattle every other fence. I could hear frequent oohs and aahs from the crowd, but didn't dare look back to see if the fences were still standing. As we came into the final double it was as though William couldn't help himself any longer, and he really clouted it. There was such a cry of disappointment that I was sure this must have been the second one we had knocked down, and was convinced that this distraction would mean that the final element would fall too. But William pulled himself together and cleared it, and then there was such

● *With everything still to play for, Steve Hadley and the Captain prepare Mary for the final phase*

Luck was on our side – with only one showjump down the victory was ours!

a roar from the crowd that I knew we had done it: we had won Badminton!

'Before there was time for everything to sink in, it was back into the arena for the prize-giving. I just couldn't believe it was really happening, even when they presented me with the trophy. When it came to the lap of honour I just wanted to go mad and gallop flat out; but managed to restrain myself, as I knew that at this stage it would be easy for William to damage himself after all he had been through.

'As we swept out of the arena we were quickly brought back down to earth by a steward who informed us that the winning horse had to be drug-tested. So Annie took William, while I was taken off for more interviews, which inevitably included questions about the tragedies on cross-country day. What can you say? You and your horse, and dozens of others, stand as proof that the course was rideable, and there was really no answer as to why three horses

● *Princess Michael of Kent congratulates Mary and runner-up Ginny Leng*

● *The Butler Bowl awarded to Mary as the highest placed British rider*

died there. All I do know is this: that William's Badminton victory will always be remembered with sadness as well as joy.

'Some degree of normality returned once we were packing up to go home – but even then the drama wasn't over. Mum and Annie had set off in the lorry ahead of David and I – we were still finding people to celebrate with! As we cruised down the motorway we suddenly saw Mum standing in the pouring rain on the hard shoulder. We pulled up to learn that William had got himself into quite a state in the lorry, and Annie thought he had colic, though by the time we reached it, things had calmed down a bit. Mum had parked in a service station and let the ramp down, and we found William and Annie serenely surveying the motorway traffic. I decided to travel with him in the lorry, and sure enough, as soon as we started off again he

began to get very restless – he would snatch at his hay, then snatch at my hand looking for food, and look round wildly in between. Eventually I found that scratching the top of his neck seemed to soothe him, and that was how we spent the rest of the journey. When we got home a vet was there to meet us, but thankfully William had, by then, settled down.

The following morning William was checked over again for any sign of injury, then turned out – and there he stayed until lunchtime. The day after that he stayed out until the evening, and the next day he was so happy in the field that he remained there day and night, left in peace apart from having his stitches bathed each day to keep the skin soft and to prevent scabbing. Mary put wound powder on the cut once it had been cleaned, to keep it free from germs and flies.

● *On the way to meet the press at the Mitsubishi tent*

● *(top right) William is lost for words!*

● *(right) William and Annie escape the crowds*

At the end of his first week of holiday, William's rest was interrupted to take him back to Badminton as all the long-listed horses had to go there for a veterinary inspection. On the way up Mary tried to catch up with her letter-writing, as she had received over four hundred letters since her victory. At the vetting the horses were checked by an equine dentist. Mary discussed William's programme with the vet, as she wanted to give him as long a rest as possible to allow him to recover mentally as well as physically from his exertions. She was advised that a horse will only start to lose muscle bulk after seventeen days without work, and so she was able to decide that she would leave William out for this length of time, and then start working him quietly from the field.

In fact William put on quite a bit of weight

during his short holiday, and once his seventeen days were up, it was obviously high time he did a little work, if only to keep his tummy in trim! This started with a few days of gentle half-hour hacks, building up over a week to an hour's walking on some of the more strenuous rides. He was brought in from the field and ridden in the morning, and then slept in his stable during the day, and was turned out again in the evening

CONTINENTAL CUP FINAL, ITALY

On 25 May, with her Badminton and Windsor successes behind her, Mary flew out to Italy for the European Cup Final at Pratoni del Vivaro; she and King Samuel had qualified for this

CCI*** competition by winning a three-day event at Le Lion d'Angers, in France, the previous autumn. She arrived to find Annie and Sammy well settled, and everyone delighted with the beautiful setting. 'I had imagined it would be hot, dry and dusty, but it was the most wonderful lush, green valley full of wild flowers and butterflies,' said Mary.

Unfortunately for the organisers there were only eight contenders for the Continental Cup, probably due to the long distance involved and the fact that many riders chose to compete at Bramham instead. However, those that made the trip were determined to make the most of it. Mary flew out with Robert Lemieux, a British-based rider who competes under the Canadian flag, while Annie and Sammy had travelled out by lorry with Mark Barry, who was representing

Ireland. Mary was the only British competitor.

'Sammy led after the dressage; he did a very bright, accurate test although he was a bit naughty and was close to boiling over. The greatest concern for all the competitors was the cross-country course, which Mark Phillips considered the biggest three-star course he had seen – and there we were all thinking we were out for a bit of holiday! In fact I was the pathfinder, as the competitor before me withdrew after the dressage.

'Sammy coped admirably well, and should really have gone clear except for an unfortunate mistake at the penultimate fence; this was a combination which involved dropping down off a bank into a road, then one and a half strides to a big hedge. I knew Robert Lemieux was planning to ride it in two strides, but that Mark Barry was opting for one long stride. As Sammy is very neat I decided to try to squeeze in two strides, but to do this I needed to make him halt at the top of the bank so that he would drop down into the road quietly and so be able to fit in the two strides. However, I obviously halted a bit strongly and he just stepped back with one hind leg – for this he was given a refusal. But he succeeded in popping in the two strides, and jumped out over the hedge quite beautifully. Robert Lemieux tried the same tactic, but unfortunately his horse decided to put in just one stride and this clash of ideas led to a fall.

'I was amazed to find that after all this we were lying second, with ten fences in hand over third place; which gives you some idea of how much trouble the cross-country caused!

'On the final day we were all very relaxed, perhaps, as circumstances were soon to reveal, a bit too much so! Mark Phillips was helping me warm up for the showjumping when for some inexplicable reason, Sammy abruptly refused the practice fence and sent me sailing over his head; as I sat in the mud, he galloped off in the direction of Rome, just as I was being called in to jump. We ran in all directions to find him and luckily the commentator kept talking, and they did not ring the bell – you have to start within 30 seconds of the bell being sounded, and I had visions of us being eliminated. After what seemed an eternity, Annie found Sammy and galloped him back to the collecting ring where I was rapidly legged back into the saddle. I didn't feel much like a Badminton winner – streaked with mud and horribly flustered – as I stopped to give my salute. We jumped a very erratic round, as neither of us had really had time to gather our thoughts and my main concern was not to stop or fall off. Despite three fences down we still held second place, and I think were very lucky to do so!'

TRAVELLING TO ITALY

For the horses, the journey to Italy for the European Cup Final involved an hour's ferry crossing and then four days by road. Annie and Sammy travelled out with Mark Barry, another competitor and two other horses. Sammy was dressed as for travelling normally at home, with a tail guard, travelling roller and breastplate, long travel boots and a leather headcollar. He did not have a tail bandage on as he does not sit back on his bottom and so is unlikely to rub his tail and Mary does not like to leave them on for longer journeys if it can be avoided.

In preparation for such a long trip Annie had put an extra-thick layer of woodshavings on the floor of the lorry, and had packed individual feeds in plastic bags to see Sammy through the whole journey. The tack she needed for everyday exercise was kept to hand, but everything for the competition was stored away safely. A well stocked first-aid kit was packed, which also contained basic veterinary drugs such as a relaxant for colic – obviously, a vet would not always be easily available.

'The most important thing when travelling horses is to have as much air as possible going through the lorry. It is better to have more air and more rugs to keep them warm than the opposite. The horses had access to hay the whole time and were offered water every half-hour. In fact the ferry crossing was only short, and they obviously found it quite relaxing! When you are first parked on board, the main thing is to make sure you have enough room to get the ramps down, as it does get very hot,' explained Annie. 'During the four days of road travel we tried to feed at the usual times, and only reduced the feed if we weren't able to work the horses that day. We stopped every five hours to let them out of the lorry to stretch their legs and to feed them. Depending on the temperature in the lorry, the horses wore either a light cotton sheet, a thermatex rug, or nothing at all.'

Although the horses travelled well and were very bright and fit for the competition, the journey was not without incident as the lorry broke down on the hard shoulder for six hours, just short of the Italian border. Annie continues: 'We were rescued by a transporter which gave us a lift to the event. But even before that, some of the windy mountain roads we had had to tackle were quite terrifying – as was Mark's driving on occasions! But we got there in the end, and Sammy was certainly none the worse for his adventures. My hopes for an Italian sun-tan were dashed, however – Sammy and I were most often to be found sheltering under his rain-sheet!'

JUNE

*J*une began with a turn in my fortunes, my roll of success coming to a halt at Bramham three-day event. I had been so looking forward to riding Apple (Star Appeal); he is a great horse and I was keen to see how he would cope with a CCI*** event. Unfortunately a skin infection in his front leg blew up just before the cross-country and we decided to withdraw him.

Then we received another blow when I was told that Conker would have to have the rest of the season off due to the tendon injury he incurred at Windsor. I had planned to ride him at the Blenheim three-day event this autumn, though luckily I will still have a ride on Samuel at this wonderful venue.

William's preparation for the final Olympic trial, to be held at the beginning of July, has gone very smoothly throughout the month, and his performance will hopefully bear this out. He was feeling as fabulous as ever, having come bouncing back from the rigours of Badminton with no apparent ill-effect.

A charity race day at Kempton Park saw myself, Ginny Leng, Katie Meacham, Jane Holderness-Roddam and Lorna Clarke (see below) competing in a flat race. My horse was a reluctant starter and was obviously 'in need of the trip' as they say in the racing world. Of greater concern was the wet weather and the speed at which my racing breeches were becoming see-through!

The Audi Masterclass series of lecture demonstrations took Robert, Blyth and myself all over Great Britain, from Derbyshire to Yorkshire to Essex – even up to Gleneagles in Scotland where I had time to enjoy the wonderful facilities of the hotel, which was a real treat! I caught the golfing bug, too, but have not had time since to follow up all that I learnt on that marvellous course.

A short break in the South of France, where we stayed at a friend's villa, came at just the right time. It gave David and me a rare chance to relax together, and I returned to England feeling fully refreshed and ready to tackle the excitement and tension which lay ahead.

FEEDING

WILLIAM

William had put on quite a bit of weight during his post-Badminton holiday, so once he was back in work his ration was kept quite low to start with; it was then gradually built up over the month to the level it had been just before Badminton. At first his ration was as follows:

Morning: 1¹/2lb (³/4 scoop) breeding mix; Provider Plus and salt
Midday: 3lb (1 scoop) stud nuts
Evening: 1lb (¹/2 scoop) breeding mix; 1¹/2lb (¹/2 scoop) stud nuts; Provider Plus and salt
Haynet: Medium (3¹/2lb) morning and evening

By the end of the month William was being fed at the following levels:

Morning: 1¹/2lb (¹/2 scoop) competition cubes; 2lb (1 scoop) breeding mix; Provider Plus and salt
Midday: 3lb (1 scoop) competition cubes
Evening: 1lb (¹/2 scoop) breeding mix; 3lb (1 scoop) competition cubes; Provider Plus and salt
Haynet: Large (5lb) morning and night

CONKER

Conker had not returned to work because of his tendon injury; he was out at grass and so was not receiving any feed.

BASIL

Basil came back into work in the first week of June and had also put on weight during his holiday. He, too, started on a reduced ration which was built up over the month as his work increased. So to begin with his ration was this:

Morning: 1lb (¹/2 scoop) breeding mix; Provider Plus and salt
Midday: 1¹/2lb (¹/2 scoop) stud nuts
Evening: 1lb (¹/2 scoop) breeding mix; 1¹/2lb (¹/2 scoop) stud nuts; Provider Plus and salt
Haynet: Large (5lb) morning and evening

By the end of June, Basil was back to competition fitness and being fed as follows:

Morning: 2lb (1 scoop) breeding mix; Provider Plus and salt
Midday: 3lb (1 scoop) stud nuts
Evening: 1lb (¹/2 scoop) breeding mix; 3lb (1 scoop) stud nuts; Provider Plus and salt
Haynet: Large (5lb) in morning, and extra large (7lb) at night

KING BASIL

Basil was brought back into work during the first weekend in June; for a few days he was just worked from the field, starting with the easier rides at walk. Mary then escaped to the South of France for a few days, leaving the horses in the capable hand of Annie, Tina and Sarah. During the second week of June, Basil's work picked up quite quickly and he was doing his first steady canter work by the end of the week. He had put on quite a bit of weight during his holiday, which Mary was pleased about; earlier in the year it had been a struggle to keep enough condition on him. Now, however, his frame was a little too stout for the rigours of eventing, and his feed and hay were reduced until he had slimmed down.

By the time Mary returned from her holiday she was keen to get back into the swing of things – besides, Basil's first event was just under three weeks away. However, when she had an initial schooling session with him over showjumps, she found that he was altogether a bit too loose, and not really sharp enough or sufficiently engaged. 'I had to ride him strongly forwards to establish a positive, sharp canter to help him create a good jump. He had reverted to his natural way of going which is to be very laid back and relaxed, whereas he really needs to be brighter and sharper,' explained Mary.

At the end of the week Basil was boxed up with William and Cuthbert (by courtesy of Annie) for the trip to Gleneagles, where all three horses were to be used in the Audi Masterclass. As it was such a long way Mary had volunteered to provide horses for herself, Blyth Tait and Robert Lemieux – so while Mary and Annie faced the ten-hour drive to Gleneagles, Blyth and Robert were looking forward to a lift in a private jet! Before they set off, Basil, Cuthbert and William were turned out in the field for half an hour to stretch their legs and get some fresh air; and at about half-way they broke the trip by stopping at a service station and leading the horses out for twenty minutes along a back lane to walk and graze before resuming their journey.

The lecture demonstration was not until the following evening, and Mary and Annie were quick to take advantage of the wonderful facilities offered by Gleneagles. The centre runs a Novice and an Intermediate one-day event, so there was a great variety of cross-country fences; Mary gave Basil a good school around the course, accompanied by Annie and Cuthbert. In fact Basil was quite spooky and green, and Mary was surprised at how backward he had become since his holiday. Annie and Cuthbert, on the other hand, were feeling very brave, and with Mary shouting advice as to whether they needed to kick on or steady up, they tackled some pretty decent fences!

For the lecture demonstration that evening, Blyth rode Basil, Robert took Cuthbert and Mary, William. Again, Mary could see that Basil had gone backwards since his holiday; he was very fidgety because of the crowd, and spooky over his fences.

On the way home from Scotland Mary stopped off at Steve Hadley's for a lesson with Basil and William; when they arrived, Steve allowed the horses to be turned out for a few hours, which they thoroughly appreciated after the long drive. And during his lesson the next day Basil became much calmer and more confident – already he was beginning to feel a different horse. Steve watched Mary ride him to some single fences in the indoor school, then they put him over a small course outside; at anything where he was the least bit sticky Mary quietly circled and asked him to jump it again so as to build up his confidence gradually.

'Basil really needs to step up a gear with all his work, now,' said Mary. 'He needs to be able to shorten his stride and become more engaged. I still tend to ride him like a young horse, and let him come to a fence on a smooth, level stride – but I must remind myself now that he needs to be kept up together more.'

Until the end of the month Basil was hacked out and schooled quietly, with fastwork every four days. The aim was for him to compete at Savernake Forest, also the venue for the final Olympic trial, on the first weekend in July; thus all he needed was for his fitness work to be increased leading up to this event.

KING KONG

Mary had been concerned about Conker's leg since Windsor. He was completely sound, but there was still just a tiny bit of heat and swelling; so he was walked out in hand for a few days. All the same, Mary made an appointment at the Animal Health Trust for him to be scanned by Sue Dyson on 9 June; almost certainly this would reveal the true nature of the problem. This worked out well as she had to go to Essex anyway with Boris for another lecture demonstration, so called in on the way.

'Sue is someone who has helped me in the past, and I trust and respect her judgement implicitly,' said Mary. 'She is very thorough in her examination, and will scan and check both front legs even though there may only appear to be a problem in one leg. She is an event rider herself and so appreciates our problems.'

Sadly, the ultrasonic scan showed that there *was* some damage to the core of the superficial digital flexor tendon of the off-fore. This structure had obviously come under significant strain, and Sue Dyson's recommendation was that Conker should not event again this autumn. As he is quiet and well-behaved in the field, she was happy for him to be turned out – though the problem with this routine was whether he would put on too much weight!

For the time being, Conker was turned out at night but kept in during the day. His front shoes were left on to help keep his hooves in good shape, but the hind shoes were removed; the farrier bevelled his hind feet as this helps to prevent the hoof breaking off round the edge. Meanwhile he would have another scan in mid-August to see how the damaged tendon was recovering.

KING WIILLIAM

Throughout the first week of June, William continued to be ridden quietly from the field. His stitches were taken out, and Mary was given a medication called 'The Lotion' to put on the wound; this was to help prevent proud flesh forming and to let the wound heal quickly without leaving a scar. It was applied as often as the girls could manage but the wound still tended to dry out, so they tried a different approach: Mary soaked a strip of gamgee in 'The Lotion' and wrapped this around William's pastern; it was then held in place with a piece of elastic bandage. This was more successful.

Before Mary went off to France William was brought in and stabled, and started on some initial schooling work: the holiday, for William, was over.

'I popped him over a few small jumps before *my* holiday – in my absence he was simply hacked out quietly, although the girls started his canter work just before I got back. The ground was getting quite firm, so they only worked him steadily, up the gallop field,' said Mary. 'In fact by the time I got back from holiday it was rock hard. Although we try to keep

During May and June, Mary's involvement with the Audi Masterclass series of lecture demonstrations kept her particularly busy; together with Robert Lemieux and Blyth Tait, she travelled to various destinations throughout the UK to present the Masterclass. The first of the series was held in front of a packed audience at Willow Farm Equestrian Centre in Faversham, Kent; its format provided a good example of what people could expect at future presentations, and clearly demonstrated the thinking behind the series.

Robert Lemieux had been closely associated with the development of the Masterclass: he was 'fed up with sitting in a freezing cold school with no facilities being bored to tears' – in other words, he was thoroughly dissatisfied with what equestrian education had to offer. It needed more entertainment, comfort and interest, he concluded. Mike Etherington-Smith, the compère for the evening warned Robert Lemieux that he would be judged on his words. But he had no need to worry – the favourable reaction of the audience proved that the series was going to provide all that it promised.

Robert, Blyth and Mary were each teamed up with a 'guinea pig' horse and rider – the decision as to who partnered whom was made by the audience and, on this occasion, they were determined that Mary should take on the youngest of the horses. The three event riders then rode their respective horse for a few minutes to assess any problems it might have in its general way of going, after which the event rider explained to the owner

and the audience how they would tackle rectifying the problems. While they did so, each owner explained what his/her horse had done, and what he/she thought its faults were. Each event rider then taught their selected pupil a simple exercise to improve the horse's way of going. Mary concentrated on accuracy, and riding the young horse forwards into a consistent contact. Robert suggested that his pupil use transitions to encourage his horse to come off its forehand, and turns on the forehand to teach it to move away from the lower leg. Blyth worked on lengthening and shortening the stride in order to 'open up' his pupil's horse; he considered it to be very talented, but felt it was only offering about 50 per cent of what it could really produce. All the event riders emphasised the importance of riding the horse forwards from the leg and seat and only using the hands to fine-tune the energy that this created.

Mary and King Samuel then gave an impressive dressage display which contained all the exercises that had been discussed. Halfway through the evening, the audience was invited to go down and meet the riders and their 'stable stars': King Kong, Just an Ace and Messiah.

The second half opened with an amusing riding and road safety display demonstrating the right and the wrong way to ride on the roads; and the latest in fluorescent safety wear and lighting was also exhibited, all modelled by Mary and Conker.

The 'pupils' then had their jumping put to the test: again, each was taught a different exercise. Robert explained one way to teach a young horse 'footwork', so that it looked at its fences and adjusted its own stride. This was done quite simply by placing four poles on the ground marking each quarter of a 20m circle. Horse and rider then trotted and cantered the circle, taking in the poles which the rider was told to ignore while the horse sorted itself out – who needs to see a stride, anyway?!

Mary used an exercise in which three fences were set up on the centre line, and then jumped in a figure-of-eight format so that the horse had to change lead over the centre fence. The rider was told simply to look towards the next fence, change his leg aids over the fence, and open his inside hand a little to encourage the horse to set off with the correct lead.

Blyth again worked on lengthening and shortening the stride, this time down a line of fences set at related distances.

The evening concluded with a Pro-Am speed-jumping challenge, in which event riders and pupils had the

● A room with a view; William's converted barn provides a light, spacious and interesting home

chance to put into practice all that had been discussed.

Mary, Robert and Blyth all thoroughly enjoyed these demonstrations. The atmosphere was always enjoyably relaxed with plenty of ad-libbing and humorous backchat, and from a spectator's point of view, their ultimate success was undeniably due to the use of 'genuine horse and rider pupils' whose good and bad points were quite obvious; this meant that any improvement they made was readily highlighted. As Mary pointed out, so much comes down to the thoroughness of the flatwork, and taking the time to teach the horse what is right and wrong. A great deal can be done by improving the transitions and general obedience; the encouraging thing about this being that any rider can work on it at home.

'The series seemed to go down well with all our audiences,' said Mary. 'We only once encountered a problem when we were given a guinea-pig horse which was really too young. He was very green, and just became more and more confused as the evening went on.' But perhaps this was not such a bad thing after all, as it showed that the training of a horse can never be rushed, even by riders of Olympic standard.

the amount of work the horses do on hard ground to a minimum, you have to subject them to it sometimes to help condition their legs so they are more able to cope with hard going when they compete. So when I schooled William I would spend the first five or ten minutes riding him in the field, and would then do the rest in the arena on the better going.

'William was feeling really good in himself. All his work is so established now that it is a case of just striving for that little bit of something extra to help us earn those higher marks.'

William travelled to Gleneagles with Cuthbert and Basil. Mary hacked him out during the first morning, and then used him for the jumping phase of the lecture demonstration in the evening.

'He was very bright and sharp during the evening, as it was his first outing since Badminton. And then the Masterclass finished with a team jumping competition, which involved jumping a small course against the clock – I hadn't given it much thought until it was too late, but I was suddenly apprehensive that with one reckless round against the clock I might be about to ruin all the hard work I had put into William. He did get very naughty and strong and had two fences down, and I resolved never to use him in such circumstances again.'

On the journey home Mary stopped off twice, at Ferdi Eilberg's and at Steve Hadley's for quick lessons on William. 'With Ferdi we concentrated on trying to make William's performance look more impressive by creating

LEG INJURIES

Like any athlete, the event horse is susceptible to tendon and ligament injuries, and in the horse these generally occur in the lower foreleg.

In structure, tendons and ligaments are very similar, but they serve different purposes: tendons link muscle to bone, while ligaments attach bone to bone. Problems occur most commonly in the flexor tendons, which run down the back of the lower leg. All tendons and ligaments are made up of bundles of tiny fibre; when the limb is over-stretched or over-loaded the fibres in the affected area are stretched or torn apart. As with any tissue which becomes strained, swelling and haemorrhage can then occur in the damaged area. Injury damage is usually found in the middle of the flexor tendon (mid-length and mid-cross-section). The temperature in the middle of the tendon increases quite significantly during strenuous exercise and it is this over-heating, combined with over-stretching, which cause most problems.

If you examine a horse's lower leg you can get some idea of where the main structures lie. Starting at the back of the leg you will feel the flexor tendons, although it is difficult to differentiate between the superficial and the deep flexor. Moving down the leg you will then come to the suspensory ligament which begins behind the knee but divides in two (about halfway down the cannon bone) and passes either side of the fetlock joint. It joins together to form a broad band at the front of the pastern, thereby creating a cradle around the whole joint. Where the fetlock meets the pastern you can feel, at either side, the two branches of the suspensory ligament. The ridge you can detect running down the front of the leg is the common extensor tendon. Other structures are not so easy to find: the lateral extensor tendon which runs down the side of the leg, and the check ligament, which starts at the back of the knee and then joins up with the deep flexor tendon. Its function is to prevent the tendon being over-stretched if possible.

SYMPTOMS

One or more of the following symptoms may indicate tendon or ligament damage: thickening or bowing of the tendon, localised heat in the tendon area, and a degree of lameness. Tendon damage is analysed using an ultra-sound scan, which produces pictures of a cross-section of the leg, taken at various points along the length of the tendon. Injuries show up on the scan as either black holes (lesions) or as a thickening or distortion of the affected structure:

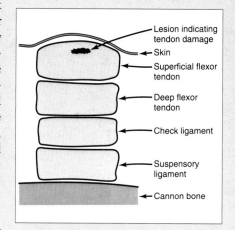

- Lesion indicating tendon damage
- Skin
- Superficial flexor tendon
- Deep flexor tendon
- Check ligament
- Suspensory ligament
- Cannon bone

The successful treatment of tendon or ligament injuries usually involves cold treatment to the affected area (either cold hosing or poulticing), along with controlled exercise such as walking out in-hand. After several weeks of treatment the injury is normally re-scanned to ascertain the state of repair. If it is progressing well then the amount of exercise will be built up until the horse is fully recovered and back in normal work. Tendon damage can take anything from a month to two years to be fully repaired. Unfortunately there are cases where recovery is never sufficient for the horse to resume eventing as a career, but advances in veterinary technology and expertise mean that, more often than not, the story has a happy ending.

● *The main muscle and ligament structures of the foreleg*

- Superficial digital flexor tendon
- Deep digital flexor tendon
- Digital extensor tendon
- Suspensory ligament
- Fetlock joint
- Extensor branch of suspensory ligament
- Deep digital flexor tendon
- Common extensor tendon

● Steve Hadley works with Mary
to improve Basil's technique

greater energy and lift in his paces. The problem is,' explained Mary, 'that once I start to ask him for more he directs all his energy forwards and becomes very strong. To overcome this we worked on downward transitions from extended to collected canter to encourage him to use the engagement of his hindquarters to steady himself, and teach him not to rely on my hand. He needs to learn to put his energy into lifting his stride rather than lengthening it and speeding up – having created the energy, he must still respect my hand and remain light in front so that the energy is contained *within* the pace we are working in.'

The following day included the jumping lesson with Steve Hadley, as the lorry gradually made its way south from Scotland. 'We jumped indoors for a while and then worked outside. William seems to be keeping much straighter since Badminton and his holiday. I rode him through a course and Steve advised me to concentrate on keeping him round and engaged and to put as much lift and life into the canter as I could, without letting him increase the speed. He felt that I needed to increase the pressure I could feel in my hand so that William

was really contained between my leg and hand on the approach, otherwise he tends to throw himself forwards over a fence without having first got high enough in the air.'

There were now just under two weeks until the final Olympic trial and Mary felt it was time to increase William's fastwork. However, the ground had become too hard to gallop at home and so she called on a friend, Simon Dutfield, who is a racehorse trainer and owns an all-weather gallop.

'Simon has a superb racehorse gallop of about a mile, which is horseshoe-shaped with an incredibly steep incline. I worked William quietly up once in trot and canter, and then went up again at three-quarter speed.'

Doddington Park one-day event for Advanced and Intermediate horses was held just a week before the final trial, and Mary had entered William with the intention of doing just the dressage and showjumping. 'I wanted to get William out in the competition atmosphere again to see how he reacted,' said Mary, 'and was expecting him to be very bright – but he was surprisingly relaxed and well behaved. He produced a super test to lead his section. He did

● *Being a relatively young horse, Apple does not show the same degree of engagement as the more advanced horses. Bramham CCCI****

then have one showjump down, but it was an impressive round for him. He stayed a lot straighter, and as we approached the fences he came on much more of a waiting stride so that I was able to ride him deep into the fence. Previously he has always rushed forwards and I have had to hold him off his fences to stop him getting too fast and flat. I felt very pleased with him, and was now confident that we were ready for the final trial and, hopefully, the Olympics.'

STAR APPEAL, BRAMHAM CCI***

Mary's programme of spring three-day events was due to finish at Bramham. As always, her schedule was hectic; having flown straight from Italy where she had ridden King Samuel into second place in the Continental Cup, she drove from Heathrow up to Uttoxeter to meet her mother and Sarah who had driven up in the lorry. That evening Mary, Robert Lemieux and Blyth Tait presented another of their Audi Masterclass lecture demonstrations; only then could she head off for Bramham with Apple.

As she had not been able to ride him for some time, they stopped en route at Michael Foljambe's estate which hosts Osberton three-day event. Apple had a good school round some of his cross-country fences before continuing the journey to Yorkshire.

At seven years old, Apple was the youngest horse competing at Bramham. He performed a very obedient test, although it just lacked some of the lightness and engagement shown by the older horses. He finished 11th out of sixty-five in the dressage. However from that point, things started to go wrong. On Saturday morning, cross-country day, a skin rash which had appeared on Apple's front heel was showing signs of infection, with swelling and heat spreading rapidly up his leg. Although he was not actually lame, after much discussion with his owners, the Pinders, it was decided not to risk him and he was withdrawn from the competition. Of course by this late stage Mary had already walked and planned her cross-country ride, and she had been looking forward to helping Apple tackle his greatest challenge to date.

'When I walked the course I thought it would be really suitable for Apple. The going was perfect, and it was a lovely, open, galloping course which would suit a big, long-striding horse like Apple. My main aim in tackling the course with him would have been to produce a happy, confidence-giving ride. For example, the first real

● *Mary is justifiably pleased with Apple's first performance at this level*

question was at fence four, where the direct route was over a big corner, but as it came so early in the course I would have ridden the long route, even though it turned out to ride well on the day. Bramham hosts the Young Rider Championship and as that section is run first the seniors get a chance to see how the course is riding before we have to tackle it ourselves.

'There was a difficult coffin, where the ground ran away from the first rail down to the ditch, and then climbed back up to the exit rail. However, Apple has always been very neat through this type of combination and so I would have taken the direct route here. Then about a third of the way round the course there was another corner-and-rails complex. As the corner was particularly awkward and the long route did not waste too much time, I would have played safe here, too – the alternative to the corner was a double of uprights to a parallel, all set on related distances which meant you could just keep riding forward in a good rhythm. At the water the quicker route was to jump a big log-pile directly into the water; or you could opt for a smaller log-pile where there was room to

land on dry ground before taking a stride to the water. As Apple is a very bold jumper but still relatively inexperienced, I did not want him to make a great big jump into the water and perhaps frighten himself, so again we would have taken the slightly longer route here.

'Nearer home there was a combination which involved a hedge and a drop followed by a stride to a very big oxer. The alternative was a step down to a combination of rails. A bold jump over the hedge and drop would take you too close to the oxer, and so we would have tackled the step and rails, but I may have changed my mind if the direct route had ridden well earlier in the day.

'Another combination near the main arena had a direct route which involved a corner followed by four strides to a brush fence. Apple is good to hold to a line and so I would have taken this direct route.

'It was a great disappointment not to have the chance to ride Apple here. He is a horse who is showing great potential and I look forward to having him fully fit again. The aim will then be to compete in the autumn at Boekelo CCI*** in Holland.'

JULY

*T*he beginning of July brought the long-awaited final Olympic trial, to be held at Savernake Forest Horse Trials in Wiltshire. My plan was to go quietly with William to make sure he finished sound and happy, which thankfully he did – and the announcement of my place in the British Olympic team was a dream come true.

All at once the Olympics were upon us. It had taken four years to produce William to this level; the preparation for the 1992 Olympics had included getting to, and competing successfully at Badminton, the main Olympic trial, after which we were long-listed for the team. I had managed to get William fit again in time for the final trial at Savernake – and this in itself had been a worry because of the close proximity of the Games – and now we had survived the event and received confirmation of an Olympic place.

I thoroughly enjoyed the team training at Badminton: Ian, Richard, Karen, Ginny and I all got on very well and a strong team spirit developed. When Master Craftsman went lame so close to the time of our departure it was devastating – but we felt that all was by no means lost as we had a very experienced reserve partnership in Karen Dixon with Get Smart.

However, it was as though the medals just weren't meant for us this time: we went out to Barcelona feeling very positive and we all tried to do our best, but things simply did not go our way. Richard and Jacana had a refusal and fall at the second water fence, and as our number one partnership to tackle the cross-country, this was not a good start. Karen then felt obliged to ride a rather defensive round on Smart to try and ensure a clear for the team, which she did. By the time William and I

were due to set off the course was proving to be riding well and the selectors gave me a free hand to choose which routes I wanted to ride.

When finally we tackled Phase D, my problem was William's exuberance – I think he was as excited as myself to be competing for his country at the Olympics! But I found myself riding an alien horse, quite unlike the calm, responsive, polite gentleman that I had ridden at Badminton Horse Trials in the spring, and my cross-country round became increasingly a nightmare. William became stronger and stronger, all the time trying to 'run through the bridle', and because of this I had to change my plans as I went along, convinced that if I tried to go the more direct routes at the water combinations, he would overjump and have a crashing fall. We went clear but collected some time penalties, though retained the fourth place which we had held after the dressage.

Ian also discovered he had a very strong Murphy Himself on his hands, so wasted time around the course trying to keep him under control; nonetheless he had a brilliant ride and at the end of cross-country day the British team were within reach of the gold medal. So when Murphy failed the last veterinary inspection it was a desperate blow for us all, and the chance of a team gold medal vanished before our eyes.

The British team position was not improved when William and I then had a bad showjumping round, despite all the hard work which Steve Hadley, Captain Mark Phillips and myself had devoted to William's jump training over the previous six months. Never mind, the team finished sixth and I finished ninth in the world – and most importantly, William was fit and sound, ready to make a bid for the 1996 Olympics in Atlanta!

● *William shows off his good form at the final Olympic trial at Savernake*

OLYMPIC PRELIMINARIES

July was to be an extremely busy month for Mary, and not least the first weekend, with the British Equestrian Olympic Fund Ball on Friday night, and the final Olympic trial at Savernake Forest horse trials on Sunday. Inevitably William was the focus of attention for the greater part of the month although Boris and Basil had their own, and for them, significant challenges ahead. Basil was competing in the Novice class at Savernake Forest, and this would be his first event of the autumn season; the cross-country was a fair-sized track, which Mary hoped would serve as good preparation for his imminent move up to Intermediate level. Boris was competing in the final trial as well as William, although he was not in contention for an Olympic place – his main aim of the season was to contest the title of British Open Champion at Gatcombe. Boris had won this title in 1990, and William had retained it for Mary in 1991; three wins in a row would surely be an achievement worthy of record!

The Olympic Ball was held at Waldridge Manor in Buckinghamshire, and crystallised the fact that this really *was* an Olympic year, and that the ultimate challenge was not far away. Mary had invited Steve and Clare Hadley, Ferdi and Gerry Eilberg, Gill and Geoff Robinson, Katie Meacham and Andrew Hoy – and, of course, David King! Gill and Geoff Robinson arrived in their luxurious mobile home, so David and Mary did not have to worry about driving home.

'The best part of the weekend,' recalls Mary, 'was being ordered to stay in bed while Gill drove me to Savernake. I didn't get up until we had arrived at the event and met up with the horses, Mum and Annie having gallantly driven them up from Devon to Wiltshire early that morning!'

Basil competed that day: he settled down quickly and produced an impressive dressage test, then jumped a double clear over a big Novice course to finish second. 'He still felt a bit sticky across country,' said Mary 'and this still leaves me wondering if he's really cut out to be a top class event horse – though having said that, he was surprisingly bold into the water. But over all, he was just a little bit too wary for it to have been a perfect round.'

The Olympic final trial

The final Olympic trial was to run over the Advanced track at Savernake Forest and all the

● *A girl can't even be left to dress in peace and quiet!*

● *Before the cross-country at Savernake, time for the showjumping post mortem with Steve Hadley*

● *William and Basil arrive at Badminton House for team training*

long-listed horses were expected to compete; other Advanced horses, such as Boris, had also been accepted in order to make up a full section.

'We had to perform the FEI dressage test which was being used in the Olympics. William did a reasonable test, although nothing like his Badminton form as he was a little bit tense; however, he finished second behind Murphy Himself on a score of 30 penalties. Boris didn't really perform at his best either, and finished with 33 penalties. With William, the showjumping result was not so good – both Captain Phillips and Steve Hadley were there to help me, but we still had two down. On the whole William didn't jump too badly round the course, but he was strong and onward-bound which never helps – he jumps best when I can ride him forwards into the fences rather than having to try to slow him down all the time.

'I took him very quietly across country. He felt great, but I didn't want to risk an injury. I knew that as long as he went clear, and finished fit and sound, he would be selected for the team. It did feel strange going so slowly, but the important thing was to look after him, and he came home sound, without any cuts or bumps. However, I did have a crack at the placings with Boris, who was clear in the showjumping: he

soared round the cross-country track, thoroughly enjoying himself, and finished second behind Murphy Himself.'

Team selection

The fifteen long-listed horses were detailed to go back to Badminton House that night; the final trot-up was to be early the next morning, after which the team would be announced. It was very nerve-racking, as there would be no second chances if anything were to go wrong at that point. However, morning came, and William bounded past the selectors as if to say that this whole thing was quite unnecessary, how could anyone imagine that he might *not* be feeling fit and well?!

'The selectors then retired for further private discussion, while we waited. Finally we were all summoned into the Stewards' Room at Badminton and Jane Holderness-Roddam, chairman of the selectors, announced the Olympic team. Although I half knew I would be chosen, it was still a great thrill to hear my name called out, along with Ginny Leng, Ian Stark and Richard Walker. Karen Dixon was named as travelling reserve and the four non-travelling reserves were Owen Moore, Lucinda

Murray, Helen Bell and William Miflin.'

The final date for submitting the named team was not until the end of the week. As the selectors needed to be absolutely sure that the horses were fit and sound, the team plus all the reserves were asked to meet in Lambourn three days later so they could be galloped and then trotted up again. Should there be any problem the selectors would then have a last opportunity to substitute any of the horses before the final declaration had to be made.

Fortunately all the selected horses finished sound and well after their fastwork in Lambourn, and all passed the trot-up the next day. The four non-travelling reserves went home, while the five team members moved lock, stock and barrel into Badminton.

Team training

'Team training is always organised at Badminton before any major championship event. It helps to develop a strong team spirit, and also keeps the riders away from any domestic worries they may have at home, as well as from the press! We get thoroughly spoilt; riders are allowed to take three horses each into training, so they can get plenty of riding and practice without using the Olympic horses too much – I took

Sammy and Basil. All the riders and grooms are given their own rooms above the stables, we are extremely well fed, and there is plenty of time to relax as well. We go swimming, play tennis, and watch videos – which is a wonderful treat for me, as we don't have a television at home!

'The official team trainer was Ferdi Eilberg, but we are allowed to have our own trainers with us as well, so Steve Hadley and Captain Phillips were on hand to help me. I only jumped William a couple of times during the eleven days we were there, and had two or three lessons with Ferdi. Every four days the horses were boxed up and taken to Lambourn to be galloped, which was fun for everyone. There was also an Open Day, when the public could come and watch us being trained and ask questions; in the course of this there was a slightly awkward moment for Captain Phillips when Ian Stark's young daughter asked if he might not find it a little difficult carrying out his duties in Barcelona as both British selector *and* official trainer to the Spanish team?

'There were press days, and one particularly exciting day when we were given all our new equipment and kit from the various sponsors of the event team, as well as the official Olympic uniform and kit. We had to keep changing in

● *William leaves his spokeslady to deal with the press*

and out of all these wonderful new things: boots, breeches and jackets for us, saddles and bridles and rugs for the horses. However, shiny new leather is not the easiest thing for humans or horses to slip in and out of, and altogether the day proved to be quite exhausting!

'A farewell cocktail party hosted by the Duke and Duchess of Beaufort was organised for all the various people who had helped to get the team this far, another evening we were shown an entertaining video of the human dope-testing technique and all that this involved. However, it was not so amusing when, lo and behold! an Olympic official turned up the following day to test us all.

'A Pedens lorry arrived on the Thursday before we were due to fly out to Barcelona, and loaded with all the spare tack and equipment. As only one small trunk was allowed on the plane with the horses, most of the kit had to be sent out early. This was also the day we galloped the horses in Lambourn again. And then the following morning we had an inkling of our Olympic luck when Master Craftsman came out lame. However, he was rested the following day and then hacked out and schooled on the Saturday, when he appeared to be 100 per cent again. On the Sunday all the horses were given their final fastwork. We used Badminton Park itself on this occasion as the going was so good

and it saved the horses making another trip in the lorry. Sadly Crafty was lame again; so then we were down to four…

'I took Basil and Sammy home to Devon on the Sunday. There was just time to give Boris a quick jump which I felt was important as I wouldn't be riding him for a few weeks, and he had several competitions lined up for the autumn, as soon as I was back home.'

Travelling to Spain

'Back at Badminton I just hacked William out quietly as the following day he would be flying out to Spain. The lorry came to pick up the horses and grooms, as well as Lord Patrick Beresford, our chef d'équipe and Brendon Murray the team farrier. It seemed funny saying goodbye to Annie and William, knowing that the next time we would all be meeting up would be in Spain. The horses were flying from Bristol. Only William and Jacana, Richard Walker's horse, had not flown before, and I was a bit concerned about William as he is quite hyper-active when he travels. However, all went well; Annie was told not to feed him any hay that morning because the flight was at 11am, and as soon as the horses were on the plane they were given their haynets – thus they munched contentedly throughout the two-hour flight.'

• Annie is left to carry William's luggage!

BARCELONA OLYMPICS 1992

'We travelled out from Heathrow that afternoon, all dressed up in our Olympic kit, and really began to feel a part of the British squad, especially as the plane was full of other Olympic athletes. On arrival in Barcelona we were met by a great crowd of Spaniards welcoming us to their country – it was all incredibly exciting! – and were ushered into a convoy of coaches; we were then driven with a police escort through the city. The first requirement was to get our accreditation papers, which would allow us into the Olympic village. This seemed to take for ever, until Scotty (Ian Stark) magically produced champagne and caviare to while away the hours! We had already met the judo team, including the infamous Big Elvis whose acquaintance we had made when he and Karen managed to spill their drinks over each other on the plane – they all joined us now, and the party proved to be the first of many.

'Once we were accredited we were free to roam the Olympic compound. Our living quarters were brand-new apartments, each apartment comprising four twin bedrooms, a kitchen, sitting-room and two bathrooms. They were quite cramped when everyone was at home, but it was all refreshingly clean and new, and we had very little to worry about as a host of cleaners

came in each day to tidy up after us. Catering was no problem, either, since the menus offered in the enormous food hall were almost beyond description: there was every type of food you could possibly imagine – hot meals, cold meals, vegetarian food, foreign dishes, enormous steaks, refrigerators full of every kind of drink, yoghurt, fruit and ice-cream: there was as much as you wanted, whenever you wanted it, and it was all free! The atmosphere in the hall was wonderful, too, with everyone dressed in the bright, vibrant colours of their country, and we kept bumping into really famous people!'

El Montanya, the site of the three-day event, was situated in the mountains north of Barcelona and was a 50-minute drive from the Olympic village. The horses were stabled on the site and the grooms accommodated in a hotel there, just a few minutes from the stables. For the first few days the riders commuted by minibus from the Olympic village to El Montanya, but once the three-day event started they stayed in a rented house in El Montanya so as to be nearer to the horses and the action.

Riders were permitted to hack about in the area where Phases A and C, the roads and tracks, would take place and there were showjumping and dressage arenas where they could school. Mary worked William quietly for the few days leading up to the event, letting him

● *Walking into the unknown –
Mary sets off to inspect the course*

● *The spectacular opening
ceremony*

take in his new surroundings and giving him time to acclimatise to the hot, humid climate. There was an area provided for fastwork but she did not consider it particularly suitable, and so did not work him at any great speed on it.

'On the Friday we had the official briefing and the first course-walk. This was still two days before the first horse inspection which is when the three-day event officially starts, and was therefore a most unusual order of events; however, it had to be done that way so as to fit in all the other Olympic commitments such as the opening ceremony. The briefing took forever, as everything was repeated in various languages and in great detail. And then at last, after the tour of the roads and tracks, came the moment we had all been waiting for: our first sight of the cross-country course. In fact, it was a pleasant surprise – the days we had already spent in El Montanya had not been particularly inspiring, everything was hot and dusty and all dried up. But the cross-country course was something else altogether, situated on a golf course and with a good covering of lush green grass. The fences themselves were bigger than I had imagined in view of the fact that so many different nations of varying experience would be tackling them, but there were plenty of alternatives. However, it all appeared to be very jumpable and I couldn't wait to meet the challenge with William – but there were still several more days to go!'

Opening ceremonies

'Karen and I went to the Olympic opening ceremony on the Saturday and I wouldn't have missed it for the world! Suddenly it made you realise that the Olympics had actually started and that you were a part of it! We all waited in a huge gymnasium which had a screen so we could see everything that was happening until we were called in. When our turn came and *Grande Bretagne* was called, we marched into the main stadium with Steve Redgrave carrying the Union Jack ahead of us; the atmosphere was wonderful! As the other countries filed in, people waved and cheered to anyone they recognised – Mark Todd was carrying the New Zealand flag, so he came in for quite a bit of stick!

'The Olympic flame was lit by an archer firing an arrow up to the torch and that was a moment I will never forget! It was followed by an incredible firework display. The finale was

● *The first horse inspection*

fantastic and moving, too – a huge rolled-up flag was carried up through the middle of all the athletes, and then it was opened out and held over the top of *all* of us, so that we were all as one, under the Olympic flag.'

THE OLYMPIC THREE-DAY EVENT

'On the day before the dressage, we were each allocated half an hour to ride up to the main dressage arena and the competition working-in areas, to experience the conditions prevailing for the dressage phase. This should have been a golden opportunity for William and I to get accustomed to the competition surroundings, but unfortunately it turned out to be quite the opposite. When it was our turn to go up to the arena, the electronic scoreboard alongside was being tested and was producing a series of whirring, clicking noises; William simply could not comprehend this strange phenomenon. He leapt around, snorting and prancing, and refused to go past it – even when I took him well away, right round to the other side, he kept looking back at it and playing up and I had not succeeded in settling him before our time was up. I was *not* looking forward to having to ride my test in that arena the next day.

'The first veterinary inspection followed, and as expected, all our team horses passed without

● (right) *One of the more relaxed moments during William's performance*

● (below) *A taste of what was to come; William strong and tense before the dressage*

● (below right) *Question and answer time*

query, William showing off to the crowd as usual and getting stronger by the minute. He was very proud and impressive, and whilst *he* may have passed the inspection easily, *I* almost did not as he happily trampled all over me in his eagerness to entertain his fans. Once the inspection was completed, the running order was drawn: we were to go fourth as a team, and I was the third rider; my Olympic number was 48! My dressage was to be on Monday evening, which I hoped would mean that it would be quieter and cooler for William.'

Dressage day

'My dressage test was not until 6.35pm on the Monday, and as William was feeling so well, I was determined to give him plenty of work before his test, especially as he would have all Tuesday to recover before he needed to tackle the speed and endurance phase.

'I rode out first thing in the morning and then met Steve Hadley in the practice arena for a brief jump-schooling session. William jumped better than I have ever known him do so before, which left us all feeling very excited. Afterwards I took him for a couple of canters round the rotavated fastwork area to complete his morning's work. In the afternoon we had an intensive dressage lesson with Ferdi, in which he worked very hard – but whilst he was performing well and being quite obedient, he was still extremely strong. By this time he had had

four hours' work, so he was taken back to his stable while I went for a very welcome swim!

'Half an hour before his test I started to work him in in the practice arenas; but as soon as we headed for the main arena he became really tense and excitable. There were still enormous numbers of people watching and milling around, flags were waving and we came into a highly charged and exciting atmosphere. The Spanish crowd was extremely enthusiastic; whereas at Badminton everyone is silent until you have performed your test, here everyone was cheering and clapping as we came into the arena – just when I was hoping for some peace and quiet to try and keep William calm! People were shouting out "Good luck, Mary!" which was really encouraging, but didn't help William's behaviour – I could feel him getting stronger and more tense, and becoming tight through his whole body. He did a reasonable

test considering how keyed up he was, and I was pleased that he had just managed to contain himself; but it had meant that I hadn't dared to ride him forwards as much as I would have liked.

'Ian and Murphy gave a brilliant performance the following morning, so at that point things were looking really good – we were lying first as a team, and individually Ian was second, Karen was third and I was fourth! Richard was further down the line, but Jacana had performed his best test ever and so he had as much to be pleased about as we did. William had a quiet day, just going out for about three-quarters of an hour to trot and canter around the roads and tracks area. I walked the steeplechase and cross-country course again that evening; usually I have my last course-walk early on cross-country day, but because of the heat and humidity I decided I would need to conserve all my energy for riding the next day – and how right I was!'

Speed and endurance day

'The big day was suddenly upon us. My start-time was nearer midday so I watched the steeplechase for a while to see how it was riding, and then went to the 10-minute box where there was a closed-circuit television so I could follow the first ten riders as they tackled the corss-country. I saw Richard's round, everything going perfectly for him until the second water; at the first element, which was a rail at the top of a steep ramp, Jacana stopped abruptly, sending Richard over the fence instead. It was desperate bad luck – had he ridden a little later in the day he would have seen how much pace was needed to negotiate the fence; but that's the luck of the draw. They were clear over the rest of the course, but had incurred a mass of penalties because of the stop, the fall and time faults.

'Back at the stables I helped Annie to get William ready. But then, just as I was all set to climb aboard, we heard that the course was being held for at least half an hour. Sitting around waiting for the go-ahead was almost unbearably nerve-racking, and I buried my head in Jilly Cooper's *Polo* to take my mind off everything.

But then it *was* time to go and off we went on Phase A with William feeling really good, relaxed but bright. It was stony in places and I was conscious of avoiding any rough areas, and I also rode in the shade wherever possible. As

• *William's new-found strength and power meant an exhausting ride for Mary*

we approached the steeplechase site William became very excited; his eyes were out on stalks and he felt like a giraffe as he took in the crowd and the atmosphere. We were met by Annie and Patrick Beresford, our chef d'équipe, who warned me that the steeplechase track was a little bit slippery on the corners, but was otherwise riding very well.

'And so we set off, with William feeling strong and keen but listening to me over the first few fences. As we went on, however, I became increasingly aware of his strength and power, and the fact that for the first time he was really using these against me – he was jumping beautifully out of his stride but was constantly trying to accelerate away. He finished easily inside the time, and sent people scattering in all directions as he roared through the channelled area where you are meant to steady up and give the horse a quick check-over. William certainly had Olympic fever, and I really had to fight to get him back to a halt. There was time for Annie to check his shoes and studs, and for me to have an Isotonic drink before setting off on Phase C. It was as important for us as riders to keep cool and drink plenty so that we didn't get dehydrated, as it was to keep the horses comfortable in the hot conditions.

'William relaxed again on Phase C, and there was quite a good breeze which made this phase very comfortable for us. Also, half-way round the roads and tracks each team had someone stationed in the shade with drinks for riders and iced water to wash down the horses again. Andrew Dixon, Karen's husband, was on duty for the British, and he gave William another quick wash-down before we continued on our way to the 10-minute box. It is here that things are a bit different when you are riding for a team rather than competing as an individual: William was taken care of by Annie and friends while I was briefed by Jane Holderness-Roddam as to how the course was riding – as is usual in an international three-day event when a British team is competing there were spotters and runners positioned around the course who were constantly relaying information back to Jane in the 10-minute box. We ran through the course together and I told Jane that my intention was to take the direct routes except at the Owl Holes, which the selectors considered dangerous, and possibly at the last water if I felt William was tired. Karen had produced a good clear round and the course, as a whole, seemed to be riding well. We set off a confident combination.

'William started off in fine style over the first fence but as we galloped on through the crowds to the second fence I suddenly realised that I had quite a different horse on my hands; he was particularly nervous of the spectators, and in one narrow section he seemed to be trying to bolt through and away from the people who were closing in around him. We hadn't even reached the second fence and he was getting horribly strong. The first five fences were relatively small and so were not really backing him off, and increasingly he was jumping dangerously flat and fast, although I did manage to get him back sufficiently for the farmyard complex at six, which was the first combination. But he accelerated away through this, getting faster and faster. The track was quite twisty and I was worried that he was going to slip up on the flat at the rate he was going.

'As we approached the first water combination, I realised with a sinking heart that it was not going to be safe to tackle the direct route.

Whilst I was just able to hold William on the approach to the fence, as soon as I released the rein to allow him to jump he just took hold and accelerated forwards. If he did this through a big combination, especially into water, he would end up having a fall. I managed to steer him through the long route and we headed on our way.

'The next big question came at the second water complex. William raced over the preceding fence, which was quite small, and just scorched down the hill towards it – as I fought with him for some control, I thought for an awful moment I was going to have to turn him in a circle to get him back, but somehow just managed to keep hold of him enough. I hadn't for one second considered doing anything but the direct route here, but with William behaving so irrationally I knew we just couldn't risk it. Even then he was still going faster than was safe to jump even the long route, and only just missed leaving my knee behind on the guiderail.

● *Taking the long route at the first water complex*

● *Still full of running, William attacks the final water*

● *William revels in the Olympic challenge*

well done at all!" As we approached the last fence I was almost completely exhausted. For the last half of the course I had had to resort to swinging William from side to side in an effort to keep control. The finish was a very welcome sight as William soared over the last fence; it was only luck that he had met it on a good stride.

'My immediate thought was that I was thrilled to have gone clear, but then I was shocked at the way William had behaved, and here, of all places. I felt dizzy and sick when I got off – whereas up to now the riders had walked off cheerfully while the horses were fussed over by the vet, this time I was the one who got fussed over by the doctor while William looked as if he was asking to go round again!

'William was washed down, and our farrier came and replaced a front shoe which we must have lost somewhere on the course. Annie then took William back to the stables to see to him properly; I stayed for a short while to watch Ian's impressive round on Murphy, then went to join Annie. We cleaned up any little cuts or grazes and covered them with Animalintex poultice, and put Ice-Tight on the remaining parts of his legs. We also bandaged a bag of ice around the hoof which had lost the shoe to reduce the amount of bruising that might result. Apart from that William seemed completely unaffected by his exploits, which is more than could be said for me; my muscles were aching all over and even a good swim in the pool did little to relieve them. However, the important thing was that William should trot up at the veterinary inspection the following morning with no unacceptable signs of stiffness or unlevelness; our precautions were vital we felt, to produce a sound horse the next day.

'As a team we were feeling really pleased at this point; we were lying second to the New Zealanders and were quietly confident that there would be a good chance of overtaking them in the showjumping to snatch the gold, as we knew that Spinning Rhombus, the New Zealand horse, is normally a worse showjumper than William. Richard was obviously feeling a bit low because of his fall, but the great thing about being a member of a team is that all the others will rally round when support is needed – we all knew that it could just as easily have been one of us if we had been first to go.

'When we checked William that evening he was a little bit stiff from having pulled and fought so much, but he was sound and well in

'As we progressed around the course I was getting weaker and weaker while William just got stronger and stronger – his mouth had probably become quite numb from pulling so much.

'We were able to take the direct route at the step up to a corner, where most people had chosen the easy alternative. It was on a good distance and uphill, and it was possible to bank the corner if things went wrong, so I decided it was safe to tackle it – I also hoped it would serve to bring William to his senses; but he continued undeterred. All the way round we were getting tremendous support from the crowd, with people shouting "Well done, Mary! Go on, Mary!" – while I was thinking "This is terrible, it's not

● *William eating up the course*

himself. Murphy showed some slight lameness, but the others were fine. Unfortunately it was Murphy's lameness which was to prove our downfall the next morning: after half an hour's hack just at walk to make sure the horses worked off any stiffness before the final inspection, it was alarmingly evident that Murphy was not improving as we had hoped, and in fact was not looking good at all. The vet had suggested applying ice to the joint, but this was not enough to help him. He was lame when trotted up, and the Ground Jury asked for him to be held over until the end; when he trotted up again he was definitely worse and so they were not able to pass him. Having been so optimistic such a short while before, it came as quite a shock suddenly to realise that our chances of any medal at all were disappearing fast.'

The showjumping test

'All the horses that were to showjump were taken by transporters down to the Polo Club in Barcelona where the final phase was to be held. It turned out to be a very long journey for them. We travelled on ahead by minibus to walk the course. When finally the horses arrived they were settled into rows of temporary stabling; we had brought some big electric fans down with us to help keep them cool, as the climate in the city was much hotter and more humid than in El Montanya.

'My main concern about the showjumping was whether I would be able to hold William after his performance the day before – Scotty had lent me a bucketful of various bits to try out. As he was not jumping till late in the afternoon I rode him out after lunch with the intention of trying out the new bits. However, I started out in his normal vulcanite pelham; we did some trot and canter work, then popped over a few practice jumps, and he felt very soft and light in my hand. Finally I decided not to risk changing his bit after all – there is always the chance that a horse will react adversely

once he is in the ring if he is not used to whatever you are riding him in.

'As the showjumping phase drew nearer I felt surprisingly relaxed; I knew William's showjumping was not his strongest point, and it helped even less knowing that the Olympic

● *The final phase begins*

● *From left to right: Gill and Geoff Robinson, Mary, Jill and Michael Thomson*

course would obviously *not* suit the less careful horses: the jumps were all the same colour, and had very little by way of fillers to make a horse back off and encourage him up into the air over them. So I was expecting things not to go well, and was quite calm about it. Had I been in pole position it would have been much worse, but in many ways I felt that lying in fourth position meant there wasn't quite so much to lose.

'When finally I got on William, I worked him on the flat for a while to get him really warmed up and supple. He was still feeling pretty bright and sharp, so we put two big wadges of cotton wool in his ears to try and muffle the noise from the crowd as he seemed to find this so distracting. The crowds were altogether very enthusiastic, and cheered and clapped *during* the showjumping rounds as well as before and after! Sadly, even over the practice fence William did not give us much cause for optimism: he was jumping very much to the left again, and I could feel that his mind simply wasn't on what he was being asked to do. When our turn came the best I can say is we went in and had five showjumps down. He had been very tense and stayed very short in his neck and although he did not get too strong his canter was too flat and free; I could not get him to relax enough so that he would round in his canter and lift his shoulders which is what he needs to do to throw a good jump. Despite this disappointment I still couldn't help feeling pleased with him in a funny way when we fin-

● *The bland, blue fences did little to get the horses in the air*

ished our round; we had got to the Olympics, we had completed and we had finished ninth in the world. My next immediate thought was how lucky we had been at Badminton, the same thing could so easily have happened. Ironically, Kibah Tic Toc and Matt Ryan, the eventual gold medal winners, had had five showjumps down at Badminton but in Barcelona he had one showjump down to win. William and I had done the reverse. The eventing world is so small that the Australians' win was enjoyed by us all, almost as much as if it had been our own. The Olympics are full of 'if only' stories – if only Murphy had passed the vet Britain would more than likely have won the gold medal, but, horses are not machines and their results and performances will always be unpredictable, and at times of defeat you can at least comfort yourself with that old Olympic ideal: "it is not the winning but the taking part" which is important (not that I agree!!).

Closing stages

'Our poor horses were then subjected to a quite unnecessarily arduous journey home: they left at 8pm and didn't return to the stables until 2am, the police escort having taken them right out of Barcelona and towards France before the drivers were able to persuade them that this really wasn't the plan at all, and that they were meant to be in El Montanya – which is only one hour's travel north of Barcelona, the city they had left six hours before. The horses were obviously very tired but fortunately unharmed, and were *more* than happy to be back in their stables again! They were not due to fly home for another week, and so William and Annie enjoyed a very relaxed holiday. Annie rode William out bareback each day up to the three-day-event site where there was plenty of grass. William grazed happily while Annie topped up her suntan;

whoever said a groom's lot is not a happy one?!

'I moved back down to the Olympic village once the three-day event was over. Ian went straight home. Karen stayed and enjoyed a few days with me, but then she had to get back. Richard stayed to the bitter end, and I'm sure he'd agree that those ten days in Barcelona until the closing ceremony were brilliant! I joined up with the British modern pentathlete team and the rowers, who had also finished their events; we went to see all the sights you were meant to see, and probably quite a few which you weren't. The atmosphere was terrific. Everyone was so friendly, and it was amazing to think that there you were, amongst the best athletes in the world. I watched as many different Olympic events as I could, finishing up at the main stadium every evening. Then it was on to the parties, which were an Olympic event in themselves, as they rarely seemed to finish before dawn.'

● *William did make a real effort over the water, a fence which ironically caused problems for others*

147

THE OLYMPICS:
BAD TACTICS OR BAD LUCK?

Taken from the original article written by Debby Sly for Eventing *magazine*

The performance in Barcelona of the British three-day-event team led to a flood of letters and articles questioning the approach and the attitude of the team and its selectors. The general feeling seemed to be that Britain had 'played safe' and lost, whereas many other nations, including some with relatively little experience of the sport, had ridden for their lives, a policy which in many cases had paid off. Whilst it is important that performances and policies are examined so that we may learn from our mistakes, this has to be done with a full knowledge of all the facts involved and should not be based on assumptions and hearsay.

Those who criticised the British team made two major assumptions: one that it was the selectors who dictated which routes each rider attempted; and two, that had all four of our riders tackled the direct routes at all the fences they would automatically have achieved clear rounds. Probably there would have been little sympathy for anyone who tried this and got it wrong – no doubt they would have been accused of selfishness, and of sacrificing the team's chances in pursuit of individual glory.

For the Barcelona Olympics 1992 Britain was widely considered to have had a very strong team; but as Jane Holderness-Roddam, chairman of the selectors, pointed out, there was always an element of doubt as to what William might do in the showjumping – also whether Murphy Himself, given his age and the fact that he is only part-Thoroughbred, would cope with the heat. Ian Stark's other horse, Glenburnie, is a Thoroughbred and was the first choice for the team, but when the time came he was recovering from a virus and was not 100 per cent fit. Karen Dixon, whilst being more than capable of a good all-round performance, did have a record of problems at water fences, as evidenced in her last three team appearances at Seoul, Stockholm and Punchestown. Richard Walker had done an excellent job as 'first man' at Punchestown, and there was no reason not to expect the same from him in Barcelona.

As far as the selection committee was concerned, the aim of the British riders was to win the *team* gold. This has long been the policy of the Horse Trials Committee, believing as they do that team success is more important than individual glory, a belief which is very much in keeping with the true spirit of the Olympic ideal. But as Richard Walker concluded, when you put four individually experienced riders into a team, whilst they will go along with the idea that the team medal is the principal aim, you do not remove from those people the strong desire to feature individually. They are proven competitors, and it is that independence of spirit which has brought them success at top level.

The riders would have walked the course several times on their own as well as with the team selectors; the selectors' role is to give advice and to make sure that each rider has considered all the possibilities. As Jane Holderness-Roddam explained, ultimately it is the rider who knows his horse best, and the final decision is one which the rider has to be happy with. The only direct route which the selectors were adamant that the riders should *not* tackle was the Owl Holes. The horses were meant to jump through a very

● *Jane Holderness-Roddam at the controversial Owl Holes*

small hole cut into a brush-type fence; however, across the top of the hole, at what would be head-height if things were to go wrong, was a solid wooden rail. The selectors considered this to be a dangerous fence, and as the alternative route did not take much longer, all the riders were quite happy with this decision.

Another fence which was much discussed was the last water complex: this involved a double of upright walls, on a downhill slope into the lake. It came at a point on the course when the horses could be very tired, and this would make it significantly more difficult. Apart from Karen, it was left to the riders to decide for themselves how they tackled this fence; they would obviously base their decision on how their horses felt at that stage of the course, and how well they had jumped the previous fences. Karen was instructed to take the long options at all three water complexes. although she herself, having been a member of the team on several occasions, felt she would have liked to have attempted the direct routes, especially as she was well placed individually when the time came, but she respected the selectors' request and agreed to make a safe clear her aim.

After the dressage phase the British team was lying in gold position; initially the competition was going really well for them. Obviously, the discussions about the cross-country course took place before the British knew they were going to be in such an enviable position – but even if this *did* lead to a 'play-safe' policy,

● *Richard Walker and Jacana having an uncomfortable jump through the direct route at the first water*

any rider who, as an individual, has led after the dressage will agree that this often causes you to tackle the cross-country differently. Knowing that there is so much to lose may persuade you not to take too many risks, as long as you are confident of achieving a good time. It is often easier to fight your way up the placings than it is to maintain a lead.

When Richard set off on the course early in the day he intended taking the direct routes through the first two water complexes and would save his decision about the last water combination until he knew how tired or otherwise Jacana was. Fence 16, the second water, came at a very tiring point in the course: from fence 8, apart from one small dip, it was a long pull up to fence 14, then a straight run to 15 before a slight slope and sharp turn to 16. There wasn't quite enough time for the horses to get their second wind, and fence 16 always promised to need a fair bit of acceleration. Richard explained what happened:

'When I turned towards the first element I had to take a pull, as I could see I was on a very long distance and I wanted to give Jacana room to fit in another stride to bring us closer to the fence. A tired horse always responds more quickly to a pull aid than to a forward aid. Jacana responded to my checking him but now, in hindsight, I can see that I did not ask strongly enough for him to go forwards to the fence again.

'He arrived at the foot of the fence with insufficient impulsion to jump it; to add to the problem his refusal was abrupt enough to send me flying over his head, thus incurring 20 penalties for the stop, and a further 60 for the fall. With the benefit of hindsight, or had I been later in the running order, I would have known to come off that corner and ride for my life.'

Richard and Jacana were clear over the rest of the course, but had incurred a significant number of penalties.

It was now even more important that Karen went clear to help bring the team score back into the reckoning. As instructed she took the long routes at the water fences but she still managed to achieve a good time which turned out to be only five seconds slower than Murphy Himself. Karen described her feelings about her performance:

'I was delighted to have achieved what had been asked of me,

● *Karen Dixon came home best of the British but was disappointed not to have been allowed to take the direct routes*

but personally, I still think the attitude of a team should be to go out and fight for it. Had I been competing individually I would definitely have attempted the direct routes – if we had been unsuccessful we would at least have gone out in style. But having said that, I have never been allowed to forget my fall at the Seoul Olympics.'

Mary had had plenty of time to see how the course was riding, and was looking forward to taking all the direct routes and achieving a good time, as would be expected of her. But this was not to be: as it turned out, William's sheer strength and power turned against her in Barcelona, when she found she simply could not control him sufficiently to feel confident about tackling the water complexes. As she explained, if they had been single fences William's scope and athleticism would probably have kept him on his feet, but taking on combinations into water with too much speed only courted disaster. William's behaviour was in almost unbelievable contrast to his gentlemanly performance at Badminton, and it is hard to know exactly what it was that led to his over-exuberance in Barcelona. However, it is perhaps signifi-cant that his build-up to Badminton was spread over four months

of constant work from January to May, his fitness programme and competition timetable tailored so that he peaked then. Afterwards there was very little time for him to have his post-Badminton rest *and* be brought up again to peak fitness for the Olympic challenge. Whilst he was more than fit enough, he had had very few competition outings, only the first two phases of the Advanced class at Dodington Park, and then the final trial itself, where he was ridden steadily to ensure he stayed sound and well.

Once in Barcelona, William did not seem to be too badly affected by the hot climate – in fact when the decision was made to reduce the roads and tracks and steeplechase, it also reduced the opportunity for some of his 'edge' to be worked off. Furthermore, as a spectator myself at Barcelona, I know that the one factor that did not come across on the television coverage was the charged atmosphere and the wild attitude of the crowd. The spectators at El Montanya were hugely enthusiastic, but the majority had no basic knowledge of horses and horse trials: they screamed encouragement, rushing forwards and waving flags not only as each horse galloped past them, but also as it approached and on its way over the fences. And their mood became almost hostile each time a rider took an alternative route, when they would boo and jeer on each occasion. The atmosphere was more

● *William's sensitive temperament and hyper-fitness left him vulnerable to the strange environment*

like that of a football match or a grand prix than that of a three-day event, and this was well summed up by the fact that the programmes needed to carry this warning: *Please do not throw things at the horses!* Obviously every horse and rider had to contend with this, the same as the next one, but it would have affected individuals differently and I am quite positive that William's sensitive temperament and his state of hyper-fitness made him vulnerable to the atmosphere he found himself in.

Mary did go clear, but with more time faults than she would have liked because of the constant fight she had had to keep William under control. Ian Stark and Murphy Himself were the last combination to set off for Great Britain. Ian had every intention of going for a fast clear round, and the crowds were treated to some of Murphy's spectacular jumping as he attacked the course. His power and scope allowed him to bounce through the first water combination, and he appeared to be still going strong as he came into the second water complex. Ian rode the direct route, but at the exit from the water Murphy suddenly realised that he was not going to make it by bouncing out and had to put

● *Murphy Himself displaying his sometimes reckless talent as he stays on his feet having misjudged the final water element*

down again quickly, which put him dangerously close to the final element. He continued in his usual headstrong manner, but by the time he was on the last third of the course it was obvious that the heat and his earlier exuberance were both taking their toll. Ian nursed him home, taking the long route at the final water as it was not the type of obstacle to tackle with a tired horse.

Ian's final comment was this: 'With the benefit of hindsight, it is perhaps time that we examine our team policy. In the past, three clear rounds would have won you a gold medal but the standard is so high now that that is no longer good enough. You need three fast clears. But at Barcelona, Karen was the only rider told to go the long ways and so I don't think the selectors deserved the criticism they have had.'

At the end of cross-country day, Great Britain was lying in second place as a team; had Murphy passed the final horse inspection, almost without doubt Britain would have won the team gold. Even counting William's expensive showjumping round, Murphy would have had to have knocked down three showjumps to lose the gold medal, and he has never had more than two fences down in the whole of his competitive life.

Undoubtedly every rider needs a degree of luck; some would say that Matt Ryan, the individual gold medallist, was lucky not to

have been unseated at the first water – equally the New Zealanders were lucky that Blyth Tait's Messiah was able to complete the event, as he was lame on the first day. Many horses finished the showjumping lame, and they were lucky that their lameness did not show up earlier, during the final inspection. Murphy Himself was not the only horse to be unsound at the end of cross-country day – we were just unlucky that he did not make it through to the final phase, whereas most of the others did. It may be that the British team veterinary and 'aftercare' facilities on hand at the event need improving so that our horses have the best possible chance of being able to complete a three-day event; hopefully this is something that will be examined during the Olympic aftermath.

When it comes down to it, I have to conclude that the British team was unlucky; each rider did what he considered best for his horse, given the circumstances on the day. Surely none of us, as mere spectators, have the right to criticise any decision a rider makes which is for the benefit of his horse. Moreover it is not uncommon, even in everyday competition for a rider to change his mind about which route he is going to tackle, as this depends on the ride his horse is giving him as he progresses round a course. There is no greater sight than a horse and rider confidently attacking a course; but equally there is nothing more sickening than watching an uncontrollable or tired horse come to grief. The safety and welfare of horse and rider must always come before entertainment value.

AUGUST

Once we had finished the three-day event we moved out of our rented house in El Montanya and back into the Olympic village. Having spent every day with William for the last month, and after all the excitement we had been through during the previous week, I found it strange leaving him as I went off to spend a horse-free ten days in Barcelona. The horses were to stay up in El Montanya for six days after the event had finished, waiting for the British dressage horses to finish competing so they could then all fly back together. Knowing that William was in Annie's capable hands during all this time allowed me to relax and enjoy the excitement of the rest of the Olympics. Annie and the other grooms also had the chance to come down to Barcelona over those last few days and get a feel of the real Olympics.

As Olympic competitors we were encouraged to stay in Spain for the duration of the competitions, and leave only after the closing ceremony; I was easily persuaded! Sadly Scotty went straight home, as he was very upset about Murphy. Karen went home after a couple of days, as she wanted to compete on her other horses – but hearing about the fantastic fun we had during the last week I think made her regret not staying on to the end. Richard and I made the most of it, as the Olympic spirit is quite intoxicating! I can honestly say that for those few days I had the best time of my life – living, eating, mixing with all the top international athletes was the experience I had been waiting for, and I would not have missed it for the world! The atmosphere within the village was fantastic – it had been built on the coast and had its own private beach, and I have never seen so many fit, tanned, muscular bodies in one place at one time! I met up with so many different competitors, and went with them to watch as many different sports as was possible. Supporting other athletes, sharing their excitements, hopes and disappointments was wonderful; this was a time I will treasure for ever. The socialising was quite something else, since Barcelona never really got going until 2am. On returning to England it was strange getting back into the routine of getting up, rather than going to bed, when dawn was breaking!

In fact coming home to a normal routine was difficult. I felt very flat for a few days, though luckily had quite a busy schedule of competing, teaching clinics, catching up on paperwork and then preparing for Gatcombe one-day event which hosts the British Open Championship. Would disappointment in Barcelona be rewarded by retaining my title at Gatcombe? With so much going on, there was no time to feel too sad about it all being over. It was disappointing to read so much criticism in the press about our Olympic performance, especially as so much of it was untrue…I started to get an inkling of what it must be like to be a member of the royal family and having to suffer in silence!

● The heat and the parties took their toll. David provides Mary and Karen with a welcome resting place!

Basil gave me a real boost when he commenced his Intermediate eventing career with super rounds across country at his first two Intermediate events. For the first time he gave me the feeling that he could become a real star. Making major errors on both Samuel and Boris at Gatcombe was disappointing particularly as, in the past, this venue has always been a happy hunting ground for me, but Pippa Nolan's win on Sir Barnaby was well deserved. Boris forgave me for misjudging the distance between fences at Gatcombe with a convincing win the following weekend at Spring Hill one-day event – good old Boris, picking me up from my down patch! Still, that's what friends are for!

TEACHING COUNTER CANTER

Once a horse's canter is well balanced, Mary would start to introduce work in counter canter, a movement required in Intermediate and Advanced dressage tests. Counter canter on the right rein, for example, involves the horse leading with the near-fore, or outside-fore and maintaining a bend to the outside; when in counter canter on the left rein he will lead with the off-fore, and still remain bent to the outside.

'I introduce counter canter by riding a small loop along the long side of the arena just a few metres in from the track. If I was cantering on the right rein, as I turn off the track to start the loop the horse would obviously maintain the right bend and continue leading with the right fore. Counter canter comes into play as you gradually ask the horse to move back onto the track, as he must continue to maintain the canter with the right lead and the right bend. I would gradually increase the size of the loop until it is at least ten metres in from the track.'

This work must be done as much on one rein as the other, so that ultimately the horse is able to work on each with equal balance and ease. It is important to give him time to get used to the new balance required in counter canter before asking him to perform very much of this type of work. Pressing on before the horse is ready will only worry him, which will lead to him

● *Basil remains calm and balanced, and bent over his inside leg throughout, as is required in the counter canter movement*

panicking and rushing. Any mistake such as changing legs or breaking into trot should be corrected by asking immediately for the correct canter lead, and trying again. Work in counter canter can be increased as the horse's overall way of going improves; eventually he should be able to perform a three-loop serpentine, the middle loop being in counter canter.

From this point you can work towards riding a full circle in counter canter. As regards your position, it is important that you sit on your inside seat bone. Your outside leg needs to remain behind the girth to keep the hindquarters straight, and a strong pushing aid is needed from your inside leg to maintain the correct canter lead and bend. You need to keep the canter round and active, but not too fast or the horse will lose his balance. If your horse comes above the bit you must re-establish a good round canter, maybe even riding him so that he is overbent for a few strides so that he understands what is required of him.

Work in counter canter can make an enormous difference to your horse's general way of going, and will particularly improve his true canter work as he will have learnt to really use his inside hind leg.

After a week relaxing in the hills of El Montanya, William and Annie were flown to Bristol; a Pedens lorry took them to Badminton House where they stayed the night, and Annie drove Mary's lorry to Sidmouth the next morning. William was thrilled to be back; as the lorry went over the little bump in the lane just before the yard, he was sticking his nose out of the window and calling to his friends in the field; he was home! As he had been let down gradually over the final week in Spain, he could be turned out straightaway – the farrier came and took off his hind shoes, so he knew then that he really *was* on his full winter holiday. Whether he spent any time reflecting on his behaviour will not be known until he has had a chance to redeem himself, Mary hoped, next spring!

Mary flew home on the Monday after the closing ceremony. 'It was another exciting and wonderful experience, but also a very sad day as it was full of goodbyes,' said Mary. 'I arrived back home in Devon at midnight only to turn round again at 5am to drive to Everdon horse trials with Boris, Sammy and Conker. The plan was to compete on Boris and then drive on to Newmarket to have Conker scanned again. I had also decided to do just the dressage with Sammy and then have him X-rayed because while I was away he had had quite an alarming experience. Sarah had fallen off him when he was doing his fastwork, and he had galloped off; he had jumped a hedge onto a road and had a crashing fall, but had got up again and galloped away in panic, jumping two cattle grids before he was caught. When the girls found him he couldn't put any weight on his hindleg, his shoes were all twisted and his saddle was round his tummy. All in all he was very lucky to have escaped apparently with just a badly knocked hock. When I got back from Barcelona he was perfectly sound although there was still some swelling there; however, he had lost quite a lot of weight; so had obviously experienced considerable pain and stress.'

Everdon one-day event

'Boris performed a very accurate dressage test, and perhaps more importantly for my peace of mind, jumped clear in the showjumping – after Barcelona, that was a tremendous relief! As he had not competed since I left for the Olympics I took him steadily round the cross-country; the course runs over ridge-and-furrow ground which can be punishing if you cross it at speed.

TEACHING REIN-BACK

By now your young horse will probably have had some experience of stepping backwards, from the everyday task of opening and shutting gates when out hacking. However, try to teach him a correct rein-back during a schooling session and he can still get into quite a muddle!

Only ask for rein-back from a good square halt, as this makes it easier for the horse to balance and organise his steps. At your first attempt it is worthwhile having someone on the ground to help, as this will avoid a confrontation with your horse if he gets confused. From the square halt, close your legs on the horse's sides but at the same time, block his forward movement by closing your hands on the reins. The energy that your legs create has to go somewhere, and if it can't go forwards, then it has to go backwards! As Mary explains…

'To begin with I would use my voice to say "Back, back" to the horse to help him understand what is required. If at the same time your assistant just pushes against his chest, then he should get the idea pretty quickly. As soon as he has taken one or two steps backwards, I would reward him with my voice and a pat, and walk forwards again. Practise the movement by stopping at different places around the arena and asking for a few strides of rein-back. If my horse comes above the bit or blocks against my hand, I make sure that I am using my legs sufficiently and vibrate my fingers on the reins to ask him to come round again. Most horses will always try and move one way or the other rather than go straight back, and this is something that must be corrected immediately. I push the horse's hindquarters back onto the straight line and then ask him to rein-back again.

● *Jill Thomson assists from the ground as Basil is introduced to the rein-back*

'Some horses want to rush backwards much too fast, and I have found that the best way to deal with this is to make them continue going backwards for further than they wish to. Once they are fed up with rushing back in reverse they will slow down of their own accord and then, after a couple of steady steps in rein-back, I would pat them and let then walk forwards again.

'When I ask for the rein-back I bring my lower leg back slightly so that the horse does not confuse it with the aid to move forwards. Some people would consider this to be incorrect but it is something I have found to work well for me. It is a matter of personal choice.'

However, he had a confident, happy clear round, and this served as a good preparation for Gatcombe, which is his main aim for the season.

'Sammy produced a stunning dressage test; this helped to convince me that there couldn't be too much wrong with him, but I still wanted confirmation that this was really the case.'

Mary stabled the horses near Everdon and drove to Newmarket the next day. Sue Dyson scanned Conker first, again being very particular to scan both his front legs before giving her thoughts on his progress. The verdict was disappointing as the healing process was apparently working only very slowly; she did not consider that he would be ready to compete again until the following autumn. Nevertheless he was booked in for another scan in three months so as to monitor his recovery rate closely.

Fortunately there was better news to come when she looked at Sammy. First of all he was trotted up in-hand: although he was perfectly level, he was tending to swing his injured leg a bit wide. When his hock was X-rayed, however, there was nothing wrong which was a great relief! Sue was happy for him to carry on with his normal work programme as long as the joint was watched closely to make sure the swelling did not get any worse. She was confident that the present swelling would disappear with work, explaining that it was an indication of the stress the joint had experienced.

It is expensive and time-consuming to have a horse scanned or X-rayed, but this is the only way to guarantee peace of mind. In Sammy's case the injury could easily have been a hairline fracture of the hock, and if this had been ignored and he had continued in work, the joint could eventually have shattered, with fatal consequences.

Mary's next involvement was to take part in a two-day teach-in at Wokingham Equestrian Centre, where it rained incessantly. 'My schedule had been hectic since the Olympics, and the weather thoroughly depressing, but it was perhaps just as well that I was away from home for a few days. The result of the Olympics had created a lot of media interest and much of it was not particularly complimentary, with accusations of defensive riding and criticism of the selectors and the team tactics – it was all the more infuriating to know that a great deal of it came from people who were completely ignorant of the facts. Apparently the phone didn't stop ringing for a week, so I was quite glad to be well out of the way.'

Wilton one-day event

Mary's first chance to ride Basil was only a few days before he was due to compete in the Novice class at Wilton horse trials.

'The girls had been hacking him out during my absence, and he was obviously fit and well. I schooled him quietly and popped him over a few showjumps, and although he lacked some of the engagement and carriage we had achieved before I left for Barcelona, overall he felt well in himself.

'At Wilton he produced a respectable dressage test, then had one showjump down. He felt a bit flat and long, but I was not too worried as I was confident this was because of the interruption to his schooling and jumping training. He gave me a really good ride across country – I was thrilled with how he went. I set off at a determined pace, knowing that he might be a bit green again, but he reacted well and in fact felt very grown-up and bold! Near the end of the course there was a big palisade and ditch where I had thought I would take the longer route, but he was going so well that we tackled the direct route and he flew it! He finished in sixth place.'

Basil's first intermediate event

Basil's next challenge was the Intermediate class at Brendon Hill horse trials in Somerset, and here the showjumping track was usually quite big; judging from his round at Wilton, Mary knew that his style would need to improve if he was to tackle a bigger course successfully. She worked him through several grids at home with the aim of sharpening up his approach and technique.

'I built the fences up to quite a decent size, and kept them at relatively short distances so that he really had to use himself properly to clear them. We finished by jumping quite an imposing treble combination, an upright to a spread to an upright, with one canter stride distance between each element; we put a placing pole on the ground in front of the first element, and a canter pole on the ground between the two elements. These ground poles encourage the horse to make the canter stride between the fences really round – he has to lift his shoulders and use himself properly, and this gives his canter *and* jump much more height.'

At this event Basil produced an exceptional dressage test, which was most gratifying since

157

this was his first attempt at Intermediate level competition. The test included shoulder-in, and work in medium canter and counter canter, all movements which he had never yet had to perform in a competition environment. His efforts earned him second place at the end of the dressage phase. As Mary had expected, the showjumping was really quite big and technical, and he had two fences down towards the end of the course; but on the whole Mary was pleased with the way he jumped.

'I did not know how he would react to the more difficult cross-country course – I knew I needed to ride him positively to give him confidence, but I did not want to overdo it and frighten him. There were alternatives at the more difficult fences, but I did not finally decide which options to tackle until we were out on the course and I could see how he was coping. His eyes came out on stalks when he saw the first of the bigger, spookier fences and he was obviously quite surprised when he realised he was going to be asked to jump them! – but he didn't hesitate, and so we tackled most of the direct routes. I rode the easy alternative rather than take on a big bullfinch spread, and also at a big, wide corner where someone else had just fallen.

'All in all I was delighted to achieve a clear round with him, but what was even more encouraging was how well he finished – the last two fences were up quite a long hill and most horses were finishing tired, but Basil was full of running over the last two which showed that he had more stamina than I had expected. His efforts earned him seventh place.'

GATCOMBE: THE BRITISH OPEN CHAMPIONSHIPS

For Sammy and Boris, Gatcombe was the ultimate aim for the 1992 season, Boris in the British Open Championships and Sammy in an Advanced section. They both did their last fast-work on the Wednesday before Gatcombe weekend, and Mary schooled them on the flat and over show jumps on Thursday. Sammy was to do his dressage on the Friday afternoon, so Mary arrived at the trials in time to work both the horses in their new surroundings. Sammy's work is technically very correct, but his temperament can cause him to become very tense and this obviously affects his performance. However, as it turned out, he produced a super test; he made one or two obvious errors, but the rest of his work was really quite spectacular.

Boris did his dressage on the Saturday morning. In 1990 he had won the British Open Champion title for Mary and it was her great hope, and that of his owner Gill Robinson, that

● *When riding the bounce it is more important than ever that the rider keeps her weight slightly behind the movement; this maintains the impulsion and allows the horse sufficient freedom to land and take-off immediately. Sammy – bold and athletic – at Gatcombe*

he should finish the season by repeating this victory. Sadly on this occasion his test was relatively disappointing – 'Maybe I worked him too much beforehand,' said Mary. 'I had given him a canter and a jump early on, and then brought him out again and lunged him before I rode him in for his test, all of which seemed to just take the edge off him. He still managed a competitive mark of 34, which left him lying about fifth.'

Sammy had to showjump that afternoon, and Mary was worried that he might be a bit tense and spooky as he had not jumped in a competition since before the Olympics; she schooled him over the practice fences before lunch. For Mary, lunch at Gatcombe in 1992 was hosted by Landrover, because at that point she was leading their three-day-event world ranking table. 'I succumbed to the temptation of a couple of glasses of wine, and these seemed to work wonders!' said Mary. 'I had to showjump Sammy in the pouring rain, but I was quite unconcerned – he flew round the course clear and took the lead in his section!'

Boris had his showjumping on the Sunday morning in the main arena, and he, too, produced a lovely clear round, moving up to fourth place. Mary began to think that perhaps things *might* work out well for him, as she knew he could go faster across country than the horses placed above him. However, her next responsibility was to Sammy, first to go across country in his section.

'I had planned to go all the direct ways except for the fence three from home, which was a palisade arrowhead with quite a wide ditch in front; it was called, quite appropriately, the Gatcombe Teaser. As I walked the course, looking at it through Sammy's eyes, I had decided it would be better to take the long route there. So off we went, and Sammy gave me a fantastic ride – he seemed to be really enjoying himself. He sailed through the Landrover feature fence, a big parallel followed by five or six strides to another parallel then a bounce to an arrowhead – this had been causing a lot of trouble, but Sammy thought nothing of it. As I jumped the fence before the Gatcombe Teaser I suddenly decided to tackle the direct route. I still don't know why I changed my mind, but in hindsight I so wish I hadn't because Sammy *did* object to the fence and ran out at the last minute. To make it worse, I was so far ahead in my section I could easily have gone the long way and still won it!

'I was still kicking myself for this error of judgement when I set off on Boris. The Landrover feature fence was proving to cause the most problems on the course; I had ridden it on five strides with Sammy, but this had meant he had had to be very athletic to clear

SIMPLE CHANGE OF LEG

A correct simple change of leg requires the horse to come from canter into walk, to walk for two to three well-defined strides, then to make a transition from walk to canter onto the opposite lead. Says Mary:

'Horses vary as to how easy they find the transition from canter to walk. A forward-going horse will really need to learn to transfer his weight from his shoulders to his hindquarters and to use his hindquarters to bring him back to walk, rather than falling onto his forehand.

'Basil, who is very quiet and settled in his canter, was easy to teach as he is always waiting for my next instruction – William, on the other hand, is always wanting to power on forwards, and is not so quick to respond to the aids for the downward transition. Before asking the horse to come from canter to walk, you must collect the canter to make sure that the horse's weight is off his forehand and that his front end is light and responsive. You do this by closing the leg and hand to steady the pace, while making sure that your leg is still creating enough impulsion to keep the canter active, but shorter than it was previously. The interaction of hand and leg required to achieve this will vary from horse to horse.

'Once the canter is collected and light, I straighten my back, sit deep in the saddle and immediately close my hands and legs. The horse can be brought to a halt straightaway, so you must be ready to soften the hand quickly so that he can walk on forwards again. During the few strides of walk which are allowed you must change the horse's bend so that he is prepared to strike off on the correct lead when you ask him. You then give a positive canter aid to ask for a direct transition from walk to canter. If the simple change has to be carried out at a specific marker as in a dressage test, you should aim to be in walk as you pass the required marker.'

● *In this simple change sequence Basil resists slightly by coming above the bit in the downward canter transition but produces an obedient transition from walk to canter*

the arrowhead bounce, as five strides meant riding the bounce on a very strong and long stride.
I had watched some other horses tackle the
combination on a shorter, more holding six
strides which had worked well for them. I decided to hold for six strides with Boris as he is not
such an athletic horse as Sammy, and this
approach I thought would make it easier for
him to bounce the arrowhead.

'Unfortunately it just wasn't my day. As I
landed over the first parallel I realised that I
would almost certainly not be able to shorten
Boris up enough to fit in six good strides. But
instead of accepting this and riding him strongly forwards for five strides, I kept holding him,
hoping we would squeeze the six strides in: in
consequence he ended up so close to the second
parallel that he had to scrabble over it and simply had no impulsion left to bounce the arrowhead. He ran out to save himself from falling. It
was a big mistake on my part; I should have ridden the combination on five strides, and being
such an honest horse, I am sure he would have
got out over the bounce somehow. I carried on
over one more fence and then retired him as I
felt there was no point making him go on; he
had no need to prove anything to anyone. It
was a tremendous disappointment, as much for
me as for Gill Robinson, who thinks the world
of him. Both she and Boris deserved to win.'

A week after Gatcombe, Basil would be tackling his next Intermediate one-day event at
Spring Hill in Gloucestershire. Sammy was also
entered in the Open Intermediate class; Mary
had intended him to do the dressage and
showjumping there as a last outing before his
three-day event at Blenheim Palace the following week. However, as he had performed so well
in these two phases at Gatcombe, Mary decided
that Boris would actually benefit more from a
relatively straightforward run round a one-day
event after his unhappy ride at Gatcombe. The
organisers kindly agreed to substitute Boris for
Sammy as they had not yet printed the programme. There are quite strict rules about sub-
stituting horses or riders: normally, horses can
only be substituted up until the ballot date for
that competition (about 4 to 6 weeks before),
whereas a rider can be substituted right up until
the final withdrawals date (a few days before).
However, organisers are sometimes able to allow
last-minute alterations as long as they have not
already printed the programme, in which every
runner and rider at an event must appear.

During the week Mary concentrated on

Basil's dressage: at Spring Hill he would be
doing a different Intermediate dressage test,
one which included rein-back and a simple
change of leg. Mary worked him through these
movements and generally tried to improve the
engagement and activity of his paces.

Spring Hill one-day event

Heavy rain during the week meant that the
going at Spring Hill was wet, slippery and quite
deep, but Mary was keen to run both Basil and
Boris; as Basil had taken to Intermediate level
work so well, Mary was hoping to qualify him
for Loughanmore CCI** in Ireland. To do this
she needed to complete three Intermediate
events without cross-country penalties; as
Loughanmore was in early October, there was
very little time in which to fit in the qualifying
runs. Boris needed the run to make sure he had
got over his upset at Gatcombe the week before.

This time Boris pulled out all the stops and
produced an incredible test for a mark of just 17
penalties. A fast double clear allowed him to
win the Open Intermediate section, and proved
that Gatcombe had done no lasting damage.

Mary was really thrilled with Basil's performance as well. 'He did a super dressage test and
produced a double clear. The showjumping had
been causing quite a lot of trouble as the arena
was cramped and involved many tight turns to
the fences, but he remained balanced and
jumped really well. On the cross-country we
took a couple of long routes to avoid a big wide
corner, and a tricky bounce under the trees.
Normally I would have been keen to let him
tackle these to gain the experience but we
needed a clear round to qualify for the Irish
three-day event, and that is what we achieved.
Basil finished in sixth place.'

Sammy was working towards Blenheim
CCI***, held in early September; Mary concentrated on his dressage, as he had made a couple of obvious mistakes at Gatcombe. 'Sammy
is the sort of horse who likes to find your weak
points as a rider and then tries to catch you out.
I worked him several times during the week to
try to show him that we were meant to be working *together*, not trying to catch each other out!
One of his favourite tricks is to tighten up in his
back during the downward transition from
extended or medium canter and then slip in a
flying change instead of coming back to the
working canter pace you want. So I worked a lot
on going forwards and coming back in canter,

● It looked like a win at Gatcombe was guaranteed but two fences later Sammy had a runout

concentrating on keeping him soft and round during the transitions.'

With only about six weeks left until the end of the 1992 horse trials season, Mary was determined to finish the year as well as it had started. Winning Badminton and Windsor and being in the Olympic team had been tremendous, but since then things had not turned out so well:

Conker was off for the season, Apple's owners wanted him to be saved for 1993, William's over-exuberance in Barcelona had let him down, and Boris and Sammy's Gatcombe bids had not been successful. But there was still Blenheim and Loughanmore to look forward to, and also Boris' last few events: perhaps Mary's luck would change again.

SEPTEMBER

Having not had a ride at the Audi Blenheim CCI last year, it was a treat to return to the Duke of Marlborough's beautiful estate and be part of this superbly presented three-day event. Sadly Sammy's strong lead after the dressage phase disappeared rapidly during the cross-country with a naughty refusal at a small alternative, and he slipped from 1st to 14th. It was most frustrating as he is such a capable horse, but his heart is not always in the right place at the right time. He was very crafty, catching me out relaxing a little too much with my mind on the next fence; my rides on him are always fascinating as you never know what he might do next! Maybe I should not really continue with him, because of his lack of generosity, but I do thoroughly enjoy riding him around courses which are not too big as long as I remember to ride him positively all the time. His dressage is of a very high standard, he is a careful jumper, and he feels neat and safe across country; plus he is tough and sound, which is worth a great deal. I feel that as long as I do not get too ambitious with the level of event I enter him for, I can have a great deal of fun and success with him. He is not the bravest, but as part of my team I feel he is a worthy member, being so good at the slightly lower level.

The last of our Audi Masterclass lectures was held on the Thursday of Blenheim and was a great success despite the weather. The heavens opened towards the end of our demonstration, but amazingly the crowds stayed – and I don't think it was just politeness! For Boris, Blenheim was a fun holiday, coming up so I could use him for the lecture evening; he got quite excited on the cross-country morning, obviously hoping that my promise of no more three-day events might not be true!

The final one-day events of the year went well, with Boris keeping up his winning form at Taunton Vale Horse Trials. He then went on to Tetbury Horse Trials for the Advanced class which was his last run of the season.

● Basil on his way to second place in the Novice Futurity Championships at Tetbury

Having led after the dressage and showjumping, he was just pipped for first on cross-country time by his fellow campaigner and friendly rival Sir Barnaby, ridden by Pippa Nolan who has had a cracking season. Good old Boris finished the season fit and sound, so all being well he will be out again for the one-day circuit next year.

Basil's preparation through September for his first three-day event went smoothly. After spending quite a bit of time getting his half-passes really established, I was rather surprised to find when I got to Ireland that the test required was not the one I thought, and in fact we did not have to do any half-passes! Never mind, he knows how to do them now, ready for next year! Basil was meant to have two runs in September before going out to Ireland, but at Taunton Vale I ended up withdrawing him due to the deep going and tricky course. Looking back it was the right decision, although hard to make at the time. Coming 2nd in the Novice Futurity Championships the following weekend was very pleasing and left me looking forward to our long journey to Loughanmore CCI in Northern Ireland at the beginning of October.

With my regular Monday evening tennis, when eight of us play religiously every week all through the year, plus David and I catching up with our entertaining, I was kept pretty busy through September with many different things. These ranged from crowning our local carnival queen to judging the floats at Sidmouth carnival, opening a health club, doing a lecture/demonstration at Hartbury College near Gloucester, as well as preparing for our third journey to Romania. For the last two years a group of event riders has driven a convoy of lorries full of supplies and equipment out to five needy orphanages. The local Devon ladies are very keen at knitting gloves, hats and scarves, in exchange for which I do an evening talk and show a video of our first journey. A few of these evenings through September helped to maintain the local people's enthusiasm and boosted our funds, our target figure being £50,000.

The competitors' briefing for Blenheim three-day event was on Wednesday, and so Annie and Mary left early that morning with Sammy and Boris; Boris was to be used for the Audi Masterclass lecture demonstration the following evening. On arrival at Blenheim, Annie settled the horses in while Mary attended the briefing.

The official tour of the roads and tracks, and the first course walk took until lunchtime, so Mary worked Sammy in the early afternoon; she wanted him to be well accustomed to his surroundings in the hope that he would remain relaxed and be less spooky throughout the event itself. The first horse inspection was later in the day and as they expected, this caused no problems – Sammy always trots out really well in hand as he has a lovely, regular, active stride.

Mary's dressage was on Friday afternoon, so she made the most of the time on Thursday to acclimatise him to the competition surroundings. He seemed very relaxed, even though there was already a good crowd of people watching the dressage. 'All Sammy's flatwork is very established,' explained Mary, 'and the only worry with him is keeping him relaxed – the opportunity to work him through the test movements in a competition atmosphere the day before his test was a great help.'

BLENHEIM MASTERCLASS

On Thursday evening Boris performed in the Masterclass held in the grounds of Blenheim

Palace: it attracted an audience of over two thousand. Halfway through, it absolutely poured with rain, but either everyone was enjoying the demonstration too much to notice, or they were too polite to leave, because they all stayed to the bitter end! The finale was a worthy spectacle, with Captain Mark Phillips and Mike Etherington-Smith persuaded to take part in the pro-am team jumping; Mike's stylish riding impressed many, but the Captain did not fare so well as people just seemed to keep getting in his way when he was trying to jump!

'We decided that Mark needed a greater challenge,' said Mary, 'so we would ride in front of the fence he was intending to jump and only move away at the last minute. He was actually doing very well until the last fence when Boris and I stood our ground for as long as we dared; with so much distraction the Captain missed his stride and knocked the fence down. This mistake particularly amused those of us who he teaches, as he is always saying that it is impossible to miss your stride if you keep the horse going forwards in a balanced, active canter! Mind you, he would not normally expect to find his fences obstructed by another horse and rider, so no doubt his theory is still correct!'

BLENHEIM THREE-DAY EVENT

Early on Friday morning Mary took Sammy for a hack, and popped him over a few practice fences so he could work off any excitement or spookiness that might have been building up in

● Knowing there were a good many arrowheads on the Blenheim course, Mary used the barrel exercise with Sammy just before the event.

Mary jumps Sammy over four upright barrels first to show him what is expected. The barrels are removed one at a time until only one remains; strangely, horses often find this offputting.

him. Later in the morning she brought him out again and worked him near the main arena until she was sure he was quite happy and relaxed in those surroundings.

'Sammy works so well on the flat that it is very easy just to sit there and let him get on with it. But I know that if I make the effort to ride him really positively and ask for just that little bit more, then he can produce some really impressive work. On this occasion he went back in his stable while I attended a lunch. Normally I have very little appetite during a competition, but on this occasion I was much more relaxed and enjoyed a good meal and a glass of wine! Sammy must have been feeling very laid back, too, because when it came to his test he produced some quite stunning work: he was very relaxed as he entered the arena – didn't spook at the flowers or the judges which is his normal reaction – and contained himself right through his test, to earn us a strong nine-point lead! On any other horse this would have left me feeling really confident, but with Sammy, you never know what he's got up his sleeve and I knew I would have to concentrate every inch of the way on the cross-country the next day. The trouble with starting the second day with a strong lead is that you know you can afford to play safe to a degree, and this can lead to you not attacking the course in the same way as you would if you were behind and trying to fight your way back up the order.'

Cross-country day turned out to be bright and sunny, and this at least was an improve-ment on the torrential rain that the event had suffered in the last two years. However, by the time Mary and Sammy had to tackle the steeplechase course the ground had become quite holding and sticky; when the ground is wet and slippery it in fact takes less effort from the horses to get through it than when it is beginning to dry out, as then their feet really do seem to get bogged down in it.

'I didn't have a very good steeplechase round – I seemed to keep seeing the bad strides, and would either be asking for an unreasonably long one, or would get right into the bottom of the fence, instead of just letting Sammy jump out of his stride. He seemed to keep getting stuck in the mud, too, so really we were both more than happy to finish, and proceed on the roads and tracks – at Blenheim, this phase is, I think, quite the most beautiful of all the events I have been to. Whilst on the subject of steeplechases, a few weeks after Blenheim I read an article by Blyth Tait in *Eventing* magazine in which he recounted a terrible steeplechase ride he had had at a three-day event, describing it as the perfect example of how *not* to ride this phase – and I thought, "Oh dear!, that sounds familiar"; our efforts at Blenheim were not exactly confidence inspiring or foot-perfect!

'However, on the day there was no time to dwell on the whys and wherefores of such an unsatisfactory round – I was more concerned about the cross-country course. Mike Etherington-Smith's course was beautifully built, *but* it did include a total of *seven* arrow-

To restore confidence and to show that it is possible, the arrowhead is then jumped from the opposite direction. Sammy understands the exercise and jumps confidently, remaining straight, over the single barrel

'The final elements of the water complex involved a step up to another, bullfinch arrowhead and I decided to play safe here, too, as bullfinches are not Sammy's favourite – he is such a careful jumper he doesn't like to touch anything, and a bullfinch is designed to be brushed through. However, I had nearly half a minute in hand over my nearest rival, and as Sammy is very quick I was confident that we could get a safe clear and not lose our lead.

'The next "question" was Coutts Complex, where I felt we were still making good time; this involved a corner followed by a sharp turn to an arrowhead bounce. The alternative was to avoid the corner and jump to the side of the arrowhead where the fence was wider with a stride between the two elements. When walking the course I had seen a short cut which involved jumping a guard rail, and had realised that this would significantly reduce the time it would take to tackle the alternative: rather than risk a silly mistake going direct over the bounce, I decided to go this 'quick' long way. Unfortunately, having jumped the first element and taken the short cut over the guard rail, I then discovered we were on a direct line to jump the arrowhead bounce: I wanted to avoid this, mainly due to the trouble it was causing but also because of Sammy's runout at Gatcombe, so I had to swing Sammy to one side to jump the alternative. This move must have confused him; he had obviously focussed his attention on the arrowhead and can't have been listening to me, or thinking about the part of the fence I wanted him to jump. By the time he *did* concentrate, it was too late; he suddenly saw a different fence in front of him and stopped abruptly. I couldn't believe it. We carried on and were clear around the rest of the course, but by then our strong lead had disappeared. One showjump down the next day meant that we finished fourteenth.'

Taunton one-day event

After Blenheim, Mary had only Boris and Basil in work; their next event was Taunton Vale where Basil would be doing the Intermediate class and Boris the Open Intermediate.

'I had not been to this event before, and unfortunately there was very heavy rain during the week before and throughout the whole weekend – so it really was wet and miserable.

I walked the course, and from Basil's point of view I was quite disappointed. It was a tricky

• *Sammy performing one of the most stunning tests of his career to take a nine point lead at Blenheim CCI****

• *(opposite) Another promising start as Sammy tackles the TNT flier early on in the course at Blenheim*

head fences which require careful riding and a genuine, straight horse. In some ways this was a pity, because when such a degree of accuracy is needed it is difficult to really attack the course – and at a three-day event a rider expects the cross-country course to need bold riding. The arena fence was a combination involving three increasingly narrow arrowheads, and it wasn't riding at all well; I took the long route here – Sammy is very neat and agile and wastes hardly any time in these situations, and I was pleased with how well he was jumping.

- (opposite top) *Sammy, infuriatingly, was clear over the rest of the course*

- (opposite below) *Boris and support team at Tetbury*

course as the fences were inconsistent in size and not always very well positioned, and the track itself was very twisty.

For a horse like Boris, who knows his job and has 'a fifth leg' I was happy to run him, but I was concerned that with Basil it might undo all that he had learnt on his last few outings. At this

level, if a horse which has just upgraded to Intermediate makes a bad mistake it can really set him back, and can take him a long time to regain his confidence.

'Boris led after the dressage and went on to jump a double clear to win his section. Basil did a good dressage test and also took the lead. I was a little disappointed with him in the showjumping, as he just felt a bit flat in himself; he jumped some fences quite beautifully, but at others felt as if he were just stepping over them, and not really bothered about clearing them at all. He only had one down, but he had definitely reverted to feeling quite green again and this confirmed my feelings about running him across country: I withdrew him, knowing that the following week he would be able to have a more suitable run over the Novice course at Tetbury Horse Trials where he was entered in the Novice Futurity Championships.'

After Taunton, Mary concentrated more on Basil's flatwork to prepare him for his first three-day event. He was entered for Loughanmnore Horse Trials, a two-star event in Ireland – 'two star' meant it would be of Intermediate standard, although the dressage would be nearer to an Advanced test. She also worked on his showjumping, building some quite spooky grids using oil drums and so on as fillers so that he had something to look at. 'I felt he just needed sharpening up, as he was beginning to feel a bit complacent,' said Mary. 'Grids make a horse really use himself, which is what Basil seemed to be forgetting to do!'

THE VALUE OF EXPERIENCE
Debby Sly's account of Taunton

It is always a difficult decision to make, whether to withdraw a horse from a competition once you have actually paid to enter and arrived at the event itself. For someone with less experience than Mary, and with perhaps less opportunity to compete than she does, it is even harder: but your first impression of a course is very important, and if you have any doubts then listen to your head rather than your heart. This was brought home to me by my own experiences at Taunton; my horse and I had only just upgraded to Intermediate level and we needed to go clear in the Intermediate class to qualify for our first three-day event. However, I did not like the course one bit when I walked it – although most of the fences were relatively small, they were not very inviting and several had to be jumped off a corner with a very short, cramped approach. My good sense said not to do it, but I was determined to qualify for the three-day event and so after a good dressage test and a clear showjumping round, we set off, with some trepidation, on the cross-country.

One of the early fences had a very awkward approach and my genuinely careful little horse ended up catching his hindlegs badly on it. There were then only a few strides to a big trakhener, and although he cleared this he had obviously given himself quite a fright. After a few straightforward fences there were several combinations in a row involving rails, banks and steps, and he just seemed to lose confidence with every one, finally refusing at a fence which normally he would not have minded at all. At this point my lack of experience became all too evident: I couldn't decide whether it was best to retire him, since he was behaving quite out of character, or whether he was perhaps trying it on because the course wasn't one which he found easy. Maybe he was hoping a display of stubbornness would mean we could call it a day. As the fences weren't actually too big for him, just not very inviting, I did him the injustice of deciding that perhaps he was trying his luck – so we continued on our unhappy way, incurring several more refusals but completing the course.

With hindsight I wish I hadn't even asked him to tackle the course, let alone insist he continue when he was obviously trying to tell me that he wasn't happy. Sadly mistakes are often made in the pursuit of experience, but at least next time I will know *not* to run my horse if my instincts tell me the course is not suitable, no matter what it might qualify us for. Luckily for me, Mighty Merchant is a very forgiving and robust character; I made sure that his next event had a good galloping track, and he rewarded me with an exhilarating clear round.

As Mary pointed out, some horses take a very long time to recover from a bad experience, and their confidence is something which should never be compromised.

Tetbury one-day event

Tetbury horse trials, in the middle of September, was the last event of the year for Boris; it also promised to be quite an exciting outing for Basil, who was entered for the Novice Futurity Championships. This competition is for five- and six-year-old horses which qualify for the final at Tetbury by being placed first or second in any Novice event during the current season.

'Basil was very relaxed in his dressage and produced a lovely test. In fact for me he was quite hard work, as I had to ask him for more energy and impulsion all the time; but the advantage of this was that I could really ride him during the test and get the work I wanted out of him, rather than having to sit there quietly in case he exploded, as is the case with William.

'He went on to produce one of his best showjumping rounds to date over the big Intermediate course; it included a water tray; and this particular fence made a good introduction to showjumping water as the tray was shielded by a low brush filler which acted as a groundline. Also, the poles over the water were not very high and formed an ascending spread, which is always inviting. So I was able to ride Basil in a stronger-than-usual canter to the fence and just let him take it in his stride. This performance put him into the lead, out of over eighty starters.

'The cross-country phase was over the novice course, so I was feeling quite hopeful. However, as I set off I was surprised to find that, once again, he was quite wavery and green, perhaps as a result of having missed a cross-country run at Taunton – I gave him a sharp reminder with my stick over the first fence to move him into a more positive gear. He improved over the next few fences, but I felt he was still not going quite straight or positively enough to tackle the half-arrowhead with ditch in front at fence 5, so I took the long route here as I wanted him to have a good jump before tackling the direct route at the water.

'He improved as we made our way round the course – and surprised me by being *over*-bold into a combination involving a rail followed by two steps down, then two strides to an exit rail: he accelerated down the steps and got too close to the final element, and we were lucky to survive! However, he jumped the corner that followed very confidently and completed the course with just one time penalty – and what an expensive one this proved to be, because we actually finished on an equal score with William Fox-Pitt! When this happens, the competitor with the cross-country round closest to the optimum time is given priority; and so we were were nudged out to second place.

'Boris was in the Advanced section, and this proved to be very competitive many of the horses aimed for Boekelo three-day event were using Tetbury as their final outing. Boris took the lead after the dressage and followed this with two foot-perfect clear rounds. But again, we were just pipped to the post: Pippa Nolan and Sir Barnaby, an old adversary of Boris' had a better cross-country time and took first place. This was Boris' last run of the season and I was thrilled that he finished fit and happy – so I can look forward to enjoying another competitive season with him next year.'

September Diary

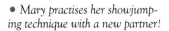
- *Boris at Tetbury – just a few seconds short of a victory, but retains a popular second place*

- *Mary practises her showjumping technique with a new partner!*

PREPARING FOR LOUGHANMORE
Basil's first three-day event

Mary's normally hectic schedule was now relatively relaxed since there was only Basil to concentrate on. Towards the end of September she increased his fittening work so that he would be well prepared for the extra rigours of a three-day event; he began doing the more strenuous road hacks, and his fastwork was increased. Every four days he was worked twice up the middle and twice up the long side of the gallop field.

'I felt he still needed a little more cross-country experience before tackling Loughanmore, so I took him to Powderham Castle which hosts a Novice and an Intermediate event. Basil found it all just too exciting. There were deer in the park which always seem to spook horses, and now that he was that bit fitter he was feeling bright and sharp anyway. The railway line to Exeter runs down the seaward side of the park, too, with trains passing quite regularly and wild ducks and geese constantly flying in for a visit – so there were plenty of distractions. I tried to settle him down by popping over some of the smaller fences before asking anything more of him. However, his spookiness was being rapidly replaced by over-boldness – he was beginning to get quite strong and wanting to rush into his fences; about four strides out he would lift his head and try to run through the bridle. It was nice to think that he was so confident but I still needed to retain some control! The next time we approached a fence, as soon as he raised his head, I asked him to halt before we reached the jump. This is something that I do not normally like to do when schooling a horse, but I felt it was important to make the point that he was not meant to rush. After doing this a few times he seemed to realise what I was trying to tell him and settled down. By the end of the session I was really pleased with him.'

Because it was now quite late in the year Basil's winter coat had started to come through; Mary decided she would need to clip him for the competition in Ireland, and that it would be best to do this once they were actually at the event as Basil might appreciate some extra warmth on the long journey to Northern Ireland. Basil himself was happily unaware of the importance of the occasion – that his performance at his first three-day event would determine whether Mary's year was to finish as it started: with success!

170

OCTOBER

*T*ravelling out to Loughanmore CCI I had mixed feelings. I was very much looking forward to seeing how Basil would cope with his first-ever three-day event, but felt sad that this was the last event of my season. Despite having gained only two clear rounds at Intermediate level, due to withdrawing from Taunton, the Selection Committee had granted us permission to compete. I travelled out with Karen Dixon, and when we arrived at Stranraer in Scotland to catch the ferry across to Larne it was rather like a British invasion, with over forty riders from England gathered at the docks. Loughanmore has established an excellent name for itself as an ideal first-timer's three-day event, so there were many people going out with their young horses. Also the Irish do know how to enjoy themselves, which is an incentive to compete there in itself! We arrived a whole day early, having left a day in hand, in case we were held up at the docks due to rough seas, so we had some time to kill. Taking advantage of this, we did a bit of sight-seeing with Karen's husband, Andrew, whose family live in Northern Ireland and had kindly invited me to stay. We went up to the north coast to the Giant's Causeway, which was fascinating, and then drove into Belfast, venturing as near the Falls Road as we dared!

We had a great week, except for the mud! Luckily the cross-country course soaked up the rain we had, and the going was amazingly good. However, Basil's showjumping round was disappointing, making me realise I must keep plugging on with as much practice as possible at this phase, in which I do not have much luck! I hope my horses discuss their problems with each other during their winter holidays, and that Boris, who has completed twelve events this year without knocking down a single showjump, gives William and Basil some useful tips!

On returning home from Ireland Annie and I had a quick swop around, unloading the eventing things from the lorry, removing the partitions, and then loading the supplies we had gathered for Romania; we then drove up to Lucinda Green's home, at Andover, which was our charity's main collection point. The next few days were spent sorting out and loading the fifty tonnes of supplies which had been donated or bought. We had collected some fantastic supplies and equipment, ranging from pallet loads of high protein meats, sugar, dried milk, tinned vegetables and soups, disinfectant, washing powder, loo paper, school and medical supplies, 5,000 pairs of good shoes, toys, trampolines, a couple of huge new commercial washing machines and driers, equipment for a new skill centre including welding tools, drills and four working car engines; we even took out a tractor for one orphanage! Somehow all this fitted into two articulated lorries and our horsebox (which Gill Robinson kindly let us take for the third year running). Lucinda's endless energy, plus a wonderful new injection of help and enthusiasm from Barry Fox, a showjumping rider who joined us at the last minute, made the loading very entertaining!

I made a quick visit to London before our departure to Romania, to present an award at the Animal Health Trust Awards luncheon, one which I had won the previous year; then on to the Horse of the Year Ball in the evening. Mitsubishi had invited David and I to be on their table, and we ended up having a fabulous evening dancing the night away – except that I was constantly trying to hide my muscley arms and unladylike hands!

Mike Cromie (event rider), Barry Fox and Brian Knight (showjumpers), Graham Coombs (mechanic), Sara Dick-Read (a friend of mine who came as cook and helper), Annie and I set off for Romania the following day in convoy – with CB contact, which was extremely entertaining! Lucinda flew out for the five unloading days, as she was sadly too busy to be away from home for two whole weeks. After a gratis trip across to Holland by Olau Ferries, it took us three days to drive across Holland, Germany, Austria and Hungary before arriving at our destination near Bucharest in Romania. There are 200,000 orphans in Romania, mainly the consequence of a law enforced by Ceaucescu their dictator, which ruled that each female had to have four children so as to increase the population of Romania. Birth control and abortions were illegal, but parents could put unwanted children into orphanages. Due to the shortage of trained staff and the lack of support by the government, these orphanages became 'hell holes'; and not until Ceaucescu was overruled and shot by his own people did this huge problem become known to the outside world. After Ceaucescu's death the law was immediately abolished, and help started to pour in from outside countries. We worked closely with a large British charity called Medical Aid for Free Romania, which took responsibility for the orphanages in an area just outside Bucharest. Seeing hundreds of unloved, dirty, sad orphans living in disgusting conditions on our first journey was extremely disturbing; it certainly convinced our group, Riders for Romania, to continue our support. However, conditions have improved enormously over the last two years, and this year it was especially satisfying to see that all the window frames and glass that we had delivered the year before, plus part of a large heating system, had been fitted by builders who had followed us out. Giving the children individual shoe-bags full of presents was extremely rewarding too; having been given so little in their lives, their appreciation was overwhelming.

Eventing, as I suppose with any sport, can become a very selfish pastime, especially for those dedicated competitors striving to reach the top. I do at times feel very guilty about the self-centred approach needed to be successful, so was thrilled to be able to get involved with this project.

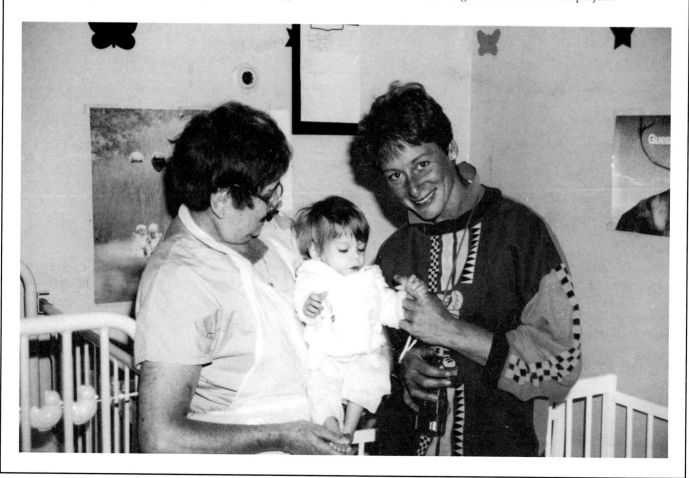

IRELAND

The first requirement for every horse travelling to Northern Ireland is a declaration of health, which must be signed by a vet within twenty-four hours of departure. As far as Basil was concerned, Monday was a day off: the vet came and declared him fit and well, then he was turned out for a couple of hours – pleasant respite before the long journey ahead. The trek to Ireland began later that day, three days before the event was due to start; they had arranged to pick up a fellow competitor, Angela Tucker and Red's Best and to travel as far as Karen Dixon's home: Barnard Castle, in County Durham. It was a five-hour drive from Angela's home in Tetbury; on arrival at Karen's the horses were given a good walk round before they were settled down for the night.

Early the next morning everything was transferred to Karen's lorry for the onward journey. The three horses, Basil, Red's Best and Too Smart were hacked out, their riders taking advantage of Karen's local hill to do some steady cantering before cooling down with a splash around in the river. Everyone was then loaded into the lorry for the three-and-a-half-hour drive to Stranraer. There were about forty-five British riders travelling out for the event, so there was quite an atmosphere at the docks. They set sail that afternoon, and just two and a half hours later were in Ireland; Basil was very relaxed throughout the crossing. Once on Irish soil it was just a half-hour drive to the event where the horses were unloaded; as at all FEI events, they were checked by the vet before they were allowed into the stabling area. The lorries were parked in a lush green field so Basil could enjoy a walk round and a graze; Mary was staying with Karen's 'in-laws' who lived just ten minutes away from the event so Annie remained on site with Basil.

Basil was quite subdued and tired the following day; in view of this Mary did no more than hack him out quietly and school him a little on the flat just to keep him supple. With only one horse entered for the competition there was plenty of time to enjoy Ireland and so Mary, Annie, Karen and her groom, Diane, were taken sight-seeing.

LOUGHANMORE THREE-DAY EVENT

The competition started officially with the briefing and trot-up on Thursday. Mary rode Basil out for half an hour before the briefing, then handed him to Annie to plait and smarten up for the trot-up while she walked the course.

'I was thrilled to find that the course was as inviting as I had remembered from last year. There were a few changes, but it was still very suitable for a young horse and I was looking forward to the next few days.

'At the trot-up it was amusing to see the young horses, all so calm and unconcerned because they hadn't a clue what was coming next! The older horses *know* that a trot-up means a three-day event, and most show their excitement and anticipation; but Basil was beautifully behaved and trotted up quietly for the Ground Jury.'

Mary worked him later that afternoon, concentrating on his flatwork. His test was not until Friday afternoon, so she did not want to do too much with him; he was extremely relaxed in himself and she felt it would be very easy to take the edge off him and produce a somewhat lifeless performance if she asked for too much now.

For Mary and Annie the social scene was very hectic; the Irish are always extremely hospitable and Loughanmore was no exception. Gill Robinson had driven over with Tina to join in the fun, which began with a cocktail party on the Thursday night. On Friday morning Mary worked Basil for just a short time near the dressage arena; he was quite unperturbed by the crowds and loudspeakers and was working very well. However, Mary was greatly surprised at this point to discover that the test she had

● *Annie, bogged down in Irish soil at Loughanmore*

As Basil's fitness work was increased in preparation for his first three-day event, his feed ration was also altered to keep pace with his increased energy requirement. Mary gradually changed the portion of his feed that had been a breeding mix to a competition mix; this particular type of feed has now been guaranteed under FEI rules, which wasn't the case earlier in the year. Spillers had also changed the name of 'competition cubes' to 'event cubes'.

One week prior to Loughanmore, and throughout the three-day event, Basil was on the following ration:

Morning: 2lb (1 scoop) competition mix; 1$\frac{1}{2}$lb ($\frac{1}{2}$ scoop) event cubes; chaff

Midday: 3lb (1 scoop) event cubes

Evening: 1lb ($\frac{1}{2}$ scoop) competition mix; 3lb (1 scoop) event cubes; chaff and salt

Hay: 9lb haynet morning and evening

● *Basil displays his scope and boldness at his first three-day event*

been practising for Loughanmore was not the test required for the competition – and she would not now be able to show off the half-passes which Basil had learnt to perform so well. In the short time available they quickly practised the movements that *were* required, one of which involved a simple change from counter canter along the short side of the arena to true canter at C. One of the reasons for counter canter is to test the horse's obedience and balance, because it is very tempting for him to change leads on a corner back into true canter; being asked to make a simple change from counter canter to true canter seemed, therefore, rather to defeat the object. However, Basil accepted this new movement quite happily – he was already accustomed to simple changes, and is very balanced in counter canter.

Basil was left to relax until half an hour before his test; Mary then just worked him quietly through a few of the movements before they were called. The going in the arena was most disappointing – thick, stodgy mud, and this was particularly unfortunate for Basil who is a loose, long-striding horse, and at that point not really toughened up enough to perform well in deep going – horses with stronger, more positive paces were coping more readily with the conditions. However, he did everything that was asked of him; his performance suffered the occasional loss of rhythm when he disappeared into the muddier patches, but he coped well enough to lie third at the end of the first day. After his test he was randomly selected for dope testing,

● *Early celebrations; Gill Robinson, Annie and Tina*

but was very obliging and in his stable quickly provided the necessary urine sample for the vet! As he had not done too much work that day, Mary changed his tack and took him over a few practice fences in the sand schooling arena.

That night an 'Irish evening' had been organised to further exhaust the competitors, though

it unfortunately did not go quite as planned because the lead singer failed to turn up – however, all party-goers enjoyed themselves enough to stay until the early hours: in Ireland the social scene is an endurance event in itself!

The next day Mary jumped Basil again, then hacked him out along the roads and tracks. She gave him a couple of good gallops up a sloping grass field and was pleased with the way he felt – she finished quite confident that he was as well prepared as he could be for the challenge that lay ahead.

By the morning of cross-country day, Basil was lying seventh out of ninety-three starters.

175

The Junior class was running first, so Mary had the chance to see how the course was riding and in fact the fences themselves seemed to be riding well; however the going had got quite heavy, especially on the roads and tracks, so much so that some of the riders voiced their anxiety and requested that Phase C be shortened. The ground jury agreed, and the reduced distance was a much fairer test for the younger horses.

Basil was quite happy to have a little snooze as he waited to set off on Phase A; he really had no idea as to why he was there! He trotted along happily on Phase A despite the muddy conditions, with Mary trying to pick the best ground and praying that all his shoes would stay on. Then on Phase B he gave Mary one of the best steeplechase rounds she had ever had.

'He was just slightly wary going into the first fence but we met it on a good stride and this gave him confidence – and after that he settled down confidently and finished easily within the time, without getting strong or silly. He recovered very quickly; after walking the first kilometre of Phase C he was keen to pick up the trot again, and finished the roads and tracks feeling strong and happy.

'Annie had been keeping alert as to how the cross-country was riding, and the reports were good – evidently the time was quite easy to achieve, too. As the roads and tracks had included quite a bit of road work, we had only fitted Basil with road studs for the first three phases; however we changed these for the cross-country and he wore chunky square studs to give him better footing in the mud. Once in the start box Basil was a different horse: his ears were pricked, and he galloped off looking eagerly for the next challenge. He was very bold over the first few fences, but there were two water complexes which came quite early on the course and one after the other, and I decided, despite how good he felt, to take the long route at the first to keep him feeling confident; we then tackled the direct route at the second water. This involved a big table followed by one stride to a step down into the pond, and as I had anticipated, I felt Basil start to hesitate as we approached the table – I'm not sure whether it was the large crowd which surprised him, or perhaps just the prospect of another water complex so soon. However, as soon as I urged him on he responded willingly, though rather "ballooned" the table; I lost my stirrup and quickly opted to take the long route out so as to have time to re-organise myself. Basil carried on

undaunted and seemed to be thoroughly enjoying himself. About three-quarters of the way round I felt him start to flag a little, but did not pressure him and just allowed him the chance to find his second wind. He finished comfortably inside the time and I was thrilled; he had jumped cleanly and carefully and had been very athletic, even over the last few fences.

'Basil seemed fine after this performance; he did not appear to have collected any cuts or bumps, although he had pulled off a front shoe. John Killingbeck, the newly appointed British team vet, helped us track down the best farrier, who tested right round the sole to make sure there was no bruising before the shoe was fitted. The vet asked for the nailheads to be rasped down to give the shoe as great a weight-bearing surface as possible, and we packed ice round the foot for half an hour as a precaution. Basil was perfectly sound when we trotted him out later.

'The final inspection was at nine o'clock the next morning. Annie had washed his legs off and tidied him up, and as he was perfectly sound when we led him out, he was left in his box until ten minutes before the final trot-up. He seemed to be quite tired, so he went straight back to his stable after he had been passed fit and well. The showjumping course was quite small, but I watched one rider after another go in and have fences down; as it turned out, only *one* of the top twenty-five horses jumped clear! Basil was lying sixth, but as this was our first three-day event together, I had no idea how well – or badly – he would jump. Some horses jump much better at a three-day event, but others perform less well if they feel tired and stiff from the previous day's exertions. Basil was jumping reasonably well in the practice arena, but his reactions were not as quick as they would have been normally. We started our round, and my heart sank as the poles started to fall – he was getting a bit stuck in the mud, and the small fences meant there wasn't a great deal to encourage him to make a real effort. We had four down, and this dropped us down the order of placings to seventeenth out of ninety-three, which was disappointing as he had started so well. Nonetheless I was delighted with the way he had coped overall, and felt very much more confident with regard to his future than I had done earlier in the season.

'We travelled back to Karen's that night, all in good spirits as Karen had finished sixth and Angela seventh. The following day we touched down in Devon again.'

● *Team spirit: David O'Connor, the eventual winner, Gill, Tina, Annie, Mary and Basil*

● (opposite) *Having warmed up on the steeplechase Basil was like a different horse on the cross-country*

WINTER MANAGEMENT

Once Mary's horses finish their last event of the season they are turned out, day and night, for their winter break. As Basil had been clipped to compete in Ireland, he was initially turned out with a New Zealand rug on; but this was taken off as soon as he had put on weight and grown more of a winter coat. The horses have their hind shoes taken off for their holiday, but are kept shod in front – the farrier comes every five to six weeks – to keep their front feet, which take so much of the strain, in good shape. Mary likes her horses to have a complete break from the artificial life that competition inevitably imposes upon them. She has to rent paddocks for their winter holidays, and keeps five horses together in one field, and two in another. Normally the fields have a good covering of grass, and they are well sheltered so the horses have no extra feed until December when they just have some Horsehage once a day out in the field. 'I feed Horsehage rather than hay at this point because it is more convenient to take in my car, plus it is much more nutritious and does not need soaking,' explains Mary. Just before Christmas they are given Horsehage twice a day, but they have no hard feed until they are stabled again at the beginning of January.

All the horses have their 'flu and tetanus boosters at the start of their winter breaks so that it does not interrupt their work schedule, and Mary sticks religiously to their six-weekly worming programme during the winter months.

● *'What do you think of it so far?' asks Debby. 'Rubbish!' says Basil*

MARY'S REVIEW OF 1992

On my return from Romania it was a great thrill to hear that William had won the Calcutta Light Horse Trophy, the end-of-year award for the horse winning the most horse trials points in the UK. I had also finished second in the Landrover World Rankings list, which was headed by Blyth Tait. These awards made me realise what a wonderful year it had been, and left me eagerly waiting for the start of next season. The horses were blissfully unaware of all this, had all grown thick winter coats while I was away and were looking fat, happy and relaxed in their fields.

'During November and December both Annie and Tina are laid off work (like the horses!) as the yard is so quiet. Sarah had left after the Olympics, Tina went off to Switzerland to stay with her sister and to work part-time until Christmas, and Annie cleared right out of the way and went to South Africa for three weeks with event riders Katie Meacham, Sophie Martindale and a Norwegian, Ivor Storli. After this she worked in Barry Fox's jumping yard until Christmas. I had let myself in for various talks and lectures during the first half of November but then flew out to join the others in Durban. Exploring the 'Garden Route' down to Cape Town, flying back up to Johannesburg, and spending three days in the Kruger Park game reserve was a wonderful experience and great fun. The only riding we did was on ostriches! This was a hilarious exhibition and good spectator sport, especially as Annie and I fell off!

'I came back to England with my batteries fully charged and raring to go. At the beginning of December Conker was due for his third scan to monitor the healing progress of his strained tendon. I took him back up to Sue Dyson at Newmarket, and the scan showed a great improvement compared to the previous one taken three months before. The plan is to bring him back into work gradually next spring, with a view to starting eventing him again in the autumn. I am really looking forward to riding him again as he is such a fun horse – naughty but nice!

'During December I spent quite a bit of time looking for a young horse to join my team for next year. Trying to find the right one is a difficult task, which doesn't get any easier, even though you become more knowledgeable. Over the years I have built up various contacts who I get in touch with, and I also keep an eye on advertisements and let as many people as possible know what I am looking for. I try to buy one or two young horses each year for Gill Robinson, so that we always have youngsters coming on. I usually know within the first year whether they are going to be top-class or not, and if I feel they haven't got what it takes, I sell them on to a less competitive home. Gill and I do get very attached to the horses so it can be an extremely difficult, and often heartbreaking, decision to sell; but in the long run it is kinder to let one go to a more suitable home than to push a horse on when he lacks the necessary ability and scope.

'I look for four- or five-year-old horses as I do not have enough land to take on anything younger. I like a horse to be between 16hh and 16.3hh, Thoroughbred or near Thoroughbred (as they have the speed and stamina required for a three-day event). Ideally the horse will already be jumping so that I can see how he performs: obviously this is the most important asset of a future top-class event horse. I look for a good shape over a jump, and expect a horse to be athletic and careful (this is especially important to me as I need as much help as possible in the showjumping phase!). A good temperament, free, workmanlike movement, natural hock activity, and correct conformation are all important points. Funnily enough, with most of my horses I have known as soon as I've seen him in the stable that he is the one I want. In my latest search the right one has not yet turned up, but when it does the long, steady, but satisfying training process will begin again.

'My main aim for 1993 is to go well enough at Badminton with William to make the team for the European Championships which are to be held in Achelswang, Germany in September. It would be wonderful to retain our European Team Gold title, and individual honours wouldn't go amiss! I am hoping that Apple will go well enough this spring for me to

consider taking him to Burghley. All along I have thought he could be the horse to follow in William's footsteps – time will tell. I plan to do quite a few OI classes with Sammy this spring to build up his confidence and aim him for Bramham, and maybe Boekelo in the autumn. Basil will be going to Windsor in May, where I hope the ground will be more forgiving than in 1992. His performance there will decide which three-day event I will aim him for in the autumn. Boris, at the age of fourteen, will carry on doing one-day events in 1993. His aim will be to regain his British Open title at Gatcombe which eluded him in 1992. Conker will rest until May when he will start walking exercise. He will then have another scan in June (six months from his last one), when hopefully his tendon will be looking good enough to do some events with him in the

● (opposite) *My dream come true…Badminton Champions 1992*
(above) *Mary and William at home*

autumn. I might leave doing a three-day event with him until 1994.

'The most important factor in training and competing, and one which often seems to be overlooked, is the enjoyment for both horse and rider. Success is the result of having built up such a relationship of mutual trust and understanding that you feel at one with your horse. The height of this success, and the ultimate enjoyment, is winning. So as far as my long term plans go – who knows! I do not want to go on eventing indefinitely but having fulfilled my ambition this year to compete at the Olympic Games, I have my sights now firmly set on a gold medal at the 1996 Olympics in Atlanta!'

ANNIE – THE GROOM'S VIEW

'I have always wanted to work with horses, and I really enjoy going eventing. It means my job is very varied; I meet some great people and go to some wonderful places. It is very rewarding watching the young horses being brought on, and improving as they go from one event to another. You can't help but get attached to the horses, and the longer they are with you the more caught up you get in how they are getting on.

'When we are not competing I'm usually in the yard by 7.30 to 7.45am to feed and muck out. We start riding out after 9am. The routine for the morning depends on which horses Mary wants to school, but there are usually two lots to ride out before lunch. The horses are turned out after exercise and so the last lot are brought back in after lunch and brushed off. In the afternoon I can be either clipping, trimming, tidying the yard, cleaning the lorry, or going wild with the strimmer to keep everything looking smart. In the summer I ride Cuthbert, my own horse, either at lunchtime or in the evening, or sometimes it works out that he can ride and lead with another horse in the morning. Mary or her mother usually feeds in the evenings, so I finish at 5pm.

'The horses are all quite different, and you get to know their personalities very quickly. Boris is every-one's big favourite; he thrives on attention and likes to think he's the man about the place. I always think of him as Cuthbert's partner in crime as they went around competing together for so long. Boris is quite bossy

● Cricket the stable cat takes a break from his mousing duties

although he never really means it, and he is lovely to ride and look after.

'Wicked Willie is now the main horse in the yard as he is at the highest level; he's the big handsome gentleman. If he were human he is the one we would all love to marry. I spent so much time with him in team training and at the Olympics that I really am very fond of him. He can be really hyper about things, but in Barcelona he tried so hard to contain it all! There were a couple of times when I seemed to be swinging from the end of his lead rope but he would suddenly realise and then look really apologetic. Although he isn't exactly a cuddly sort of horse he loves being groomed, clipped and trimmed.

'Apple is like a young teenager and can get quite boisterous, although he tries very hard to be nice about it. Despite his liveliness around the yard he is like a police horse to ride out – very calm and safe. He can be persuaded to co-operate about most things, but he still won't let me clip his ears!

'I am very fond of Super Sammy because when he came to us he was a really nervous, puny little horse; you wouldn't believe how much he has changed. He has grown into a really nice horse and has much more confidence in himself, and when he puts his mind to it he can be a real star. He likes to have a cuddle when no-one else is looking – if anyone saw it would spoil his image! Now that he has been with us a while he is good to clip and handle but he is a real monkey to catch. The village is often treated to me shouting and cursing after he has disappeared to the other end of the field. But he's very good and clean in the stable, so that makes up for it.

'As for Conker the Plonker…well, there always has to be one who loves making life difficult! He's really messy in the stable; when you open the door in the morning half his bed pours out around your feet. If he's tied up and gets bored he will pull back and break free. He is regularly caught with things disappearing down his throat, so you have to watch where you leave your coat or jumper! He really is very cheeky, but then he looks at you with those glorious big eyes and all is forgiven.

'Basil hasn't been with us that long compared to the others, but he has really improved and grown up over the year. I was really proud of him at Loughanmore; it was his first time abroad and his first three-day event, and he behaved so well. He is a nice horse to ride and a nice person to have around so I hope he progresses well and stays with us.

'Bertie [Cuthbert] is my main man. He's like an angel in the stable but a Hell's Angel to ride sometimes! He's seventeen now and very proud of the fact that he was second at Burghley. Now that he's mine I hunt him throughout the winter and do riding club competitions. He's nice to work with in the yard and fits in with all the other horses. I am really grateful that I have him; Gill Robinson gave him to me when he retired and Mary lets me keep him in her yard, and so it couldn't have worked out better for him or me!'

DRESSAGE TRAINING WITH MARY
by Ferdi Eilberg

'I have worked with Mary now for over ten years, so our basic thinking about how things should be done has been established and between us we have developed something of a system. Over the years Mary has obviously achieved a good 'feel' as regards bringing on her own horses, but she usually brings them up for me to see after their winter break so that we can assess their standard and consider where there might be any particular problems. Training horses is very much a two-way affair, and Mary knows her horses far better than I do; she must therefore tell me if she is having difficulty with anything and I then watch the horse working and try to pick up on the cause of the problem – then I can help her develop a series of exercises to overcome it.

'Before the start of the eventing season we work mainly on getting the basics right: free forward movement, and smooth and resistance-free transitions. After that it is a case of helping in the build-up to the main events that she is aiming for. As the event horse becomes fitter in his build-up to a three-day event it becomes increasingly difficult to persuade him to accept the arena discipline, and stay steady enough. When Mary comes here for help, usually at least one of the horses will be so full of himself that she just has to work him on her own until he settles – we may canter and even jump the horses before expecting them to concentrate on dressage. I do not believe in forcing a horse to concentrate on flatwork if he is over-excited; otherwise he may associate the telling off he gets for being too enthusiastic with performing the actual movement, and then he will become worried about it.

'I do not often ride Mary's horses; she is a very capable rider, and if I can achieve what I want in the horse through Mary, this is far more constructive as it means she has done it herself and will be able to do it again. However, if something is not coming through properly, or if I cannot understand the problem Mary thinks a particular horse has, then I will ride it. For example I did enjoy working with King Boris, who always looked

● *With Ferdi at the Olympics*

as if he was working well – but Mary would say it felt as if he wasn't really going forwards. In this case I rode the horse, and realised what Mary was talking about straightaway – I had to work quite hard to make Boris open up and use himself properly, though then he responded well. In fact although he is harder work to ride, it is far better to have a horse that you can really ride through the test than to have one like William or Conker who are almost too keen and onward-going.

'I also rode William at Badminton during the team training – he is a particularly onward-bound horse, and is better if he is made to do quite a lot of collected work; otherwise he becomes too strong and takes charge when Mary asks for certain movements, which means she cannot then ride him forwards properly in a test. It is easy for me to get on him and demand a little more engagement and collection, as I am used to that from riding pure dressage horses – and it never hurts to ask a horse to work at a higher level than the one at which he is actually performing. At Badminton this year we had it just right as William waited for Mary's commands and allowed her to ride out the movements.

'Inevitably I take an interest in the rest of the horses' work – it is no good having an event horse which is superb on the flat but not bold enough on the cross-country! King Cuthbert, who is retired now, was probably the greatest character Mary has had to date – he was very cheeky. All horses present a different challenge and so they are all rewarding in their own way. Currently William is probably the most scopey of Mary's horses, and he is now very capable in his flat work; in fact Mary had done well in helping him to organise himself, as he used to be all over the place – but he has always been very brave and honest across country, so he is an exciting horse to work with.'

● *The Captain with Mary and Ferdi*

An Observation On Jump Training
by Captain Mark Phillips

'The two most important things when jumping a horse are to have him going forwards and to keep him balanced. It is the same for a horse as it is for a human: if you are in balance physically your performance is uninhibited, but if you lose your balance it becomes limited.

'What the rider actually does on the approach to a fence depends on whether the horse is going forwards and how well balanced he is. If you have the power and he is in balance you can move him up to the fence and soften the hand on the last couple of strides to allow him to lower his head and neck, and bring his shoulders up to produce a good, round jump; but if the horse is not balanced then the shoulder will not come off the ground, although you can protect most horses by keeping a firmer contact, thus helping them to produce a good jump.

'William's problem is that he has a very high head carriage and his shoulder does not come off the ground very well. If you hold the front end too firmly to protect him from the fence he inverts himself and throws a flat jump – but if you don't hold firmly enough he also throws a flat jump. If you put him too deep he jumps to the left: if you hold him too far off the fence he again tends to jump flat. Add to that his propensity for rolling poles off, and it all adds up to him being a very complex character to deal with. Nevertheless I'm sure that as he gets older and stronger the quality of his canter will improve, and this will help his showjumping.

'Mary is very professional in her approach and all her horses are a little different to work with. From my point of view it is an honour and privilege to work with someone who is so talented and open-minded; with a

person of Mary's calibre you are striving all the time towards that last little bit of perfection. Nevertheless, however much development takes place, a great deal of improvisation is still required on the third day of a three-day event.'

A Trainer's Thoughts on Showjumping
by Steve Hadley

'I like a rider to be able to put his horse in a long, low outline on the flat. For jumping I like to see a round, swinging canter, with the horse on the bit and the hocks engaged. In an ideal world, the rider would have the ability and the eye to move the horse powerfully forwards from a long way out and to put the horse deep into the fence. Some of the top eventers, Mary included, can see a stride from far enough out, others cannot; but it is a skill which I try to help riders of every standard to achieve.

'Of Mary's horses, Conker would be my favourite; he is a real workmanlike horse and a natural jumper – the showjumping phase will never be his problem. He has a good technique and the right attitude; when he is faced with a line of jumps his attention is focussed on the top rail, he backs himself off and his mind is set on clearing it. In his preparation him for next season, as far as the showjumping is concerned he really doesn't need any extra work. Rather it is important to retain the innocence and freshness in his jump – you want him to come into the ring and be looking at what he has got to do; you don't want to give a good horse the excuse to become complacent about his work. I hope that he has the scope to tackle the cross-country at the top level as I do not see the other two phases being a problem for him at all.'

● *Steve jumping Basil*

● *Gill receiving the Calcutta Light Horse Trophy from John Tulloch, as owner of the horse gaining the most trials points in 1992*

AN OWNER'S INVOLVEMENT
by Gill Robinson

'My first involvement with Mary was through sponsoring her in the name of the Carphone Group, the company owned by myself and my ex-husband Graham Thomas. We were introduced to her by Tadjik Kopanski, director of the Pony Club, who had just sold her a horse; we all met for supper and were straightaway the best of friends.

'Not long after, Graham Thomas left for Australia and six months later the Carphone Group was sold; however, the new owners continued to sponsor Mary as she had a twelve-month contract which they felt compelled to honour. When this came to an end I tried very hard to find new sponsorship for her, but none was forthcoming; so I told her that we would see if we could get by somehow with just myself as sponsor.

'I think our team is quite unique – we are all such good friends yet manage not to step on each others' toes, and we are extremely lucky in having Tina and Annie: they are very special people, and have never once let Mary down. And where any of us would be without Mary's mother, Jill Thomson, I really don't know – she is an endless source of help, encouragement and resourcefulness...and wonderful food!

My relationship with Mary has always run so smoothly that I cannot imagine developing such a suc-cessful relationship with any other rider. Mary is always 100 per cent honest with me about the horses; she is scrupulous about their care, fitness, feeding and training, and I know she will always do what is best for them. She always chooses the horses herself, so in that respect she is perhaps luckier than many other riders who are handed a horse to ride which someone else has chosen, and which may not suit them very well. I am not particularly ambitious myself, nor do I think are Annie or Tina, but we put our efforts into wholeheartedly supporting Mary in her ambition.

'Eventing is a wonderful sport; I have made many lifelong friends, and have never before had so many laughs and so many tears – it is certainly a sport that teaches you a lot about life. At Badminton in 1991 Boris had looked to have victory in the bag but then tipped up in the lake; I ran to the finish to meet Mary, and as she came out of the weighing-in room we looked at each other and just said 'Damn!'. A few years ago I would certainly not have taken such a disappointment so lightly, but horses teach you that *nothing* is guaranteed! Always, the main concern is that both Mary and the horse finish sound and happy, because as long as they do there will always be another day and another chance.

'I have many happy memories and love all the horses dearly – but King Boris is something special. I don't really know how to describe how I feel about him, other than it has been like a continuing love affair! If only there were more men around like Boris – though I shouldn't really say that as I have only just re-married; but I'm sure Geoff doesn't mind the four-legged threat! Boris is just such a funny, loveable thing; Annie is always telling me that when I watch the other horses competing I look very serious about it all, but when Boris is performing I just have a big grin on my face, although Badminton 1991 was an exception – that was really serious stuff! I'm sure Boris thinks the yard is run

entirely for his benefit. He has such a tremendous heart, and always gives 150 per cent. He wouldn't be the fastest galloper but he is very nimble, and fast over fences as he sets himself up and never has to be checked; at least, that's what *he* tells me, but I'm sure Mary's got something to do with it!

'Boris' victory at Gatcombe in the British Open Championship is my happiest memory, even more so than Mary's Badminton win. Throughout his career, a lot of people have been sceptical about Boris and felt he was not good enough, but when I watched him over the first three fences at Gatcombe I *knew* he was going to win. I could hear the commentators saying that he didn't seem to be going fast enough, and I could see Captain Mark Phillips shaking his head, but Boris and I knew better. I don't quite know what I will do when he retires for good; I think *I* will have to write a book – *Life after Boris!*'

AN OWNER'S THOUGHTS
by David King

'Mary and I have known each other since about 1982, when we met at a New Year's Eve party in Honiton, Devon. At the time Mary was not sponsored, and it wasn't long before I found myself the proud part-owner of an event horse, King Boris. However, when Mary was signed up by the Carphone Group, Gill fell in love with Boris and I sold her my half-share; though this transaction didn't let me off the hook as Mary was by then expanding her string of horses and they were fast becoming a major part of both our lives.

'I have always liked horses, although I have never been that enthusiastic about actually riding them. I am a keen racing man, and previously owned shares in two race-horses, Steel City and Wild Geese – the latter even man-aged to win a couple of times at Wincanton! I *can* claim to have sat on Boris once, but beyond that I am happy to be a spectator; and as Mary has become more and more successful, my enjoyment and involvement in the sport has also increased – especially as I own half of William!

'Mary's win at Badminton, was without a shadow of a doubt, the greatest thrill of them all. I had a lucky feeling about Badminton; Mary was wearing number 38, which was my age at the time, and it was 10 May, and my father's 80th birthday – even though I am not normally lucky when it comes to gambling I felt confident enough to decide to put a bet on Mary winning, . A friend and I went off to find a bookie, but unusually for us, we couldn't track one down, so the bet was never laid, which is probably just as well. Being involved with event horses can also bring great disappointments; for example in one year, Mary was lying first and third with Cuthbert and Boris at Burghley on the final day. On both horses she rolled the last showjump pole and ended up second and fourth. But as everyone keeps telling me, that's horses!

'For me, the horses can only be an enjoyable interlude, as I have my own farm and business to run. My father and I have a beef farm, and I also work as a livestock agent, buying and selling beef cattle. This involves going to market five or six days a week and organising the transport of cattle all over England and Scotland.

'Despite our hectic schedules, Mary and I still find time for an equally hectic social life; we both enjoy tennis, skiing and watersports and catching up on the rounds of dinner parties!

'I realised long ago that owning event horses would never make me a rich man; the trouble is that they are either worth nothing or they're worth a small fortune – and the horses that are worth a fortune are the ones you never want to sell!'

 Mary and David

INDEX

INDEX

AUTHORS' ACKNOWLEDGEMENTS

Mary: 'I would like to thank my mother for all her calm support; my father for putting up with being such a long-suffering horse widower; Annie and Tina for their loyalty and hard work over the years; Ferdi, Steve and Mark for helping me to achieve my aims; David, for his continued encouragement, understanding and good humour; Debby, for all her enthusiasm and patience.'

Debby: 'I would like to thank Steve Hadley, Captain Mark Phillips and Ferdi Eilberg for their contributions and for allowing me to join their training sessions; John Killingbeck MRCVS; Gill Robinson; David King; Jill and Michael Thomson for allowing the numerous invasions of their home; Martin for coping with the disruption to our home and horses over the last year; Mary for her time and patience; and Sue Hall (editor) and Sue Cleave (designer) of David & Charles, for taking us on!'

PICTURE ACKNOWLEDGEMENTS

The authors and publishers would like to thank Kit Houghton for supplying most of the photographs for this book. Thanks are also due to the following people for their photographs: Barn Owl Associates pp6, 10; Equestrian Services Thorney pp8-9, 166; Fiona Peters/Hoofprints Photography pp10-11; Srdja Djukanovic pp18-19, 114, 190; Peter Ayres pp50-1, 88-9; Nick Morris pp91, 92, 93, 94, 108-9, 110-11, 116-17, 126-7, 184; Hugo Czerny pp94-5; the 'Sponsorship Workshop' pp122, 123; Debby Sly p132 (margin); Barbara Thomson pp 136, 137; Bob Langrish pp138, 144, 146, 162; Trevor Meeks /Horse & Hound p148; Gypsy Joe p189; and to the unknown photographer who took the picture on p13 – thank you!